# Canadian Financial Markets

# Canadian Financial Markets

## 3rd Edition

W.T. Hunter

**broadview press**

# Cataloguing in Publication Data

Hunter, W.T.
      Canadian Financial Markets

3rd ed.
Includes index
ISBN   0-921149-48-4

1.   Capital market — Canada.   2.   Securities — Canada.   3.   Money market —
Canada.   I.   Title.


         HG185.C2H8  1991         332.6'0971         C91-094872-0

broadview press                    OR                    broadview press
P.O. Box 1243                                            269 Portage Rd.
Peterborough, Ontario                                    Lewiston, NY
K9J 7H5    Canada                                        14092    USA


                        *printed in Canada*

# Table of Contents

*FOR DORIS*

# preface

This slim volume attempts to provide an introductory overview of the various Canadian financial markets to readers with a rudimentary understanding of basic economics. It is not a "how to" manual providing instruction in management finance or personal finance. Instead the objective is more modest—to leave the reader better able to understand the news reports and quotations in the financial press.

A key theme throughout is the way in which these markets adjust to change. The changes wrought by inflation in the 1980s are traced in the earlier chapters, and in the latter chapters the integration of Canadian financial markets into world markets is emphasized in the light of the changes brought by advancing technology, deregulation and the increasing importance of institutional investors.

While changes in tax regulations, the deregulation of Canadian financial markets, the stock market break of October, 1987 and other developments have necessitated a revision of the initial text, the objectives remain the same.

The author would like to express his gratitude to the following people for their generous assistance: James Cole who perused the initial manuscript with great care and made innumerable helpful suggestions; Dean H.H. Binhammer of Royal Military College and an anonymous reviewer who made many helpful comments; Stephen Henderson and Gail Crawford of RBC Dominion Securities; David Adamo of Scotia McLeod Fixed Income Research; and Don LePan who helped throughout the writing of all editions with great style. As always, the author remains entirely responsible for the resulting product.

# CHAPTER ONE

# introduction

THOSE READERS WHO HAVE ENDURED AN INTRODUCTORY COURSE IN economics may remember the simple macroeconomic model in which the national income is in equilibrium when planned savings equals planned investment. The leakage out of the circular flow of income into savings is just offset by the injection of investment into the circular flow. The capital market is where the leakage from households gets turned into investment in physical capital by business firms. This book is about the capital market and its various parts.

Of course, reality is more complicated than the simple model, and saving is done not only by households, but also by businesses and governments, and it can arise as well from the international transactions in the economy. On the other hand, investment in the sense of the formation of fixed capital can be a result of business, household or government initiatives as well as arising from international activities. Consequently, the sources of funds for the capital market are various and can be thought of as coming from surplus units whose current income exceeds their current expenditure. The users of funds, on the other hand, are likewise various and can be thought of as deficit units in the sense that their current expenditure exceeds their current income.

The capital market can then be defined more formally as the place where the funds of surplus units are transferred to deficit units, and in the process non-monetary financial assets are created. As well, the capital market facilitates changes in the ownership of existing non-monetary financial assets.

The transfer of funds in the capital market gives rise to various evidences of debt and ownership which can be referred to as non-monetary financial assets. The money for which they are typically exchanged is obviously a key ingredient of the market and crucial to its operation. However, we will not be concerned here with the creation of money or the control of the money supply; this is usually treated separately under the rubric of money and banking.

The non-monetary financial assets created are claims to some future stream of payments, and may also be referred to as securities. The surplus units may lend directly to the deficit units in return for primary securities, which are obligations of the borrower. However, it is much more likely that the lending will take place indirectly through some financial intermediary that transforms the direct claim on the borrower into an indirect security that is the liability of the financial intermediary. For example, the seller of a house may loan funds directly to the buyer of the house on the security of a mortgage. On the other hand, the seller of the house may not wish to have all the proceeds tied up in a mortgage that may be relatively difficult to turn into cash, and prefer instead to put his money into a guaranteed investment certificate issued by a trust or mortgage loan company. This intermediary, in turn, could re-lend the funds to the buyer of the house on the security of a mortgage.

By transforming direct claims into indirect claims, financial intermediaries offer advantages to both ultimate lenders and ultimate borrowers. The indirect securities which are the liabilities of the financial intermediary offer greater flexibility and convenience to the lender. The guaranteed investment certificates in the preceding example can be in almost any amount and in a number of different terms to maturity. Thus small pools of saving can be tapped for eventual investment in real assets. The lender is spared the expense and difficulty of assessing the property and drawing up the necessary legal documents. Because the intermediary invests in a number of different primary securities, risk is reduced through diversification, and the indirect security of the intermediary is consequently a less risky investment than the primary security of the ultimate borrower. The intermediary has greater expertise and experience at its disposal and should improve the quality of investment decisions. Similar benefits in terms of flexibility and convenience accrue to the borrower as he is able to approach a variety of competing lending institutions in an impersonal manner.

Financial intermediation increases economic efficiency within the financial system by reducing the costs of transferring funds from surplus units to deficit units. It does this by taking advantage of economies of scale which are not available to the individual borrower or lender, in this way increasing productivity in this sector of the economy. Moreover, through product differentiation, financial institutions increase the diversity of non-monetary financial assets available to borrowers and lenders.

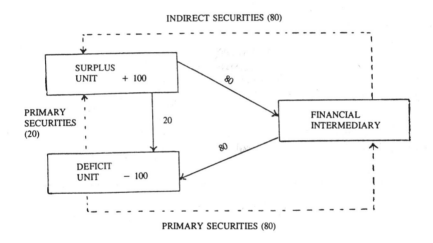

The preceding diagram illustrates the process of financial intermediation. In this diagram, the flows of funds are depicted by solid lines, while the movements of securities are shown by dashed lines. The surplus unit, such as the seller of a house, has funds of 100 (representing, perhaps, the $100,000 that he received for his house) while the deficit unit, in this case the buyer of the house, needs 100 to finance the excess of his expenditures over his income. Perhaps the . seller lends 20 to the buyer directly on the security of a second mortgage, and this is shown by the solid arrow as a flow of funds equal to 20 from the surplus unit to the deficit unit, with a corresponding movement of primary securities (the second mortgage) in the opposite direction. The surplus unit invests the other 80 of his funds with a financial intermediary, say in the form of a guaranteed investment certificate issued by a trust company. The solid line from the surplus unit to the financial intermediary shows this flow of funds, and in return the trust company issues indirect securities of 80 in the form of a guaranteed investment certificate, which is its liability. The buyer of the house, in turn, obtains the other 80 of funds that he requires by borrowing at the trust company against the security of a first mortgage. The flow of funds in this transaction is depicted by the solid line from the financial intermediary to the deficit unit, with the corresponding flow of direct securities (the first mortgage) shown by the dashed line in the opposite direction.

One result of financial intermediation is immediately obvious from this diagram. The process has increased the stock of non-monetary financial assets available. Funds made available by surplus units and used by deficit units total 100, but non-monetary financial assets are equal to 180, composed of the primary securities issued by the deficit unit in the form of first and second mortgages (80 + 20) as well as the indirect securities issued by the financial intermediary in the form of a guaranteed investment certificate (80). Consequently, the total of non-monetary financial assets is not an accurate indication of the relative importance of the financial industry. What we do know is that the assets of financial institutions as a percentage of Gross National Product have grown fairly steadily over the past century.[1] In the absence of "layering" (the holding of one financial institution's liabilities by another financial institution), this indicates that the benefits of intermediation to both lenders and borrowers have resulted in a greater proportion of the transfer of funds taking place in this indirect manner.

On the other hand, there has in recent years been a trend toward securitization which in a broad sense refers to the development of a variety of instruments that permit the ultimate borrower to bypass intermediaries and borrow directly from ultimate lenders. More narrowly, securitization refers to the process of converting loans of various sorts into marketable securities by packaging the loans into pools and issuing securities collateralized by the pool of loans.

Financial intermediation increases liquidity in the financial system. Liquidity is the ability to realize the value of an asset in money, and should take into account not only the time and transaction cost of converting the asset into money, but also the degree of certainty of being able to do so without loss of capital. Marketability is a slightly different concept involving the ability to sell an existing asset in an organized market. Mortgages are not very marketable securities since there is no well developed secondary market for mortgages, and because it is difficult to realize the value of a mortgage in terms of money, mortgages are also described as illiquid securities. On the other hand, Canada Savings Bonds are not marketable, since they cannot be sold to another person, but they are probably the most liquid non-monetary financial asset, since they can be redeemed for their par value at any time. Intermediaries enhance liquidity in the financial sector by holding assets in the form of primary securities (which may themselves be rather illiquid), while at the same time creating more liquid indirect securities which are then held by the ultimate lenders in the economy.

To the extent that financial intermediaries accomplish this feat of increasing liquidity by borrowing short and lending long, as trust companies might do if they issued guaranteed investment certificates for one year terms and lent money on twenty year mortgages, this creates the possibility of financial collapse if there were a crisis of confidence in the institution. It would be impossible to liquidate the underlying assets in the form of primary securities sufficiently quickly to obtain the funds required to redeem the much more liquid indirect securities which are the obligations of the intermediary to its creditors. Another problem could arise in this situation if interest rates rose and the intermediary had to borrow new funds in the short term at rates that exceeded the return on their longer term assets.

Crises of confidence are an ever present threat to financial intermediaries, and one of the reasons why governments intervene through regulation is to attempt to maintain confidence in the system. However, recent difficulties in the Canadian financial sector have not always been simply problems of liquidity, and efforts to maintain confidence through direct rescue operations have been misplaced when the underlying problems are really ones of insolvency resulting from assets that will never be recoverable.

In addition to transferring funds from surplus units to deficit units, the capital market also facilitates changes in the ownership of existing assets. Primary markets are where deficit units originally sell primary securities and intermediaries sell indirect securities, while secondary markets are where outstanding financial assets are traded. Secondary markets are necessary to provide the marketability referred to earlier, so that holders of existing securities can sell them to someone else on short notice. The existence of secondary markets which provide marketability for outstanding securities also enhances the operation of primary markets, since lenders will be more willing to acquire primary securities if they know that there is a market where they can dispose of these issues at a later date. The better developed the secondary market, the greater the promotion of the corresponding primary market.

Financial intermediaries, such as banks, trust companies, credit unions and insurance companies take the savings of surplus units in return for claims upon themselves. Market intermediaries such as investment dealers facilitate the change in the ownership of financial claims. Market intermediaries may perform a brokerage function, acting as agents or go-betweens in bringing together the buyers and sellers of securities. Thus stockbrokers typically act as agents in bringing together buyers and sellers of stock in the secondary market, and they charge a commission for their services. Dealers, or jobbers, on the other hand, buy securities from one party and sell them to another in the secondary market, and in so doing act as principals. Bond dealers and money market jobbers work in this way, hoping to make money from the difference between the prices at which they buy and sell. Dealers and jobbers perform an important function by reducing fluctuations in the prices of securities and reducing the spread between the prices at which it is possible to buy and sell.

This, then, is the capital market, where funds are transferred from surplus units to deficit units, often via financial intermediaries, where non-monetary financial assets are created, and where changes in the ownership of non-monetary financial assets are facilitated. These jobs are accomplished in pursuit of the basic function of the capital market: to elicit funds for investment and to allocate these funds among competing uses.

One way of studying the Canadian capital market would be to look at the participants in it, and in particular to examine the range of financial intermediaries. The most important of these are, of course, the banks, which play the basic role in the payments system, are central to the control of the money supply and are increasingly becoming involved in market intermediation. As already noted the creation and control of the money supply are normally the stuff of courses in money and banking, and for this reason we are going to avoid this important area. To treat the other market and financial intermediaries on their own, on the other hand, would be rather like doing *Hamlet* without the Prince. This is one reason for approaching the subject in a way that cuts across institutional lines, that is by markets rather than by institutions.

Moreover, the distinctions between the various intermediaries are quickly becoming increasingly blurred through mergers and new undertakings. In the process of securitization referred to above, the commercial banks have been bypassed, and consequently they have tried, where allowed, to move into investment banking, or market intermediation, in which they act as agents and receive a fee for their services. Merchant banking carries the process a step further and involves the bank investing some of its own capital into the venture. On the other hand, investment dealers provide banking services.

In the United States there has been a movement in recent years toward department stores of finance, as single institutions provide banking, investment, insurance and other services. This development, along with the movement of banks into brokerage and brokers into banking, has taken place within the existing laws, but reforms proposed in 1991 would allow financial holding companies that could have subsidiaries involved in both commercial banking (financial intermediation) and investment banking (market intermediation), thereby overcoming the restrictions imposed by the Glass-Steagall Act of 1933.

Deregulation hit Britain's financial markets with the Big Bang on October 27, 1986, as commissions were no longer fixed, dealers could take positions in, as well as buy and sell, securities, trading in British govenment bonds was opened up and foreign firms were allowed into the industry.

In Canada we had our own Mini Bang on June 30, 1987 as the traditional barriers to ownership of securities firms by other financial institutions and foreigners were removed. By 1988, all the major Canadian banks had acquired a controlling interest in a securities firm.

These ongoing developments make it difficult to write something that will still be current by the time it is read. A similar problem arises if the approach to the capital market is through a description of the instruments in it. The emergence of stripped and zero coupon bonds, the introduction of mortgage-backed bonds and Toronto index participation units (TIPs), the rise of interest and exchange swaps, new instruments in the Euromarkets such as note-issuance facilities and floating rate notes, the proliferation of futures and options contracts, and of options on futures are all illustrative of the same difficulty of providing a catalogue which is at once both current and complete.

Instead, the organization of this introductory overview will be to describe the various financial markets which together comprise the Canadian capital market. Basic to any market is price, and our starting point will be a discussion of prices in the capital market. The price of money is the rate of interest, but the prices of non-monetary financial assets are usually compared in terms of yield, or rate of return. We start, then, by discussing yields, how they are determined and why they differ, as well as the ways in which yields are altered by taking into consideration inflation and taxation.

We then move on to a description of the component parts of the capital market, the various markets for different types of non-monetary financial assets. We start with those for fixed income securities: the bond market, the money market and the mortgage market; then move on to securities which have variable incomes as exemplified by the stock market; and arrive finally at markets which provide facilities for hedging and where any returns are highly speculative and dependent largely upon capital gains, such as the options and futures markets.

Finally, we examine the international dimension of the Canadian capital market. We begin by discussing the foreign exchange market which is not strictly speaking a part of the capital market where non-monetary financial assets are traded, but rather a necessary adjunct to international borrowing and investment. We will describe how the Canadian capital market is integrated into world capital markets, both through the long standing connections between Canadian and other national markets, particularly that of the United States, and also through the more recent evolution of supranational capital markets exemplified by the Euromarkets. The effect of this worldwide integration in terms of competition and regulation will be an underlying theme of the penultimate chapter, where we assess the efficiency with which financial markets operate in Canada and the way in which they are controlled. The concluding chapter will discuss the Stock

Market Break of October, 1987 in terms of the developments discussed in earlier chapters.

# Note

1   Neufeld, E.P. *The Financial System of Canada*. Toronto: Macmillan of Canada, 1972. p. 24.

# Further References

Department of Finance, Government of Canada. *The Regulation of Canadian Financial Institutions: Proposals for Discussion*. Ottawa: Minister of Supply and Services, 1985. Appendix 1.

Economic Council of Canada. *A Framework for Financial Regulation*. Ottawa: Ministry of Supply and Services, 1987. Chapter 1.

Hood, W.C. *Financing of Economic Activity in Canada*. Study for The Royal Commission on Canada's Economic Prospects. Ottawa: Queen's Printer, 1959. Chapter 2.

Neufeld, E.P. *The Financial System of Canada*. Toronto: Macmillan of Canada, 1972. Chapter 1.

Shearer, R.A., Chant, J.F. and Bond, D.E. *The Economics of the Canadian Financial System*. Second Edition. Scarborough, Ontario: Prentice-Hall Canada, 1984. Chapter 1.

Van Horne, J.C. *Financial Market Rates and Flows*. Englewood Cliffs, N.J.: Prentice-Hall, 1978. Chapter 1.

Williamson, J.P. "Canadian Capital Markets" and "Canadian Financial Institutions." Government of Canada, Department of Consumer and Corporate Affairs. *Proposals for a Securities Market Law for Canada*. Vol. 3. Ottawa: Minister of Supply and Services, 1979. pp. 1-133; 719-946.

**CHAPTER TWO**

# yields

NON-MONETARY FINANCIAL ASSETS ARE HELD AS A STORE OF VALUE AND for the return that they are expected to provide. They represent a claim on an expected future stream of payments. In the case of a bond, that stream of payments is made up of interest coupons along with the repayment of the principal amount at the maturity date. In the case of a stock the payment is in the form of a dividend which may or may not be paid and which may or may not be constant in value, along with the final value of the stock when, and if, it is sold or redeemed. The yield on a financial asset is the discount rate which equates the present value of the expected future payments with the current market price of the security.

The rate of interest is the amount the borrower contracts to pay for the use of money. Simple interest is computed by taking the amount of money lent and multiplying it by the rate of interest times the number of periods. Thus:

Value of a sum at simple interest = $V + V(i \times n)$

Where:  $V$ = principal
  $i$ = rate of interest
  $n$ = term (number of periods)

If the principal amount is \$1,000, the rate of interest is 10% per annum and the period of the loan is three years, simple interest would be:

$1,000 (.10 \times 3) = \$300$

and the total value of interest and principal at the end of the period would be:

$1,000 + $1,000 (.10 x 3) = $1,300.

Compound interest allows for interest on interest, and thus increases the amount of interest paid, with the difference between this and simple interest becoming greater, the greater the number of periods involved. Consequently, the more often the interest computation takes place, the greater the effect of compound interest.

Returning to the example above, and using the same principal amount, rate of interest and time period, compound interest gives the following result:

Value of interest and principal after one period:

$1,000 + ($1,000 x .10) = $1,100     $1000 (1.1)$

Value of interest and principal after two periods:

$1,100 + ($1,100 x .10) = $1,210     $1000 (1.1)^2$

Value of interest and principal after three periods:

$1,210 + ($1,210 x .10) = $1,331     $1000 (1.1)^3$

Thus we see that allowing for compounding increases the value of principal and interest by $31 after three years, in this example. More generally, the value of $1 invested at interest rate i over three periods can be given as:

Value of interest and principal after one period:

$1 + [1 \times i] = 1 + i$

Value of interest and principal after two periods:

$[1+i] + [(1+i) \times i] = (1+i) \times (1+i) = (1+i)^2$

Value of interest and principal after three periods:

$[1+i]^2 + [(1+i)^2 \times i] = (1+i)^2 \times (1+i) = (1+i)^3$

Thus: value of a sum at compound interest $= V(1+i)^n$

Applying this to the above example, the value of interest and principal at the end of three years would be:

$1,000 x $(1.10)^3$ = $1,331.

If we know the final value and the present value, but wanted to find out the rate of interest that equates the two we could easily do so. In the preceding example we found that:

$1,000 x $(1+i)^3$ = $1,331

by rearranging:

$1,000 = $\dfrac{\$1,331}{(1+i)^3}$

and solving for i would give .10, or 10%.

More generally, any future value after n periods can be brought back to its present value, or discounted, by dividing by $(1+i)^n$. While the rate of interest is generally shown as i, the rate of discount used in finding present value is usually shown as r, so that the divisor becomes $(1+r)^n$. If the rate of discount, r, is known, then the present value of any future amount can be computed; and if the present value is known, the rate of discount involved can be computed. This rate of discount, then, would be the yield, which was defined earlier as the discount rate which equates the expected value of future payments with the current market price of the security.

## Fixed Income Yields

The preceding definition of yield talks of future payments in the plural, and typically financial assets yield a stream of such payments, all of which must be discounted, as contrasted with our earlier example when there was simply one final payment at maturity. In the case of a bond which bears annual coupons and which has a fixed value at maturity, the following equation would hold:

$$P_o = \frac{C_1}{(1+r)} + \frac{C_2}{(1+r)^2} + \frac{C_3}{(1+r)^3} + \dots \frac{C_n}{(1+r)^n} + \frac{VM}{(1+r)^n}$$

where:     $P_o$ = the current market price
           $C_t$ = the expected interest payment in period t (coupon)

VM = the value at maturity
n = the term to maturity (term)
r = the yield to maturity

For example: a $1,000 bond with 20 years left to maturity, an annual coupon of $60 and selling at a current price of $894:

$$\$894 = \frac{60}{(1+r)} + \frac{60}{(1+r)^2} + \ldots \frac{60}{(1+r)^{20}} + \frac{1000}{(1+r)^{20}}$$

$$r = 7\%$$

The mechanics of solving for r are too complicated to warrant discussion in an introductory overview. Moreover, if the interest payments are semi-annual, as would normally be the case with a bond, the expression is even more complex. In any event, the solution for r is readily available from yield books or computer programmes, although some interpolation may be necessary. Yield books do not always provide for the relatively high interest rates that have been experienced in recent years, often going only as high as 10% or 12%. Moreover, in recent years such books have gone the way of the horse and buggy as modern computer technology has taken over.

Note that in the above example, the coupon of 60 represents a rate of 6% on the par value of the bond, or $1,000. However, the yield is 7%, or higher than the coupon rate of interest, in part because of the additional yield provided by the capital gain resulting from buying the bond at less than its eventual redemption price, and in part because the fixed interest payments represent a higher percentage return on the discounted price. When the bond was originally issued, 6% may have been the going rate for that type of security and with that term to maturity. At the present time, however, the going rate is higher, and consequently the already issued bond must fall in price in order to bring the effective yield to maturity into line with market rates of interest. When interest rates rise, the prices of outstanding bonds fall; and when interest rates fall, the prices of outstanding bonds rise.

Yields are thus seen to vary inversely with bond prices, and this is only logical. The two components of yield are the interest payments which are fixed in amount, and the difference between the present value and the value at maturity. If the value at maturity is higher than the present value, or price, then a capital gain will be realized at maturity, while if the value at maturity is less than the present value, a capital loss is incurred. When bond prices fall, the value of the fixed interest payments, or coupons, rises as a percentage of this new lower price, so that the effective return on this component of yield increases. Moreover, the lower the price of the bond the greater the capital gain, or the smaller the capital loss, at maturity, and so the second component of yield is also increased. Consequently, both elements of yield increase when bond prices fall, while the reverse is true if bond prices rise.

The rate of interest can be a confusing term here. The rate of interest established when the money was originally borrowed is reflected in the coupon, whose amount is fixed for the term of the bond. Rates of interest in the marketplace change, and when they do bond prices change in order to bring effective yields into line with these going rates of interest.

When a bond is selling at par, i.e. $P_o = 100$, the yield is equal to the coupon rate. Most bonds have semi-annual coupon payments. However, if we ignore the effects of semi-annual compounding, the coupon rate in this case is really equivalent to simple interest. Canada Savings Bonds are always redeemable at par, and thus the coupon rate of interest is the yield on these bonds. When there have been large changes in interest rates, the coupon rates have been changed on Canada Savings Bonds in order to keep them competitive, since with these bonds price changes are not a possibility.

The coupon rates reflect market rates of interest when the bond is issued. Different bond issues may have similar maturity dates but very different coupon rates reflecting different dates of issue, and consequently they will sell at very different prices. For example, the Government of Canada has two bond issues outstanding which are due to mature on March 15, 1998, one bearing a 3.75% coupon, and the other a 10.75% coupon. As of June 21, 1991, the 3.75% bond was quoted at 72.65 to yield 9.30% until maturity, while the 10.75% bond was quoted at 103.50 to yield 10.02% until maturity. The difference in yields on the two bonds is a result of taxation rules, as explained in the next chapter. These examples also illustrate the general proposition that when a bond is selling above par, or at a premium, the yield is lower than the coupon rate, and when a bond is selling below par, or at a discount, the yield is greater than the coupon rate.

Yield is a function of price, coupon and term. We have seen that bond prices and yields vary inversely, but there are also relationships between price movements and term, and between price movements and coupon, which are important. As bond prices fall to a greater discount, more of the return or yield comes from the capital gain realized at the end of the period. This has two important implications. In response to a given rise in interest rates:

(a)        The longer the term is, the further the price will fall, for otherwise comparable bonds (i.e. of equal coupon rate and quality). This is because the longer the term, the greater the discount on that portion of the return which is only realized as a capital gain at maturity.

(b)        The lower the coupon is, the further the price will fall, for otherwise comparable bonds (i.e. of equal term and quality). This is because with a lower coupon more of the return comes from the capital gain which is only realized at the end of the period, and which is therefore subject to a greater discount than interest payments in the interim would be.

It follows, then, that when interest rates rise, the prices of bonds with low coupons and long terms will fall furthest, and conversely when interest rates fall, these bonds will have the most dramatic price increases.

The total return on a bond is made up of the repayment of capital at maturity, regular interest payments and money generated from the reinvestment of interest payments. A measure known as duration takes into account not only the interest payments themselves, but also *when* they are to be received, realizing that earlier payments have more value than those received later. It is a weighted average of the present value of the principal at maturity plus the present value of all interest payments in the interim, assuming that they can be reinvested at the original yield to maturity. It thus gives a measure in years of the average life of a debt instrument on a present-value basis.

Duration was formulated in 1938 by Frederick Macaulay as a more accurate measure of the life of a coupon bond, and it has come into greater prominence in recent years as computer technology has allowed greater ease of calculation. When interest rates change, bond price movements differ depending upon the coupon and term, as was explained earlier. Since duration takes into account both coupon and term, it may be a more useful indicator than just maturity. If there is a single payment, duration equals maturity, but if there are interim payments duration is always less than maturity. For example, a 20-year, 10% issue priced at its face value has a duration of only 8.4 years. The lower the coupon, the closer its duration is to its maturity.

When somebody invests in a bond he cannot be sure his realized return will equal the yield promised at the time of purchase, even if there were no default. Since bond prices changes as market rates of interest change, the investor runs a price risk if he has to sell before maturity. If the maturity equals the desired holding period there will be no price risk. However, the rate at which coupons can be reinvested will vary as market rates of interest change, and the investor will have a coupon reinvestment risk even if maturity equals the desired holding period. The two risks vary in opposite directions. For example, if market rates of interest rise, bond prices fall and price risk increases, but coupons can be re-invested at higher rates and coupon reinvestment risk declines. The investor can be sure of a realized return equal to the yield projected at the time of purchase by having duration equal to the intended holding period. Only in this case will the bond be "immunized," so that any change in interest rates causes the return from price and the return from coupon re-investment to change by equal amounts, but in opposite directions.

The zero coupon bonds and stripped bonds which have been developed recently can be discussed in terms of these distinctions. Zero coupon bonds are bonds issued without any coupons, and as such are just like long term non-interest bearing notes, or promises to pay. Their yield is simply the discount rate which gives the note a present value equal to the current price. Stripped bonds are similar, except that they originally carried coupons which have since been removed and sold separately. In both cases the coupons are not just low but are reduced to zero, and if the bonds have a long term they will exhibit very volatile prices in times of changing market interest rates. Moreover, since reinvestment of coupons is not a factor, the realized return will always equal the expected return at purchase, as long as the holding period coincides with the maturity.

While yields on bonds are readily available from the financial press, or from yield books or computer programmes, it might be useful to show how one might compute the rough yield on a bond in the absence of such resources. One approximation is to take the interest return on an annual basis, add to it a portion of the capital gain or loss pro-rated over the term of the bond, and then express this total return as a percentage of the average of the present price and the value at maturity. For example, for a bond maturing in four years, bearing a 10% coupon and priced at 92, the approximate yield would be:

interest per annum: 10.00

annualized capital gain: $\dfrac{8.00}{4} = 2.00$

total return per annum: $10.00 + 2.00 = 12.00$

average value: $\dfrac{92.00 + 100.00}{2} = 96.00$

approximate yield: $\dfrac{12.00}{96.00}$ x $100 = 12.50\%$

This result can be compared with the exact result of 12.62% obtained from a computer programme. Note also that the yield is above the coupon rate of interest, which is what one would expect with a bond selling at a discount.

## Stock Yields

Up to this point we have discussed yield entirely in terms of fixed income securities, and in particular bonds. It is possible to compute the yield on the stream of future payments because these payments are fixed in amount. With equities the stream of future payments is uncertain. Dividends on common stock may or may not be declared, and if declared their size will depend upon the profits of the company and the decision of the Directors. While dividends on preferred stock are normally fixed in size, they too will only be paid if declared by the Directors. With both kinds of stock there is no definitely fixed maturity date, and so it is not possible to define a term to maturity or a value at maturity. As a result, yields on equities are normally computed by taking only the indicated annual dividend at current rates as a percentage of the current market price. For example, a stock selling at $50 and currently paying a quarterly dividend of 25 cents would have an indicated annual dividend of $1 and would thus have a yield equal to 1/50 x 100 = 2%. A more concrete example would be BCE (formerly Bell Canada Enterprises) selling at, say $40.00 per share and paying a dividend of .64 per quarter, or $2.56 per year, thereby yielding 6.40%.

Published yields on equities are usually below those on bonds in spite of the fact that they carry greater risk. One reason for this is that stocks are bought in anticipation of capital gains and/or increased dividends, but these are not included in the calculation of yield because they cannot be known.

It is possible to compute a holding period yield for a stock by establishing a terminal value and a terminal date for the holding period. For example, using the stock selling at $50 and paying an annual dividend of $1, assume that the dividend remains constant but the stock rises in price to $70 after three years at which time it is sold. Then one could compute a holding period yield as follows:

$$50 = \frac{1}{(1+r)} + \frac{1}{(1+r)^2} + \frac{1}{(1+r)^3} + \frac{70}{(1+r)^3}$$

r = 13.67%

This sequence of events is not entirely implausible, and the yield is much higher than the 2% figure which results from using only the indicated annual dividend. However, it is a yield that can only be known with certainty in hindsight.

## Differences In Yields

### *Risk Premiums*

We have seen that yields may change over time as market rates of interest change. We now turn to differences in yields at a given moment in time, and what explains these differences.

Up to this point we have discussed yields on bonds as if they were free of any possibility of default. Bonds of the Government of Canada can be considered default-free since in the final analysis the Government could resort to printing the money required to pay the interest and the amount owing at maturity. While the lender would undoubtedly suffer a loss in purchasing power due to inflation if this were to happen, he would receive the nominal amounts contracted for and in this sense there would be no default. Payments on the bonds of other borrowers are not so assured, however, and lenders must therefore make some allowance for the possibility that they will not receive their money.

Investors thus demand an additional return as an allowance to compensate for the risk of default. If markets worked perfectly, this allowance would be exactly equal to the difference between the promised rate of return on this security and the promised rate of return on a default-free security. There would be, then, a risk premium built into the promised rate which would equal the expected loss due to default.

These risk premiums are estimated by bond rating agencies. In Canada two bond rating agencies have appeared in recent years: the Canadian Bond Rating Service and the Dominion Bond Rating Service. In the United States this has been done for many years by Moody's and Standard and Poor's. While their notation differs slightly, triple A is the top rating, and all bonds rated above the fourth rank, the top B rating, are considered medium grade or above and of investment quality. Issues below this are considered speculative. Junk bonds are bonds rated below investment quality, and they have acquired prominence in recent years as a result of a spate of leveraged buyouts where one company takes over another by buying the equity with the proceeds from bonds issued against the collateral of the acquired firm's assets. This leads generally to a more highly levered capital structure, and therefore greater risk in the event of rising interest rates or depressed sales. Both of these misfortunes hit Campeau Corporation.

Risk premiums tend to vary with the stage of the business cycle. In times of recession investors are more conscious of the possibility of default and they become more concerned with safety. This may result in a "flight to quality" as investors sell riskier bonds and buy default-free bonds. Such a development has the effect of increasing the yield on riskier bonds relative to default-free bonds. In other words, the risk premium demanded increases in a time of recession. Conversely, at times of business expansion and prosperity there is less fear of default and less concern with safety, and so the risk premium is reduced.

## Term Structure

If one holds default risk constant and looks at how yields on bonds differ in relation to the term to maturity, one sees the term structure of interest rates. This is most often done with Government of Canada bonds since they are of equal risk, in this case being considered default-free, and since there are a large number of bonds outstanding and therefore a large number of observations. If these bonds are put on a two-dimensional diagram where the vertical axis depicts the yield and the horizontal axis shows the term to maturity, we get what is referred to as a yield curve.

Why might yields differ with respect to term to maturity? Or put in another way, what explains the shape of the yield curve at any given moment? There are a number of rival hypotheses on this score, but the ones which seem to be best supported by the evidence revolve around uncertainty and expectations.[1]

Uncertainty is held to be greater in the long term than in the short term. We have already seen that bonds of comparable coupon and quality vary more in price the longer the term to maturity. It follows that a lender can be less certain of what he might receive for his bond if he should have to sell it before maturity, and in this sense he has a less liquid security. Consequently, he demands a liquidity premium to compensate for this loss, and this liquidity premium on longer term bonds causes higher yields in the longer term and an upward-sloping yield curve. Another way of looking at this would be to say that lenders prefer to lend short whereas borrowers prefer to borrow long, and a premium is required to overcome this mismatching of desires in the market.

However, we must also consider the role of expectations. A basic assumption often employed is that the long term rate of interest is an unbiased average of the current short term rate and future short term rates expected to prevail during the longer term. If future rates are expected to be the same as present rates, then the long term rate will be an average of identical numbers, the long term rate and the short term rate will be the same, and the yield curve will be horizontal. Alternatively, if future short term rates are expected to be higher than present short term rates, the long term rate will be higher than the short term rate and the yield curve will be upward-sloping. Finally, if future short term rates are expected to be lower than current short term rates, the long term rate will be lower than the short term rate and the yield curve will be downward-sloping.

Combining the presumption that the yield curve will be upward sloping as a result of the liquidity premium with the foregoing generalizations based on expectations, we could get yield curves of any shape.

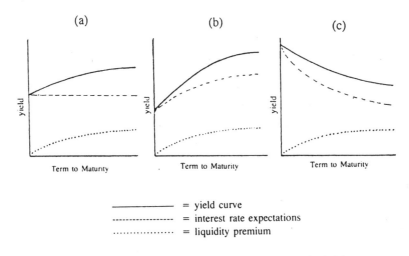

(a)    (b)    (c)

———————— = yield curve
------------------ = interest rate expectations
.................. = liquidity premium

In the preceding diagrams, different shapes of yield curves are derived by combining a constant liquidity premium with curves depicting different expectations about future interest rates. In panel (a), future short term rates are expected to be the same as curent short term rates, or expectations are neutral, and the resulting curve for expected interest rates is horizontal. Combining this with the liquidity premium which increases with term to maturity, the resulting yield curve is upward-sloping. When future short term rates are expected to be higher than current short term rates, as in panel (b), the curve for interest rate expectations is upward sloping, and the combined yield curve when the liquidity premium is added slopes up even more sharply. If, however, the expectation is that future short term rates will be lower than present short term rates, the curve based on expectations will be downward sloping, and if it slopes down sufficiently sharply to more than offset the liquidity premium which rises with term to maturity, the resulting yield curve could be

22

downward-sloping. In panel (c) we see that the yield curve does indeed slope down.

These possible shapes for the yield curve may be compared with what has in fact been observed over time. Usually, at the trough of the business cycle interest rates are low and expectations are that they will be higher in the future; we normally observe an upward sloping yield curve such as in panel (b) during such periods. On the other hand, when the business cycle is at a peak and interest rates are high, expectations are that interest rates will be lower in the future, and in such periods we may observe a downward sloping yield curve such as the one depicted in panel (c).

Yield Curves, Government of Canada Bonds

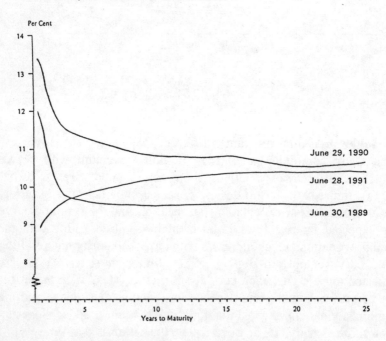

Source: Scotia McLeod, Fixed Income Research

The yield curves shown are mid-year observations for 1989, 1990, and 1991. The yield curve was inverted throughout 1989 and 1990. The peak of the business cycle did not come until the first quarter of

1990, so that the inverse yield curve was well ahead of the change in economic activity and persisted well after the turning point in the cycle. Moreover, interest rates were up to two points higher in the latter year. The trough of the business cycle appears to have been in early 1991, and by mid-year the more usual upward-sloping yield curve was in place.

One practical use to which yield curves can be put is identifying relative bargains in bonds. Points plotted above the curve represent yields higher than the smooth best-fit to the range of observations, and would mean higher than average yields and a better buy, every-thing else being equal. Observations below the curve represent poorer buys. Of course, everything else may not be equal. For example, tax considerations to be discussed in the next chapter might lead to higher or lower pre-tax nominal yields, in order that after-tax yields would be comparable, and thus give rise to outlying observations.

## Other Factors Which Affect Yields

Another set of factors which may explain differences in yields at any given moment in time are the various non-coupon features that may be attached to bonds.

### (a) Callability

If a bond is callable it means that the borrower has the right to call in the bond before the normal maturity date, and might well do so if market interest rates fell and money could be saved by refinancing. If interest rates have fallen, the prices of already issued bonds would have risen in line with the decline in interest rates, but the rise in price would be limited by the possibility of the bonds being redeemed before their normal maturity date. Consequently, this feature is a disadvantage to the investor and he will demand a premium in the form of a higher yield to offset this. The callable feature is usually deferred for a certain period of time after the bonds are issued, and normally the borrower has to pay a premium upon calling the bonds, the size of the premium declining over time. Concern with this feature is greatest when interest rates are high and expected to fall, and least when interest rates are low and expected to rise.

## (b) Extendibles/Retractables

Another feature which was common in the early 1980s was the possibility of extending or retracting the term to maturity. An extendible bond is one which has a relatively short term when issued, perhaps five years, but which allows the lender to extend the term, perhaps to ten years, if notice is given in time (usually three to six months before the initial maturity date). The Government of Canada issued a number of these extendible bonds in the early 1980s as an added inducement for lenders at a time when the borrowers were having difficulty interesting lenders in bonds. An example would be the 14.5% bonds originally due May 1, 1986, but extendible to May 1, 1991, a bond referred to as Canada 14.5, May 1 86/91. Since investors would be expected to extend the term if current market rates were less than the coupon rate, this means that when the bond is selling at a premium (reflecting the fact that current market interest rates are less than the the coupon rate of interest), the longer maturity date is the proper maturity date to consider, and the effective yield is computed to that date. When the bond is selling at a discount because current market interest rates exceed the coupon rate of interest, the presumption is that the term will not be extended, and the effective yield is computed to the shorter maturity date. In the case of the Canada 14.5, May 1 86/91 referred to earlier, the bond in 1986 was selling at a premium and the vast majority of holders did opt to extend the date of maturity.

A retractable bond is similar except that here the original term of the bond is longer, but the lender can retract the term to maturity if notice is given in time. These bonds are more typically issued by corporations, but once again represent an inducement to attract lenders at a time when there is little enthusiasm for long term bonds. An example was Reichhold Chemical 11.25% bonds due February 15, 1996 but retractable to February 15, 1986 at the holder's option exercisable after June 15, 1985 and prior to December 15, 1985. This bond was referred to as Reichhold 11.25, Feb 15 96/86. As with extendibles, the yield on retractables is computed to the initial or longer maturity date if the bond is selling at a premium, and to the shorter date if the bond is selling at a discount. In the case of the Reichhold bond the coupon rate was close to the market rate at the time that holders had to make their decision, and in the event 69% of the bondholders opted to retract the date of maturity. The bonds were also callable after the retraction date, and the company announced that they were calling in the remainder of the issue in March, 1986 at a price of 105.25 plus accrued interest.

## (c) Convertibles

Still another feature of a bond that might affect its relative yield is the possibility of convertibility. Corporations may issue bonds or debentures that are convertible into the common stock of the company. This privilege normally extends over a period of years, and the terms of conversion into stock involve a price which is initially above the current market value of the stock. Consequently, when the bond or debenture is originally issued, it sells mainly on the basis of the interest coupons, with the possibility of conversion into stock in the future as an added inducement to the investor. If the stock rises in price close to the point where the market price is equal to the conversion price, or in other words the market value of the shares into which the bond or debenture can be converted is equal to the par value of the bond or debenture, the convertible becomes a "two-way" security, where the interest coupons provide a relatively secure return, but there is a prospect for capital gain if the stock continues to rise in value. As a result, the yield on such a bond or debenture may be below that of other bonds or debentures that are otherwise similar. Once the stock rises above the price implicit in the conversion feature, the bond or debenture will sell at a price reflecting the value of the shares into which it can be converted, and consequently this higher price will mean a drop in yield.

The fact that the stock into which the bond may be converted is worth more than the par value of the bond does not guarantee that the bond will in fact be converted, since the yield in terms of interest coupons may be greater than the corresponding yield from dividends, if any, on the stock, a comparison that may be further complicated by tax considerations. Consequently, there may be a call provision in the terms of the bond which allows the borrowing company to effectively force conversion by allowing the company to redeem the bonds in this situation.

In summary, the callable feature is a disadvantage to the investor and should be reflected in a yield which is slightly higher, everything else being equal. Government of Canada bonds are not normally callable. Extendible, retractable and convertible bonds are advantageous to the investor and this should be reflected in yields which are marginally lower when they are issued, everything else being equal. Once they are outstanding and trading in the secondary market, however, these extendible, callable and convertible features will affect prices and therefore yields in the ways described above.

# Note

1   Van Horne, J.C. *Financial Market Rates and Flows* Englewood Cliffs, N.J.: Prentice-Hall, 1978. p.112.

# Further References

Shearer, R.A., Chant J.F. and Bond, D.E. *The Economics of the Canadian Financial System*. Second Edition. Scarborough, Ontario: Prentice-Hall Canada, 1984. Chapter 5, pp.74-87; Chapter 7, pp.125-31.

Van Horne, J.C. *Financial Market Rates and Flows*. Englewood Cliffs, N.J.: Prentice-Hall, 1978. Chapters 3-7

Wood Gundy Securities Limited. *Bond Values*. Toronto: 1968, 1970. (These are yield books which only deal with yields up to 12%.)

CHAPTER THREE

# inflation and taxation

T HE DISCUSSION OF YIELDS IN THE PRECEDING CHAPTER WAS IN TERMS of nominal rates of return. These rates have to be adjusted for inflation and for taxation in order to arrive at the real after-tax rates of return upon which lenders base investment decisions, and the real after-tax costs upon which borrowers base their financing decisions.

## Inflation

If prices are rising, the interest received on money lent does not all represent increased command over resources; some of it simply provides for the maintenance of purchasing power in real terms. Consequently, it is important to distinguish between *real* and *nominal* rates of interest, where the former represent the real increase in purchasing power, while the latter are the rates of interest observable in the marketplace.

It is also important to distinguish between *expected* and *unexpected* inflation. Lenders and borrowers adjust interest rates to take into account the expected rate of inflation. If the actual rate of inflation that occurs is different, this is unexpected inflation. The real rate of interest, then, is the nominal rate of interest minus the expected rate of inflation.[1]

If inflation is correctly anticipated, neither lenders nor borrowers lose. For example, if inflation is expected to be 5% and nominal interest rates are 10%, the real rate of interest is 5%. If inflation turns out to be 5%, as anticipated, lenders receive back a principal amount that has 5% less purchasing power, but also interest of 10%, half of which is a real gain in purchasing power and half of which goes to replace the lost purchasing power of the principal. Borrowers pay back the loan in dollars that are worth 5% less, but they have to make up for this by paying a higher interest rate of 10%, so that their real cost is still 5%.

However, if inflation is not correctly anticipated, and turns out to be higher than expected, borrowers gain and lenders lose. If, in the previous example, prices had increased at a rate of 10% instead of 5%, then the interest payments received by the lender would just make up for the loss of purchasing power of the principal, and there would be no real increase in purchasing power and no real return from lending. Conversely, borrowers would be paying back a total in principal and interest that would be equal to the purchasing power of the money they received at the beginning of the period, and would incur no real cost.

In the above example, one might conclude that the real rate of interest was 0%, but then the question would arise as to why anyone would lend money in this situation. It could be argued that the lender would have been even worse off if he had not lent, since inflation would have still eroded the value of his money and he would have received nothing to offset this. However, it seems more likely that both lenders and borrowers operate on the expectation of positive rates of interest when they enter into the contract. Thus we distinguish between *ex ante* real rates of interest based on expected rates of inflation, with such rates always being positive, and *ex post* real rates of interest based on the actual rates of inflation, which may well be negative.

Since the expected rate of inflation is not observable, *ex ante* real rates of interest, upon which lending and borrowing decisions are based, are not observable. Consequently, the real rates of interest that we often see in the press are really *ex post* real rates, where the actual rates of inflation are subtracted from the nominal interest rates agreed to at an earlier date. This is a crude calculation which tends to make people look stupid or clever, depending upon whether actual inflation exceeds or falls short of expected inflation, and upon whether they are lenders or borrowers.

Clearly, it would be preferable to have a measure of the rate upon which decisions are based. By definition these rates are not observable, but attempts have been made to measure them by estimating expected rates of inflation, either by looking at published estimates of anticipated inflation, or else by inferring the expected rate of inflation as the difference between recorded nominal rates of interest and the historic long run real rate of interest during periods of stable prices. The evidence points to a definite adjustment of nominal interest rates in line with expected inflation, although there are differences of opinion as to how closely this adjustment approaches a one-for-one basis, (that is, every one percentage point change in expected inflation brings a one percentage point change in the nominal interest rate).

The rapid adjustment of nominal rates of interest to expected rates of inflation was emphasized in recent years as a result of the prominent role played by the money supply watchers. Increased acceptance of the doctrines of monetarism in the later 1970s meant increased concern with the rate of growth of the money supply. In more traditional analysis, an increase in the money supply would be expected, at least initially, to lower the rate of interest in line with the laws of supply and demand. Monetarists, however, stressed that any such increase above the long run real growth potential of the economy would give rise to inflation, and that once this inflation is anticipated, there will be a rise in nominal interest rates precisely equal to the expected rate of inflation, so that real rates would not change at all. Consequently, attention was focused on the rate of growth of the money supply as given by the weekly release of statistics by the Federal Reserve Board in the United States, and when the change was felt to be above the amount required for non-inflationary growth, this gave rise immediately to expectations of rising inflation, which in turn caused traders in the bond market to mark down bond prices and thus bring about a rise in interest rates. The effect of changing expectations about inflation was immediately reflected in nominal interest rates in the marketplace, and increases in the money supply increased the rate of interest rather than decreasing it. This phenomenon was exasperating to those in charge of monetary policy, and may have been one of the contributing factors in the decision to abandon strict adherence to monetary growth targets.

A second, slightly different, consequence of persistent and accelerating inflation is sometimes referred to as inflation risk. Rising rates of inflation may cause lenders to lose because of unanticipated inflation; if properly anticipated in the nominal rate there would be no loss. However, even if the current rate of interest correctly anticipates the rising inflation, the value of outstanding bonds issued at lower nominal rates falls as nominal rates rise, and as a result the values of existing portfolios decrease. In this way, accelerating inflation, even if correctly anticipated currently, increases risk, and lenders may require an added premium to offset this risk. On the other hand, they may react to this added risk by avoiding it through not lending on fixed interest terms, particularly in the long term market where the effect of rising interest rates on the prices of outstanding bonds is most marked.

During the 1970s, inflation accelerated so that each new peak of business activity saw prices increase more quickly than the past one, and the level of inflation to which the economy receded in the troughs was at a higher plateau than the one previously experienced. Lenders lost from unanticipated inflation and also from inflation risk, and the memory of these losses seems to have lingered. Rates of inflation decreased sharply from 1983 to 1985, but nominal interest rates did not decline as quickly because of expectations that inflation would once again increase, with further losses from inflation risk. There was a shift from negative *ex post* real rates of interest in the 1970s to *ex post* real rates of interest in the 1980s that were very high by historic standards, with traumatic results for borrowers, whether they were houseowners, corporations or third world governments.

Since lenders clearly lose from unanticipated inflation and from inflation risk, they would benefit from bonds where the rate of interest was tied to some index of price increase, thereby fixing the *ex post* real rate of interest. Such indexed bonds have been introduced in some countries, in particular in England, but they have not yet appeared widely in North America. The first bonds linked to inflation introduced in the United States in January, 1988 carried a real rate of interest of 3%, to which an allowance for inflation was added. Governments could more easily shoulder the risk inherent for the borrowers in not knowing the rate of interest that they will have to pay, but private financial intermediaries could only avoid this risk if they could arrange to have both assets and liabilities similarly indexed. For example, a trust company could issue indexed guaranteed investment certificates and invest the proceeds in indexed mortgages. The fact that private markets have not given rise to such securities may be partially attributable to the difficulties of innovating in two markets simultaneously. Government authorities may resist the introduction of indexed bonds because they feel that they would institutionalize inflation and cause greater acceptance of it. However, the Liberal Party in Canada showed some interest in the idea when borrowers, especially the government, were being penalized by high *ex post* real rates rather than being rewarded by negative *ex post* real rates. In early 1991, the debt managers of the federal government floated the idea of indexed bonds, presumably in the belief that the actual rate of inflation experienced in the future plus a real rate of, say, 3%, would mean lower interest rates than they were then having to pay. However, as of June 1991, nothing had come of the idea.

One recent development of interest here is the introduction of floating rate debentures and preferred shares, where the rate of interest is tied to another rate of interest which moves with the market, such as the banks' prime lending rate. This does not ensure any particular level for the *ex post* real rate of interest, but to the extent that market rates of interest do move in line with inflation, the securities do resemble indexed bonds, and they certainly reduce inflation risk.

## Taxation

Governments at all levels in Canada raise revenue through a myriad of taxes, many of which affect the financial markets in complex ways. There will be no attempt here to provide a complete catalogue of such influences; but a brief introduction will be given to some of the principal ways in which taxes, and in particular income taxes, alter the decisions which borrowers and lenders make.

Where individuals are concerned, personal income tax covers all income, whether earned or from investments, whether Canadian or foreign. A resident of Canada is required to report total income from all sources, and after subtracting certain deductions and exemptions, to compute the tax payable by applying progressively higher rates of tax to the remaining taxable income. Certain tax credits may then be allowable against the tax payable. Tax reforms which became effective in 1988 reduced the number of tax brackets from ten to three, and largely replaced the system of personal deductions and exemptions with a system of tax credits. The exemptions and brackets in the tax schedule are indexed for inflation, although beginning in 1986 this was limited to inflation in excess of 3% per annum. The basic federal tax payable, before any federal surtax, is subject to a further provincial income tax, except in Quebec where there is a separate provincial income tax system.

Since the rates of taxation are progressive, that is they increase in line with the tax base, the rate that affects decision making is the marginal rate—the rate that applies to the last dollar of taxable income. In 1990, the basic maximum rate of federal income tax was 29%, and it applied to all taxable income in excess of $56,550. In addition, there was a surtax of 5% on tax up to $15,000, and an additional 3% surtax thereafter. The provincial income tax in Ontario in the same year was 53% of the basic federal tax, and there was a surtax of 10% on tax over $10,000. Thus the maximum marginal rate, including surtaxes, for residents of Ontario in 1990 was 48.2%.

However, when it comes to computing taxable income, not all income is treated equally. Capital gains, which result from disposing of assets for more than they cost, are not fully taxable. The rationale for this preferential treatment is to encourage risk-taking, and possibly to offset that part of capital gains which simply reflects inflation. There can be little doubt that in Canada it also reflects the fact that until the 1987 tax reform in the United States capital gains there were only taxed at half rates.

From 1971, when capital gains taxation was introduced in Canada, until 1987, only half of those capital gains subject to tax were actually taxable, in effect cutting in half the tax rate on capital gains. Furthermore, in 1985 the Minister of Finance introduced a personal lifetime tax exemption on up to $500,000 of capital gains, to be phased in over the years 1985 to 1990. The reforms introduced in 1987 capped this exemption at $100,000, although it remains at $500,000 for qualified farm property and certain private corporations. Beginning in 1988, two-thirds of capital gains were to be taxable, with the inclusion rate rising to three-quarters in 1990. Assets are deemed to have been disposed of upon death and leaving the country, so that capital gains are subject to taxation for the year in which such events occur. Personal property is subject to capital gains tax within certain rules, the most notable exception being for a principal residence. Capital losses are allowable against capital gains.

The fact that interest income is fully taxable while only part of capital gains is taxable complicates the computation of effective after-tax yields. In the preceding chapter we outlined a way of computing the rough yield on a bond without using a yield book or computer programme, and we found that for a bond maturing in four years with a 10% coupon and priced at 92, the yield was roughly 12.50% (see p. 17). If we assume a marginal rate for federal and provincial taxes combined of 50%, we might be tempted to say that the yield after tax was 6.25%. However, account must be taken of the fact that part of the return here is in the form of a capital gain which is taxed at reduced rates and may not be subject to tax at all.

If we assume that three-quarters of the capital gain is subject to tax, and that the person's marginal rate for federal and provincial taxes combined is 50%, one method for computing the after-tax yield without using a yield book or computer programme would be as follows:

interest income per year after tax $= 10.00$ x $.5 = 5.00$

capital gain per year after tax $= 2.00 - (2.00$ x $.75$ x $.5)$

$$= 2.00 - .75$$

$$= 1.25$$

total return per annum $= 5.00 + 1.25 = 6.25$

value at maturity $=$ maturity value - capital gains tax

$$= 100 - (8.00 \text{ x } .75 \text{ x } .5)$$

$$= 100 - 3.00 = 97.00$$

average of purchase price and value at maturity $= \dfrac{92 + 97}{2} = 94.50$

approximate after-tax yield $= \dfrac{6.25}{94.50}$ x $100 = 6.61\%$

On the other hand, if the person had not exhausted his exemption from capital gains taxation, none of the capital gain portion of the return would be subject to tax, and a rough approximation of the after-tax rate of return might be given by the following computation:

interest income per year after tax = 10.00 x .5 = 5.00
capital gain per year after tax = 2.00
total return per annum = 7.00

$$\text{average of purchase price and value at maturity} = \frac{92.00 + 100.00}{2}$$
$$= 96.00$$
$$\text{approximate after-tax yield} = \frac{7}{96.00} \text{ x } 100 = 7.29\%$$

It can be seen, then, that the after-tax yield on bonds selling at a discount is higher than it would be if we assumed that the total return was subject to tax at a marginal rate of 50%, because the capital gain portion of the return is taxed at lower rates, or not at all. If the capital gain portion is effectively taxed at three-quarter rates the after-tax rate of return is 6.61%, and if the capital gain is completely exempted from taxation, the after-tax rate of return rises to 7.29%.

The greater the proportion of the return in the form of capital gains, the higher the after-tax yield relative to the before-tax yield. It follows that deep discount bonds, which have a substantial capital gain component in their total return, will be particularly appealing to taxpayers in high marginal tax brackets, and this explains why such bonds normally sell at lower effective pre-tax yields than bonds of comparable quality which have higher coupons or shorter terms. Any remaining capital gains exemption will obviously increase still more the attractiveness of such investments. On the other hand, bonds with high coupons selling at large premiums will have a much lower relative after-tax yield, since all the coupon interest is subject to tax, unless the owner has taxable gains against which to write off the capital losses at maturity on such bonds. This comparison was illustrated on page 14 by the case of two Canada bonds with identical maturity dates but very different coupons.

Another provision of the tax act as it affects individuals has important effects on the flow of funds in the capital market. This is the dividend tax credit, which reduces the effective taxation on dividends from Canadian companies, and which therefore raises the after-tax yield on Canadian stocks relative to those on bonds, debentures and non-Canadian stocks. Since this is a tax credit it reduces the tax paid by directly reducing the taxes payable, as opposed to reducing taxable income through increasing deductions.

As of 1990, dividends from eligible Canadian companies were grossed-up, or increased, by 25% when reported as part of taxable income. Then 13 1/3% of the grossed-up amount (or one sixth of the actual dividends paid) was deducted from tax payable. The net result of all this is to reduce the effective tax rate on dividends, and for taxpayers with the top marginal rate, the tax rate is reduced by about one-third on dividends from eligible Canadian companies.

The logic of the dividend tax credit is to integrate the personal and corporate income taxes and avoid double taxation of the same income. Since corporations have to pay taxes on income before paying dividends, tax on the dividends when received by shareholders represents a second levy on the same income. It is also designed to promote risk-taking, particularly with respect to investment in Canadian companies. While at one time the dividend tax credit made it possible to have substantial dividend income without paying any tax at all on it, the reduction of the benefit to one third in 1987 meant that a single person with income only from dividends living in Ontario would be liable for taxes on amounts in excess of approximately $24,000. (Before the 1987 changes the figure had been in the neighbourhood of $45,000.) Moreover, the introduction of the alternative minimum income tax has helped to eradicate this seeming inequity.

The dividend tax credit, then, helps to encourage investment in stocks rather than bonds, and is another factor which helps to explain the higher before-tax nominal yield on bonds compared to stocks, even though the bonds carry less risk. Of course, as previously noted, the fact that yields on stocks are computed on the presently indicated dividend does not allow for any capital gains or increases in dividends, and undoubtedly understates the expected rate of return. The standard rule of thumb in the investment community is that there should be about a 5:4 ratio between nominal yields on bonds and stocks in order to equalize after-tax yields for individuals in the maximum tax bracket. For example, a 10% yield on a bond or debenture is roughly equivalent to an 8% yield on a stock for people paying the maximum marginal rate.

The changes in the way in which different types of investment income have been treated as a result of the tax reforms which became effective in 1988 and 1990 can seen in the following table. It is based on the situation of a person living in Ontario, paying maximum marginal rates including surtaxes, and who has exhausted any capital gains exemption.

|  | 1987 | 1988 | 1990 |
|---|---|---|---|
| interest income | 52.5% | 46.1% | 48.2% |
| dividends from Canadian companies | 35.7% | 31.2% | 32.6% |
| capital gains | 26.3% | 30.8% | 36.2% |

There has been a reduction of rates on both interest and dividend income, which while eroded by surtaxes, has been roughly comparable in proportional terms. The major alteration in relative rates has been the increase in tax on capital gains. This, combined with the capping of the lifetime exemption, represents a distinct shift in philosophy on the part of the government, which introduced the lifetime capital gains exemption in 1985 as a way of encouraging risk-taking. It undoubtedly reflects the influence of the American tax reforms, which now treat capital gains in the same way as other income. One would expect the changes in Canada to have the effect in the capital market of increasing the relative attractiveness of stocks paying high dividends, while decreasing that of growth stocks where profits are re-invested rather than distributed. As well, it will decrease the relative attractiveness of deep-discount bonds for those in maximum tax brackets.

There are also a number of provisions available to taxpayers which allow them to deduct from taxable income contributions made to plans providing for retirement income. A registered pension plan (RPP) is a pension plan run by an employer to which both employers and employees may make contributions, and any such contributions made by an employee are deductible from her income before tax is computed. A deferred profit sharing plan (DPSP) may also be set up by employers as an additional form of compensation for employees in the future, and while contributions to such plans are normally paid by employers and thus deductible as a business expense, they may also be made by employees and are then deductible from their income for tax purposes. A registered retirement savings plan (RRSP) is a plan set up by an individual to provide for income at a later date, and contributions into such a plan are deductible from income for tax purposes up to certain limits. The limits depend upon the amount of earned income, whether or not the person is self-employed, and if an employee, on the amounts paid into other plans and the types of plans they are. There are also provisions for lump sum payments into an RRSP in respect of past service, and such contributions also escape tax in the year in which they are made. An RRSP may be de-registered at any time, but must be terminated in the year in which the taxpayer reaches age 71. When disbursements are made from these plans they are, of course, taxable.

All of these plans place funds in trust with an intermediary. Not only are contributions to such plans deductible from income in the years made within the limits prescribed, but all income earned and capital gains realized on funds invested are not taxed until the plan is terminated and the proceeds disbursed. Consequently, such plans provide for a significant deferral of tax, as well as a reduction of tax payable at the present time. If a taxpayer is at maximum earning power and thus at high marginal rates at the present time, but likely to be receiving less income in the future and therefore subject to tax at lower marginal rates, the total tax payable is reduced, in addition to the saving involved in deferring payment. The result of these provisions, then, is to promote the flow of funds into these vehicles and thus into the capital market.

There are other tax provisions which promote the flow of funds into different types of investment. In Quebec, the Quebec Stock Savings Plan (QSSP) allows residents of that province to claim an income tax deduction for purchases of new equity issues of Quebec-based companies. In 1985 the allowance went from 50% of the value of the shares to as high as 150% for small companies, although it has since been modified. It has been suggested that the federal government should adopt a similar set of incentives.

A slightly different type of plan was the Indexed Securities Investment Plan (ISIP) introduced by the federal government in October, 1983. The objective here was to exempt from taxation that part of any capital gain which only reflected rising prices. Securities placed with an institution under such a plan were to be valued at the end of each year, and from the difference between this value and their cost or their value at the end of the preceding year, was subtracted an amount corresponding to the increase in their value that resulted from inflation. The resulting amount was a measure of real capital gain.

25% of this amount was subject to taxation as a capital gain, whether realized or not, with the remainder of the tax deferred.

For example, if a person held securities in an ISIP which were valued at $10,000 at the beginning of the year and which were valued at $14,000 at the end of the year, and there were 10% inflation during the year, then the real capital gain would be the difference between the two valuations, or $4,000, minus the inflationary factor of $1,000 (10% of the beginning value of $10,000) = $3,000. Under then existing laws half of this amount, or $1,500, would be a taxable capital gain, even though it had not actually been realized in cash, and 25% of this, or $375 would be subject to taxation.

It can be seen that this plan, unlike the RRSPs for example, is not one which defers taxes so much as one that avoids taxation on inflationary capital gains. Indeed, to the extent that it makes tax payable on capital gains even if they are not actually realized but only accrued, it increases taxes in the current period compared with what they would have been in the absence of such an arrangement, although it does defer some part of the taxes if the gains are actually realized. The fact that current taxes might have increased under these plans may have discouraged the movement of funds into ISIPs, and along with the declining rates of inflation experienced after their introduction may explain their limited popularity. In any event, the government repealed the ISIP provisions as of January 1, 1986.

The provisions of the tax act just discussed apply to individuals, but corporations and institutions also provide funds to the capital market and their decisions are affected by the tax provisions as well. For example, Canadian corporations do not pay tax on dividends received from other Canadian corporations, since the funds from which such dividends are paid have already been subjected once to corporate income tax. On the other hand, interest income from investments in other corporations is subject to corporate income tax, since the interest has been allowable as a deduction from income before taxes for the borrowing corporation. Consequently, corporations may be willing to buy preferred shares, the dividends from which escape further tax, at rates well below prevailing yields on bonds and money market instruments, and such shares with dividends tied to a percentage of the banks' prime lending rate were popular for a while; they are an example of the floating rate securities mentioned earlier. Some institutions such as pension funds may not have to pay any tax on investment income if it is held in trust, and for them there is no distinction between pre-tax and post-tax rates of return.

Borrowers are also affected differentially by the tax provisions. Governments, of course, do not pay taxes, but corporations and individuals are affected by the extent to which the expenses of borrowing can be deducted as costs of earning income. As a rule of thumb, the corporate income tax rate approaches 50% in Canada, although there are reductions for manufacturing and processing and even larger reductions for small business, with further complications arising from surtaxes, federal concessions to make way for the provinces, and so on. Corporations can deduct interest expenses from revenues in arriving at taxable income, whereas dividend payments are made out of income after taxes. Consequently, from the tax point of view, debt financing is preferred to equity financing, since $1.00 in dividend payments after taxes is roughly equivalent to $2.00 in interest payments before taxes. This tends to favour the supply of bonds in the market, whereas we have seen that provisions such as the dividend tax credit and the capital gains tax favour the demand for equities, with the result that bonds sell at lower prices and higher yields because of the effects of the tax system on both borrowers and lenders.

On the other hand, individuals may or may not be able to deduct interest expense when arriving at taxable income. Ownership of a house is a major expense for many taxpayers, but in Canada, unlike the United States, interest charges on a mortgage are not deductible from income. Interest costs incurred in earning investment income are deductible from investment income but not from capital gains. At one time, interest on funds borrowed for an RRSP was deductible, but this is no longer the case.

## Inflation and Taxation

In comparing alternatives, then, lenders should try to maximize real after-tax rates of return. If, for example, nominal interest rates are 10%, the expected rate of inflation is 5% and the lender has a marginal tax rate of 50%, the real after-tax rate of return is zero. Since the person has to pay one half of the 10% earned as interest in tax, this leaves only 5%, and this is completely used up in compensating for the loss of purchasing power if prices rise by 5%.

Should the rate of inflation actually experienced rise to 6%, then the *ex post* real rate of interest after taxes would be negative, or -1%. If the expected rate of inflation rose in line with the rate actually experienced, nominal interest rates would rise. In the above example, if the expected rate of inflation rose to 6%, the nominal rate of interest would rise to 11%. However, the real after-tax rate of return would still be negative, since in the 50% tax bracket 5.5% would go in taxes, leaving only 5.5% to compensate for the inflation of 6%. The *ex ante* real rate of return after taxes would be -.5%. In the light of this, one might expect that nominal interest rates would rise more than one-for-one with expected inflation in order to keep real after tax rates of return positive. Yet this has not usually been the case, and this may be partially explained by the fact that not all lenders are subject to maximum tax and some, such as pension funds, are not subject to tax at all. Moreover, some other institutional lenders are constrained to buy bonds regardless of real after-tax yields by regulations that govern their investment practices. Perhaps the interaction of inflation and taxation could be a partial explanation of the continuing high *ex post* real rates of interest in the 1980s, however.

It might be thought irrational to lend money if real after tax rates of return are negative, but of course some return to help offset the loss of purchasing power due to inflation is better than none. However, such circumstances certainly make lenders more reluctant to purchase fixed income securities. A bond with interest indexed to some measure of inflation, or a term deposit offering any positive *ex post* real rate of interest would be attractive in these circumstances, if taxes were only levied on real returns, since whatever the marginal tax rate there would be some return left after taxes.

Borrowers are concerned with after-tax real costs of debt, and here differential tax rates and high nominal interest rates resulting from high rates of expected inflation interact to affect borrowers very differently. For example, (taking a situation which prevailed in late 1981[2]), suppose nominal interest rates were at 22%, inflation was at 12.5% and the tax rates shown are the combined federal and provincial rates prevailing for the class of borrower indicated (see the table on the following page).

| Borrower | Tax Offset | After Tax Cost | After Tax Real Cost |
|---|---|---|---|
| LARGE RETAILER | 48% | 11.4% | -1.1% |
| LARGE MANUFACTURER | 42% | 12.8% | 0.3% |
| SMALL MANUFACTURER | 22% | 17.2% | 4.7% |
| MORTGAGE PAYER | 0% | 22.0% | 9.5% |

Since interest costs are deductible from income for the first three classes of borrowers, the real cost in after-tax dollars is reduced by the percentages indicated as tax offset. If the rate of inflation is then subtracted from the resulting figures, we get the real cost of the debt after taking into consideration both inflation and taxation, and it can be seen that in spite of the very high nominal rates of interest, debt costs were actually negative for at least one class of borrower. This example also shows how inflation and taxation interact to produce distortions in the demand for funds, in this case depressing the demand for housing because of the very high real cost of mortgages. When this occurs, the government may take additional measures to counteract the distortions, and in this case the federal government gave grants and the Ontario government offered interest-free loans to assist people buying homes.

The foregoing are just two examples of how inflation and taxation interact to affect the flow of funds in the capital market. These problems have not been resolved by the tax reforms enacted thus far.

Moreover, the taxation system has been held to discourage both savings and investment. The Economic Council of Canada has argued that taxing income on an annual basis discourages savings, and that taxation of inflationary gains is unfair. If a person could shelter savings from taxation when they are earning high incomes and consequently subject to high marginal rates, and then realize the income later when their earnings and their marginal rates are lower, they would pay lower taxes based on lifetime income, and be inclined to save more. Thus the Council advocates full indexation of tax brackets, deductions and exemptions, and greater provision for registered savings so that income is taxed on a lifetime income basis. They also advocate a lowering of tax rates along with a broadening of the tax base by complete taxation of capital gains.

With respect to corporate taxation they advocate lower and more uniform rates, reduction of capital cost allowances to correspond more closely to actual capital costs, and indexation of other costs by re-establishing the inventory allowance adjustment and restricting interest deductions to real, rather than nominal, expenses. Allowing an inventory allowance adjustment for inflation would increase costs in an inflationary environment, while restricting interest deductions to real, rather than nominal, expenses, would decrease costs. The Council holds that overall this would both encourage investment and lead to reduced distortions in its allocation.

The personal income tax reforms adopted have generally reduced rates, primarily with an eye to being competitive with those in the United States after tax reform there. However, they have not eliminated the distortions that arise from treating capital gains differently from other income, a reform that has been enacted in the United States. There has been provision for an increase in allowable savings under RRSPs for some groups, but this has been done in an attempt to provide equitable treatment of people under different plans, rather than to provide in a substantial way for taxing on a lifetime income basis. Indexation of tax brackets, deductions and exemptions continues to be limited to inflation in excess of 3% per annum, and the Indexed Securities Investment Plan (ISIP) has not been re-introduced. The move away from exemptions to tax credits is progressive, since the benefit is the same dollar amount for all taxpayers, as opposed to a benefit based on marginal rates on exempted amounts, with the benefit being greater the higher the marginal rate.

Corporate income tax rates have also been reduced, once again with an eye to being competitive with the United States, while broadening the tax base by reducing capital cost allowances, which is consistent with the Economic Council's proposals. However, the rates continue to discriminate between types of industry and there is no adjustment for inflation in the form of inventory allowances or restriction of interest deductions to real expenses.

The assumption seems to be that the distortions caused by inflation at present rates are not serious enough to warrant the complications, and revenue loss, introduced by indexation. It is argued that the better course is to eliminate inflation. While this is undoubtedly true in an ideal world, the assumption that inflation at present rates does not introduce serious distortions is questionable, and it is apparent that there will be greater problems if there is, in fact, a resurgence of inflation. If one defines income as an increase in the real wealth of the income owner, and not just what is necessary to maintain the value of existing capital, the taxation system taxes investment income more as inflation rises, so that the real after-tax rate of return on both debt and equity decreases. This policy will have serious implications for the economy if it discourages investment.

# Notes

1   Actually, the value of a sum, 1, at the end of one period, taking into account both the expected rate of inflation and the real rate of interest would be given by $(1+p)(1+i_r)$; where p = the expected rate of inflation; and $i_r$ = the real rate of interest. The resulting product is $1 + p + i_r + pi_r$, and to say that the nominal rate of interest equals the expected rate of inflation plus the real rate of interest ignores the last term which is the product of the two, and which could be significant if the expected rate of inflation were high.

2   This example is taken from an article by John Bossons entitled, "It is the tax system that prevents monetary policy being effective" in the *Globe and Mail Report on Business*. Toronto: 19 October, 1981. p.B2.

# Further References

Economic Council of Canada, *Road Map for Tax Reform: The Taxation of Savings and Investment*. Ottawa: Minister of Supply and Services, 1987.

Grady, P. "Indexation and the Taxation of Business and Investment Income." Discussion Paper No. 283, Economic Council of Canada. Ottawa: 1984.

Jenkins, G.P. "The Role and Economic Implications of the Canadian Dividend Tax Credit." Discussion Paper No. 307, Economic Council of Canada. Ottawa: 1986.

Pesando J.E. *The Impact of Inflation on Financial Markets in Canada*. Montreal: C.D. Howe Research Institute, 1977. Chapters 1, 2.

Shearer R.A., Chant J.F. and Bond, D.E. *The Economics of the Canadian Financial System*. Second Edition. Scarborough, Ontario: Prentice-Hall Canada, 1984. Chapter 7, pp. 132-45.

# CHAPTER FOUR

# the bond market

A BOND MAY BE DEFINED AS A "WRITTEN PROMISE TO REPAY A SPECIFIC sum of money at a fixed time in the future, and to pay interest at a specific rate, secured by a pledge of assets which may be forfeited if interest payments are not made or the loan is not repaid".

There are many different types of bonds, which may be distinguished by the class of borrower or the type of asset pledged as security. Bonds and debentures are usually treated together, although the distinction between them is that bonds are secured by a pledge of specific assets whereas debentures represent a general charge against the borrower. When the federal government borrows money, the instrument issued represents a general charge against the Consolidated Revenue Fund of Canada, and not a pledge of a specific asset such as the Peace Tower. In line with the preceding distinction the securities of the Government of Canada should be called debentures, but they are always referred to as bonds, and thus the classification breaks down as soon as it is applied to the most important borrower. Consequently, we will tend to use the terms bonds and debentures interchangeably.

It is important to distinguish between the primary bond market and the secondary bond market. The primary market is where bonds are originally sold to raise money for governments, corporations, municipalities, religious institutions, hospitals, etc., while the secondary market is where the trading in bonds already outstanding takes place. This secondary market is also called the "over-the-counter" or "street" market, and it enhances the liquidity of bonds by providing a way of transferring the ownership of existing bonds, and by giving a guide to their values. By performing these functions it in turn promotes the primary market, since the initial purchasers will be less reluctant to buy if they know that they can subsequently sell their bonds readily at a fair price. Of course, these functions are performed better for some bonds than others, so that liquidity is high for the bonds of the Government of Canada, but much lower for municipal debentures where the market is much thinner. The secondary market is simply a network of telephone lines, telex machines etc., rather than a physical location like a stock exchange, and in Canada it is concentrated in Toronto, and to a lesser extent in other centres. The secondary market is dominated by institutional trading.

Bond dealers, or investment dealers, work as principals; that is, they own the bonds they buy or sell rather than working as agents on commission. In order to do this, they keep inventories of bonds which are financed in large part with borrowed funds. They quote a price, or bid, which indicates what they are willing to pay for a specific bond, and another price, or ask, which is the price at which they are willing to sell the same bond. For example, a Government of Canada bond might be quoted at 98 ¼ - ½. The difference between the bid and ask prices is the spread, and it constitutes the dealer's margin. The width of the spread reflects the breadth of the market for that bond, the wider the spread the thinner the market.

The basic unit of denomination in bonds is $1,000 par value, but prices are always quoted in relation to 100—that is, as percentages. For example, a bond selling at a discount of 5% is quoted at 95, and a $1,000 bond would cost $950. On the other hand a bond selling at a premium of 5% would be quoted at 105, and a $1,000 bond would cost $1,050. The minimum subdivision in price quotations is normally ⅛, or $1.25 on a $1,000 bond, although sometimes bonds selling close to par value may be priced to the nearest decimal place, for example 99.40. Bonds are identified by the borrower, the coupon rate and the maturity date. For example, Canada 9 ½s of '01 refer to the bonds issued by the Government of Canada bearing 9 ½% coupons and maturing on October 1, 2001.

In the secondary market, the standard trading unit for bonds depends upon the issuer, maturity and type of bond. $250,000 par value is the trading unit for Treasury Bills and Government of Canada bonds maturing in less than one year; $100,000 for Canada bonds with terms of one to three years; $25,000 for longer Canadas, provincial, municipal and corporate bonds and debentures; and $5,000 for convertible debentures or bonds and debentures with warrants, rights, etc. attached. Purchases can, of course, be made in much smaller amounts, and there has been active promotion of Treasury Bills to individual investors in denominations as low as $1,000.

The normal settlement date for bond transactions is the fifth business day after the transaction, except for Government of Canada bonds under three years, which are settled on the next business day and Treasury Bills, which are settled on the same day. Bonds are sold with an adjustment for accrued interest. For example, if a bond with a maturity date of October 1 were purchased on July 25 for settlement on August 1, the purchaser would pay in addition to the purchase price the interest accrued from the last semi-annual interest date on April 1, which in this example would be computed as $122/365$ of the annual coupon (29 days in April, 31 in May, 30 in June, 31 in July and 1 in August).

Bonds may be registered, in which case the ownership is recorded in the books kept by the trust company that acts as transfer agent, and interest is paid by cheque to the registered owner. On the other hand, they may be bearer bonds, in which case they are negotiable by the holder, and interest coupons are attached to the bond. These are clipped and presented for payment on the due dates. A hybrid of these two forms would be bonds registered only as to principal, with interest coupons attached.

There were domestic bond issues in Canada prior to World War I, but there was no significant trading in outstanding bonds. The federal government financed the First World War effort primarily by borrowing, with limited reliance on the newly-introduced income tax, and this helped to develop the Canadian bond market. World War II provided a further stimulus to the market, although about half the war effort in this case was financed by taxes. Between these wars other borrowers entered the market, although the Great Depression limited business. In the first decade after World War II, these other borrowers greatly extended their activities, while the federal government was running budget surpluses and using them to reduce its outstanding debt. However, since 1957, the federal debt has increased in most years, and federal issues of new bonds have almost pre-empted the primary bond market in some years, just as they did during the Second World War, with the feds consistently coming to the market with new issues in excess of a billion dollars a month since 1983.

Millions of dollars

Gross amount as at 31 December

| | 1979 | 1980 | 1981 | 1982 | 1983 | 1984 | 1985 | 1986 | 1987 | 1988 | 1989 |
|---|---|---|---|---|---|---|---|---|---|---|---|
| **Government of Canada direct and guaranteed** | | | | | | | | | | | |
| Canadian dollars only | 50,462 | 56,377 | 68,804 | 81,450 | 94,956 | 109,876 | 129,333 | 137,558 | 158,149 | 169,153 | 168,313 |
| Other currencies | 3,406 | 3,352 | 3,590 | 4,891 | 4,337 | 4,411 | 7,163 | 9,821 | 9,004 | 7,356 | 5,070 |
| **Provincial direct and guaranteed** | | | | | | | | | | | |
| Canadian dollars only | 49,504 | 58,353 | 66,454 | 76,104 | 85,785 | 94,704 | 102,088 | 111,468 | 119,206 | 127,901 | 135,630 |
| Other currencies | 27,135 | 27,788 | 32,589 | 38,644 | 42,545 | 46,971 | 54,933 | 63,710 | 65,816 | 59,510 | 59,287 |
| **Municipal direct and guaranteed** | | | | | | | | | | | |
| Canadian dollars only | 11,974 | 13,070 | 14,470 | 16,457 | 18,152 | 19,525 | 20,273 | 21,482 | 22,384 | 24,229 | 26,046 |
| Other currencies | 4,202 | 4,086 | 4,007 | 4,198 | 3,980 | 4,064 | 4,395 | 4,329 | 3,855 | 3,134 | 2,712 |
| **Corporate Financial** | | | | | | | | | | | |
| Canadian dollars only | 7,584 | 8,020 | 8,657 | 8,194 | 7,984 | 8,074 | 8,326 | 9,806 | 10,011 | 10,658 | 12,567 |
| Other currencies | 4,660 | 5,797 | 7,091 | 8,522 | 9,523 | 10,352 | 14,260 | 21,421 | 24,053 | 27,073 | 29,857 |
| **Non Financial** | | | | | | | | | | | |
| Canadian dollars only | 19,323 | 20,457 | 21,555 | 22,160 | 23,010 | 23,725 | 24,820 | 26,894 | 29,634 | 32,113 | 36,984 |
| Other currencies | 10,335 | 11,657 | 14,603 | 18,262 | 19,353 | 20,885 | 23,788 | 26,485 | 28,279 | 27,414 | 29,868 |
| **Institutions** | | | | | | | | | | | |
| Canadian dollars only | 1,023 | 1,072 | 1,051 | 1,217 | 1,169 | 1,111 | 1,185 | 1,172 | 1,069 | 1,106 | 1,041 |
| Other currencies | 18 | 19 | 18 | 35 | 36 | 37 | 63 | 113 | 94 | 113 | 137 |
| **Foreign debtors** | | | | | | | | | | | |
| Canadian dollars only | 128 | 278 | 342 | 405 | 570 | 770 | 1,140 | 1,139 | 914 | 951 | 851 |
| **Total** | | | | | | | | | | | |
| Canadian dollars only | 139,999 | 157,628 | 181,332 | 205,988 | 231,626 | 257,784 | 287,165 | 309,519 | 341,366 | 366,111 | 381,432 |
| Other currencies | 49,755 | 52,698 | 61,898 | 74,553 | 79,784 | 86,719 | 104,603 | 125,878 | 131,101 | 124,605 | 126,931 |

Source: *Bank of Canada Review*, October 1990.

THE BOND MARKET

The figures on the preceeding page for bonds outstanding give some indication of the relative magnitude of the various classes of borrowers. While the federal government has dominated the primary bond market in Canada in recent years, the provinces in aggregate have accumulated more debt. However, these figures for the federal government do not include Treasury Bills, which have been a major source of its new funds in recent years. If they were included the federal government would have the largest outstanding debt. Corporate, commercial, and financial paper with terms to maturity of less than one year are also excluded.

It can also be seen that the federal government has relied less on foreign currency issues than have the other classes of borrowers, and that consequently the debt of the federal government denominated in foreign currencies is relatively small. The provinces, on the other hand, have consistently issued from a third to more than half of their debt in foreign currencies, while the proportion for companies in recent years has risen to more than two-thirds for financial corporations, and more than half for non-financial ones. This corporate foreign borrowing has the perverse effect of keeping up the value of the Canadian dollar and making it more difficult for Canadian companies to compete internationally. The small entry for foreign debtors results from issues sold in Canada by foreign borrowers such as the World Bank.

In recent years the importance of the United States as a supplier of funds has declined relative to other sources, principally the Euromarkets. The greater use of off-shore financing has been based on more favourable rates of interest, and reinforced by interest rate and currency swaps introduced in the 1980s. An interest rate swap is an arrangement in which two or more borrowers exchange their interest-servicing liabilities, normally trading fixed rate payments for variable rate payments, thereby each paying a lower rate than they would have if they had borrowed independently. A currency swap, on the other hand, involves the exchange between borrowers of the entire borrowing commitment, with the repayment of principal at maturity being re-exchanged at a pre-determined currency rate. These new mechanisms are illustrative of the internationalization of capital markets that has taken place in recent years, and will be discussed in more detail in Chapter Ten.

While Canadian borrowers have relied on capital markets outside Canada, they have raised most of their funds in the Canadian market. However, debt issued in Canadian funds may also be purchased by non-residents, and about one-third of all Canadian bonds, or a total of $179 billion, was held by non-residents at the end of 1990. In recent years, there have been significant foreign purchases of federal government Canadian dollar debt, and 38% is now held abroad. At the end of 1990, the Americans accounted for 30% of foreign holdings of all Canadian bonds, while the rapidly-increasing share held by the Japanese stood at 25%.

Bonds issued by Canadian entities denominated in foreign currencies, as well as those denominated in Canadian dollars but held by foreigners, are both in a sense foreign debt. However, the former require foreign currency to service the debt while that latter do not, so that the fact that a high proportion of the Canadian debt is held by foreigners does not imply the same potential for debt servicing difficulties as that faced by many third world countries, whose debt is almost entirely denominated in foreign currencies. Of course, if foreign bondholders choose to sell their Canadian bonds and repatriate the proceeds, or to repatriate the proceeds upon payment at maturity, this may cause balance of payments difficulties and downward pressure on the Canadian dollar. Moreover, it should also be remembered that Canadian holdings of debt of other countries have also grown with the internationalization of the capital market, so that foreign assets have grown along with foreign debt. For example, holdings of foreign currency by the federal government greatly exceed the foreign currency liabilities of the federal government, so the government of Canada, in this sense, does not have a net foreign debt.

The figures below for net new issues placed in 1989 and 1990 give net amounts of money raised after repayments through all the major issues of primary securities by Canadian borrowers, and by foreign borrowers in the Canadian market, in those years. Here the dominance of federal government borrowing is apparent. This figure does include Treasury Bills, but as it is net new issues it does not include new money borrowed to pay back outstanding bonds. If it did, that would make the federal government figure even higher relative to the others. The sharp decrease in new issues in 1990 reflects the depressed economy, and there is also a greater reliance on the American market which is a reversal of the trend of recent years to rely more on Euromarket financing.

The figures on net new issues indicate that for all borrowers in the aggregate, bonds are a much more important source of funds than stocks in the primary market, and the value of trade in outstanding bonds in the secondary market is also greater than that in stocks listed on the

| *Net New Security Issues Placed in Canada and Abroad:* | | |
|---|---|---|
| | (millions of dollars) | |
| | *1989* | *1990* |
| Government of Canada | $22,799 | $21,847 |
| Provinces | 10,704 | 11,877 |
| Municipalities | 1,492 | 380 |
| Corporations — Bonds | 13,868 | 9,007 |
| Corporations — Stocks | 13,519 | 4,449 |
| Other Institutions and Foreign Debtors | -140 | 11 |
| Short Term Paper | 7,883 | 1,263 |
| **Total** | $70,126 | $48,835 |
| | | |
| Of which placed in: Canada | $62,715 | $38,716 |
| U.S.A. | 1,729 | 9,644 |
| Other | 5,683 | 475 |
| **Total** | $70,126 | $48,835 |

Source: *Bank of Canada Review*, April, 1991. Table F5.

Canadian exchanges, in spite of the latter's higher profile. For example, figures from the Canadian stock exchanges for 1990 put the value of stock exchange trading at $84.1 billion, while figures from the Investment Dealers Association valued trading in bonds and debentures in 1990 in the Canadian secondary market at $640.3 billion.

## Government of Canada Bonds

The Government of Canada borrows money to repay maturing debt and to make up the difference between its expenditures and its revenues, that is, to cover the budget deficit. If the budget is in surplus there will be no need to borrow for fiscal reasons, and the surplus may be used to help repay maturing debt. However, even in these circumstances it is unlikely that the Government will avoid new borrowing entirely, since the need to repay maturing debt will normally outrun any budget surplus. Since the Government usually just rolls over maturing debt, paying back the oustanding issues with the proceeds from new issues, gross debt issues for this reason alone are substantial, and when there is also a large deficit, as there has been in recent years, new Government issues

*Government of Canada Debt as of December 31, 1990:*

|  | (millions of dollars, par value) |
| --- | ---: |
| Treasury Bills | $135,400 |
| Bonds under 3 years to maturity | 42,216 |
| Bonds 3-5 years | 26,827 |
| Bonds 5-10 years | 31,383 |
| Bonds 10 years and over | 42,196 |
| **Total** | $278,022 |
| | |
| Loans, drawings under standby facilities and U.S. pay "Canada Bills" | 1,122 |
| Non-market securities: | |
| Canada Savings Bonds | 34,406 |
| Other | 3,494 |
| Matured and Outstanding | 45 |
| **Total** | $317,087 |

Average term to maturity of marketable debt — 4 years: 0 months

Source: *Bank of Canada Review*, April, 1991. Table G6

*Who Holds this Debt?*

| | |
| --- | ---: |
| Bank of Canada | $20,364 |
| Chartered Banks | 19,456 |
| Government of Canada Accounts | 5,116 |
| General Public—Canadian residents | 201,298 |
| —Non-residents | 70,854 |
| **Total** | $317,087 |

Source: *Bank of Canada Review*, April, 1991. Table G5.

dominate the market. We have already noted how the federal government's securities account for the majority of new issues in the primary market; they also account for the majority of trade in outstanding issues in the secondary market.

The figures in the preceeding table show the Government of Canada marketable debt, divided between Treasury Bills and bonds ranged according to term-to-maturity, as well as non-market sources of funds and bank loans. The major non-market securities are Canada Savings Bonds, which will be discussed below, while the bank loans, drawings under stand-by facilities and U.S. pay "Canada Bills" usually arise from the need for American dollars with which to intervene in the foreign exchange market in support of the Canadian dollar.

The various securities issued by the federal government are obligations of the Government of Canada, but the Bank of Canada is very much involved in their sale and distribution. Since the Bank may also buy the Government's securities, and in the final analysis might be forced to do so if they could not find any other buyers, the Government can always sell its securities and thus find the money to repay maturing debt. It is in this sense that the Government's securities are free of the risk of default. However, if the Bank of Canada buys up Government of Canada bonds they increase the money supply in the process. If this is done in an excessive manner it will lead to inflation, with the result that the money used to repay maturing debt will be worth considerably less in terms of real purchasing power than the money originally lent.

The Bank of Canada acts as debt manager for the Government, advising it on the terms of new issues, including the coupon rates of interest, the terms to maturity and the actual selling prices, which may not be exactly at par. To do this the Bank must know the maturity structure of the existing debt, the preferences of potential buyers of the bonds as to term, and the state of the market at the time of issue, in order to determine a price which will allow the bonds to be sold but which will not be any lower than necessary. The Bank delivers new bonds, redeems outstanding and maturing issues, pays interest, registers bonds and acts as a transfer agent. It also manages the Purchase Account, which buys up outstanding bonds as they approach maturity in order to facilitate the refunding of this debt.

Treasury Bills are short-term debts of the Government of Canada and the provincial governments, with maturity dates up to one year. As such they are part of the money market and will be dealt with in the following chapter. It will be sufficient here to note that the Government of Canada auctions Treasury Bills at a competitive tender each week, normally on Thursday. As can be seen from the preceding figures, this constitutes a significant, and what is more, a rapidly growing component of the federal debt. In recent years, the federal government has increasingly frequently auctioned bonds to the primary distributors, feeling that this is a cheaper method of financing its requirements than to pay commissions. The federal government also engages in interest rate swaps, both in international markets, and beginning in 1988, in the domestic Canadian market.

The Government comes to the bond market at least once a month with a new issue of bonds, the proceeds of which may be used to roll over maturing debt or for the general purposes of the Government of Canada. When it is a fixed-price offering, the Government will give an indication of when it plans to come to the market, and the Bank of Canada will give a few days' advance notice of the terms of the issue to the financial community. On the actual date of the offering, usually a Tuesday, the Bank of Canada informs the banks and investment dealers, who are the primary distributors, of the prices of the bonds and the amount that they have been allotted. In some cases, the primary distributors are allowed to apply for additional bonds in proportion to their original allotment.

As an example of this process we can look at the the issue of $1,700,000,000 of bonds dated offered Tuesday, June 18, 1991 for settlement on July 1. The issue was in four different maturities, to appeal to the preferences of different buyers, and the division of the total between the various maturities is decided upon according to the response of the market, but within stated limitations. The bonds offered in this case were:

- 9.25% bonds due December 15, 1994, priced at 99.40 to yield 9.45%
- 9.25% bonds due October 1, 1996, priced at 98.40 to yield 9.64%
- 9.75% bonds due December 1, 2001, priced at 98.90 to yield 9.93%
- 9.75% bonds due June 1, 2021, priced at 96.55 to yield 10.12%

The Bank of Canada agreed to buy a minimum of $100 million. The bonds were non-callable, as is normally the case with Canadas.

The coupons on these bonds ranged from 9.25% to 9.75%, increasing with term to maturity in line with the yield curve which was in existence at the time, but the bonds had to be priced sufficiently below par to bring the effective yield up in each case. These prices proved relatively attractive, and all of the bonds were sold by the end of the day. However, as reported in the press the next day, some of the bonds were simply being held in inventories, in the hope that interest rates would fall and quick capital gains could be realized, rather than being in the hands of investors who wished to retain them. It was later announced that the division of the issue between maturities was (in millions of dollars) 25, 75, 950 and 650 from the short term to the long term respectively.

### Canada Savings Bonds

Treasury Bill auctions are a weekly event; auctions of other bonds occur at regular intervals; fixed-price offerings are now occurring less frequently; and the other major sale of government debt in the form of Canada Savings Bonds is an annual event, with the bonds dated November 1 of each year, and the annual interest payments made on that date.

Canada Savings Bonds are a unique type of security in a number of ways. They grew out of the Victory Bonds which were issued during the Second World War to help tap the savings of individuals to finance the war effort. They are consequently designed for individual investors, although trusts and estates may hold them under certain conditions. The purchasers must be resident Canadians, and the amount they are allowed to purchase is limited, although the limitation has ranged from as little as $1,000 to as high as $75,000 of purchases additional to present holdings of maturing issues. While they are always redeemable at par, they cannot be sold to anyone else, and thus are non-marketable.

The bonds have been in two forms since 1977, both of which are registered at the Bank of Canada. Regular interest bonds have annual interest paid by cheque to the registered owner, or by direct deposit into the registered owner's deposit account. Compound interest bonds provide for the interest to accumulate and earn additional interest, with the whole amount of interest and principal payable at maturity. However, tax is payable on the interest at least as often as the end of every three years. Compound interest bonds are available by instalment purchase at some places of employment. If Canada Savings Bonds are redeemed before maturity, interest is paid up to the end of the month preceding the date of redemption, except in the first three months after purchase. In the case of compound interest bonds, compound interest begins to accrue one year and one month after the date of issue, so that if this type of bond is cashed after that time, the holder gets the compound interest accrued to the end of the preceding month.

The normal pattern of CSB holdings was for there to be a sharp rise each November 1 when a new issue was sold, and a gradual decline thereafter until the next November 1, as holders cashed in bonds to make major purchases or meet emergency needs, in line with the design of the bond as a savings vehicle for individuals. However, when rates of interest in the market rose markedly in the 1980s, holders often cashed in the bonds and reinvested the proceeds at more attractive rates of interest, especially in Treasury Bills. Given the large proportion of the federal debt held in this form, the potential for a really significant cash drain forced the Government to raise the rate of interest payable on Canada Savings Bonds during the year to forestall redemption.

The interest rate paid on the bonds was traditionally somewhat above the best rate that could be obtained on savings deposits at financial institutions, for that was the holding with which Canada Savings Bonds were thought to be most directly competitive. However, with the increase in sales of Treasury Bills to individual investors, the rate on CSBs was for a while kept more or less in line with the T-Bill rate. Now, as the government has come to rely less on this type of financing, the interest rate has gone back to being competitive with other savings instruments. Since the price of Canada Savings Bonds cannot vary from par, interest rate changes have to be substituted for the price changes that occur with marketable bonds. What has evolved is a bond cashable at par with a rate of interest that may go up if market rates rise, but which will not go below the guaranteed minimum. However, in recent years, the government has only guaranteed the rate for the current year.

In order to market CSBs the rate has to be set in advance of November 1, and the government has sometimes found itself promising rates that turned out to be excessively generous. In 1981, the rate was set at 19.5% two months in advance of November 1, and by the time the bonds were actually sold this was about 2% higher than needed. Since this rate was offered not only on new bonds but also on existing ones to forestall conversion, this mistake cost taxpayers hundreds of millions of dollars. In 1987, the government waited until two weeks before the date of issue to set the rate of interest at 9%, but was still caught by a dramatic decline

Changes in Canadian dollar Government of Canada securities outstanding, 1986-90

Billions of dollars (par value)

|  | 1986 | 1987 | 1988 | 1989 | 1990 |
|---|---|---|---|---|---|
| Treasury bills | +10.3 | +4.5 | +20.9 | +25.5 | +14.9 |
| Marketable bonds | +11.3 | +11.2 | +11.0 | +9.9 | +15.6 |
| Canada Savings Bonds | −4.3 | +8.6 | −0.5 | −10.8 | −8.1 |
| Total | +17.3 | +24.3 | +31.4 | +24.6 | +22.4 |

Table 2

Proportion of debt

|  | 1986 | 1987 | 1988 | 1989 | 1990 |
|---|---|---|---|---|---|
| Treasury bills | 33.9% | 32.3% | 36.4% | 42.2% | 43.9% |
| Marketable bonds | 44.1% | 44.3% | 43.2% | 42.9% | 44.9% |
| Canada Savings Bonds | 22.0% | 23.4% | 20.4% | 14.9% | 11.2% |
| Total | 100.0% | 100.0% | 100.0% | 100.0% | 100.0% |

Source: Bank of Canada, *Annual Report*, 1990, p. 41.

THE BOND MARKET

in interest rates resulting from the injection of liquidity into the system by central bankers to counteract the potentially disastrous effects of the Stock Market Break of October 19. That year, CSBs became the most attractive investment around, and the government then limited purchases of the new issues to $20,000 per person.

CSBs are a relatively expensive way of raising money, since sales agents are given generous commissions. This cost, combined with consideration of the other problems outlined has led the government to place less reliance on Canada Savings Bonds. The relative changes can be seen in the above table. The proportion accounted for by CSBs has been cut in half, while Treasury Bills now account for a much larger proportion. One consequence of this is that the average term to maturity of the marketable debt has been greatly reduced, standing at just 4 over years at the end of 1990. When short term rates rise, this can greatly increase the cost of servicing the debt, and this was the government's fate in the later 1980s as the yield curve became inverted. On the other hand, when short term rates fall as they have dramatically in 1991, this has a pronounced beneficial effect on the cost of servicing the debt.

Canada Savings Bonds are by now an institution in Canada, and as long as there is a ready market for them, the Government will undoubtedly continue to tap that market, even if less agressively than in the past. Moreover, the fact that there is a ready market for this type of vehicle has led some of the provinces to introduce provincial savings bonds, including British Columbia and Quebec in 1988.

## Provincial Government Bonds

As shown earlier, the provinces issued more than 10 billion dollars of new securities over and above refundings in 1989 and 1990. They are an important supplier of bonds to the bond market. Traditionally, the provinces borrowed mainly in the longer term and primarily for capital purposes, but continuing budget deficits have caused them to tap the short-term market in recent years, and most of the provinces issue Treasury Bills, some on a weekly basis. The provinces also guarantee the securities of provincially-owned utilities. For example, Ontario guarantees the bonds of Ontario Hydro. The provinces have frequent recourse to foreign bond markets. Quebec, for example, has a longstanding relationship with the New York market, and many of the provinces have in recent years tapped the Euromarkets.

Provincial bonds may be sold by competitive tender, but more commonly the selling is done through a fiscal agent. The agent, or agents, are investment dealers who normally have a permanent advisory relationship with the province concerned. They form a banking group, or syndicate, to underwrite the issue and perhaps also a selling group to achieve even wider distribution. This process will be explained more fully in the section below on underwriting.

Unlike the Government of Canada, the provincial governments do not have captive central banks and the assurance of a market for their bonds that goes with this. Consequently, they can only borrow money as long as they can find someone to buy their securities, and they are not free from the risk of default. Indeed, Alberta defaulted during the 1930s. Consequently, the yields on provincial issues start above those on Government of Canada issues, and the differences in yields reflect the credit ratings of the provinces. These ratings depend in turn upon the amount of debt per capita already outstanding, income per capita and the fiscal management of the province. Alberta, even with a record of default in its history, attained a high rating by virtue of its very low outstanding debt after not having had to borrow for many years. Newfoundland has traditionally had a low standing, but this has been enhanced somewhat by the Hibernia oil discovery off its coast. Ontario usually has the highest credit rating, but it lost its AAA rating November 1985, regained it in July 1988, and had it taken away again in 1991 when the government budget projected a record deficit.

## Municipal Debentures

As the earlier figures illustrated, municipal debentures account for a relatively small part of the bond market. This is true of the primary market, although the figures for new issues of provincial bonds include municipal debentures guaranteed by the provinces. The relative insignificance of municipals is even more pronounced in the secondary market, so that municipal debentures are quite illiquid securities. The purchasers of municipals are mainly institutions, although a municipality may sell some of its own securities to local individuals in the over-the-counter market. Often municipalities borrow from a provincial municipal loan fund, in which case the issue requires provincial approval. The bigger municipalities may use fiscal agents, and they may also have recourse to the New York market or the Euromarkets. Smaller municipalities usually sell their securities through competitive tender.

Often municipal debentures come in serial form, with a portion of the principal coming due each year over, say, a twenty year period. The maturities may not be evenly spaced, with the result that there could be a larger amount, or "balloon," coming due at the final maturity. The rationale behind the serial bond is to appeal to the preferences of different buyers, so that banks and trust companies might purchase the shorter maturities, while life insurance companies and pension funds might be interested in the longer terms. The need to pay back a certain amount of the loan each year also serves to impose fiscal prudence on the municipality.

Yields on municipals normally start above those on provincials, and reflect credit ratings which are based on taxable assessments, type of industry, population patterns, fiscal management, etc. However, there may be anomalies in the yields, such as in Nova Scotia and New Brunswick. In these provinces provisions of the Trustee Act have forced certain institutions to buy municipal debentures, thereby providing a captive market for these borrowers, and keeping municipal yields below corresponding provincial yields.

## Corporate Bonds and Debentures

Corporations have a variety of ways of raising money, and usually issue bonds or debentures to finance the acquisition of capital assets having a relatively long life expectancy. Since bond interest is deductible as an expense from income for tax purposes, while dividends are paid out of after-tax earnings, debt is viewed by corporations as a cheaper way of raising money, as long as they are making profits. However, the interest on debt must be paid and the principal repaid, regardless of earnings, so that too great a debt load relative to equity can cause problems for a company in times of reduced earnings; a highly levered capital structure can cause a company to come to grief. This lesson is always most evident during times of depression, and many Canadian companies went into receivership in the 1930s. An example would be Abitibi Paper.

Traditionally, short term funds for financing inventories and receivables are provided by bank loans, while longer term financing is provided by bonds and debentures, but if lenders are reluctant to enter the long term bond market, firms may have to go to the banks for longer term credit. However, this type of longer term loan is usually made at variable rates of interest, just like short term credit, which is tied to the prime rate. When interest rates rose dramatically in the early 1980s, many firms experienced great difficulty in servicing this debt. More recently, the trend has been to securitization, as markets have been developed for a variety of instruments that permit the ultimate borrower to bypass banks and other financial intermediaries and to borrow directly from lenders.

The various types of bonds issued by corporations can be distinguished by the type of security pledged. First mortgage bonds are secured by the pledge of property and equipment, while second mortgage bonds may be secured by the same assets, but with the provision that in the event of default the obligations to the first mortgage bondholders are satisfied before the second mortgage bondholders get anything. Collateral trust bonds would be issued with a pledge of financial assets as security, while equipment trust certificates might have as security the rolling stock of a railway.

Corporate bonds and debentures have a number of features in addition to the basic security backing them. Most corporate bonds are callable, and to make bonds more saleable in the reluctant markets of the early 1980s many were given a retractable feature whereby the lender could shorten the term to maturity if interest rates rose in the interim. This is similar to the extendible feature that was more common with Government bonds. One effect in both of these cases is to reduce the original yield below what would have been necessary to sell the bond in the absence of these features, as discussed above in Chapter Two. The retractable feature can also be viewed as an offset to the callable feature in that, when a bond is both retractable and callable, both the lender and the borrower are able to shorten the term to maturity if interest rates move to their advantage. Corporate debentures may also be convertible into stock of the company, with effects on yield as discussed in Chapter Two.

Another feature designed to help sell corporate bonds and debentures, is to attach warrants to them. Warrants provide the holder with the opportunity to buy additional securities of the company. Warrants might also be attached to other securities, such as preferred shares, in which case they could confer the right to buy stocks or bonds, and they could even provide the right to purchase the securities of some other company. An example would be the issue of preferred shares by Canadian Utilities in 1982 that carried warrants to purchase common shares of Transalta Utilities. The purpose of this was to allow Canadian Utilities to comply with a court order to get rid of its interlocking shareholding with Transalta Utilities. When the warrants confer the right to buy common stock, it is usually on the basis of one share for each warrant. When warrants to buy stock are issued with a bond or debenture, the price of the stock on the market is normally below the price at which the stock can be purchased with the warrant, so that the warrant has no intrinsic value. However, the warrant is usually valid for several years and thus has a time or speculative value which provides an added inducement to buy the bond or debenture. Warrants can be separated from the security to which they are attached and traded independently in the stock or over-the-counter markets where there are price quotations for them. Since warrants confer the right to purchase shares worth many times the value of the warrant, warrants possess a great deal of leverage and hence speculative appeal. Because of this, they trade above their intrinsic value, but will approach this value, if any, as they approach their expiry date and lose their time value.

Another important provision with many corporate bonds and debentures is the sinking fund. This is an arrangement which ensures that the corporation is putting aside each year a certain amount towards meeting the cost of repayment. The corporation is required to deposit each year with the trustee a certain amount of money which can be accumulated in order to redeem the bonds at maturity, or else used to redeem each year a certain number of bonds drawn by lot by the trustee. The corporation may also be able to meet its obligation by presenting a certain number of bonds, and will do this if they can purchase the bonds in the market below their par value. Alternatively, the trustee could use funds to purchase bonds in the marketplace if this were cheaper than drawing by lot for redemption at par, and if the bonds were available.

It would be impossible to give all the different features that corporate bonds and debentures might possess, and new wrinkles are continually being devised to make securities more attractive. As we have seen, accelerating inflation makes lenders wary of buying fixed income securities since they may lose from unanticipated inflation as well as inflation risk. Corporations have added such features as retractability, convertibility and warrants to bonds and debentures to overcome this reluctance. An even more recent development is a feature that allows investors to cash in their bonds if a hostile takeover looms against the company that issued the debt. Since acquirers typically incur heavy debt when they buy a company or the company increases its debt to resist the takeover, the ratings on the company's existing debt are downgraded, the market value of outstanding bonds falls, and potential lenders seek protection against this possibility. Still another recent innovation is notes and debentures issued by oil companies with interest payments tied to the price of oil. Assessing the merits of all these features and such other provisions as callability and the risk of default is a complex job, but it is essential to making an informed investment decision.

## Underwriting

Underwriting is the process in which investment dealers bring a new issue of securities to the primary market and accept the risk of getting them sold. The securities might be bonds, debentures, preferred stock, common stock, or some package, usually called units, containing various of these elements. As we are discussing the bond market here, we shall describe the process in terms of a corporate bond underwriting.

The lead underwriter will advise the corporation as to the type of issue which is best suited to its requirements and the state of the market at the present time. The investment dealer who is to be the lead underwriter may have a long-standing relationship with the corporation based on past underwritings and may be represented on the company's Board of Directors. Once it is decided to make a public offering of securities a prospectus is required by law. There are different prospectus requirements for each of the jurisdictions in which the securities are to be sold, but if the requirements of, say, Ontario are met, the other provinces will normally accept this as meeting their requirements.

A preliminary prospectus may be issued outlining the type of issue and some of the information on it, and this could be used by the investment dealer to gauge interest in the issue. However, a final prospectus containing detailed information is required, and this information must include complete details on the terms of the issue, its price, the margin to the underwriter, complete information on the operation of the company, its officers and Directors, and financial statements including *pro forma* balance sheets which show the finances of the company after the securities have been sold. The purpose of the prospectus is to provide complete and detailed information to the potential investor in order to facilitate an informed investment decision. However, the result is usually a rather daunting document the size of a small book, couched in technical and legal jargon. Moreover, the requirement for a full prospectus greatly increases the time and expense of selling securities. Consequently, there was a move in 1982 toward a short form of prospectus called a prompt offering prospectus (POP) which may be used in conjunction with the filing of an annual information form, and which simplifies and streamlines this procedure.

Another important document that is required with a bond issue is a trust deed, which is drawn up between the borrower and a trust company acting on behalf of the bondholders. This trust deed sets out the details of the security being pledged, the restrictive covenants which limit the borrower's ability to buy and dispose of assets or issue further securities, the provisions for the seizure of assets in the event of default, the sinking fund requirements, provisions for redemption and transfer of the securities, and other similar information.

The lead underwriter will form a syndicate, known as the banking group, to share in the underwriting risk. If wider distribution is desired, additional firms will be invited to assist without sharing in the underwriting risk; they are known as the selling group. This group could include banks or any of the investment dealers in Canada. The compensation to each of the groups involved in the process of selling the securities will vary according to their reponsibility and the risk undertaken. For example, the borrowing corporation might receive $98.50 for every $100 par value of bonds sold to the public. The banking group might get their bonds for $98.75, with the difference between this and the proceeds to the borrower going to cover expenses of the syndicate. The selling group, in turn, might pay $99.25 for their bonds, the higher price and margin reflecting their smaller risk, since they only take the bonds which they can sell and have no obligation beyond this. The total margin between the price the public pays and the proceeds to the borrower in this example, assuming the bonds are sold at par, would be 1.5%. The usual margin on a public offering in Canada is the range of 1.5%-2.5%.

The lead underwriter in conjunction with the banking group will decide upon the division of the issue between the various groups. Some portion will be set aside for exempt institutions, who are exempt in the sense that they will be approached by one member of the syndicate on behalf of the whole banking group. Another portion will be set aside for the selling group and the remainder will be left for the banking group. However, the members of the banking group are responsible for the whole issue according to their proportional participation, and share in expenses and in the profits from sales to exempt institutions as well as those from sales by the selling group, in proportion to this participation.

If the bonds are not all drawn down, the head of the syndicate may allot them, or create a "pot," and allow members of the group to sell all the bonds they can, drawing them down as needed. The members of the banking group and selling group sign agreements which ensure that they do not offer bonds for sale below the agreed price. There are other terms to these agreements along with a penalty clause for any violation of them. Such agreements, of course, constitute an agreement to fix prices, a practice which is normally illegal in Canada under the Competition Act, but for which there is a specific exemption in the case of underwriting securities. The lead underwriter, on the other hand, is allowed to buy bonds or sell them short in the market in order to offset speculation and stabilize the market, in this way facilitating the sale of the issue. In the event that the bonds simply cannot be sold at the issue price even after a reasonable period of time, the lead underwriter may have to release the banking group from the terms of their agreement and allow the sale of the bonds at whatever price is possible.

Participation in banking groups is jealously guarded, and the division of the issue can be very contentious. When the issue is formally announced in the financial press in an advertisement known as a "tombstone," the first names on the list of investment dealers responsible for the underwriting are those of the lead underwriter(s), and then come the members of the banking group listed in order of their proportional share from top to bottom and from left to right. The financial community is acutely conscious of the pecking order displayed and any changes in it. Such advertisements often appear only as a matter of record after the issue has been sold, rather than as an attempt to attract orders, and then a statement to that effect will appear in the advertisement.

An example of such a tombstone is shown, in this case for an issue of common shares sold in Canada and the United States. The syndicate leader is Nesbitt Thomson, the other members of the banking group are shown in larger type, and the selling group in smaller type, descending

New Issue

# TransCanada PipeLines Limited

## 15,500,000 Common Shares

Price: $17.25 per share

### 9,750,000 Common Shares

This portion of the offering is being offered in Canada by the undersigned.

Nesbitt Thomson Inc.

Burns Fry Limited     ScotiaMcLeod Inc.

RBC Dominion Securities
Inc.
   
Wood Gundy
Inc.
   
Gordon Capital
Corporation

Bunting Warburg Inc.     Midland Walwyn Capital
Inc.
   
Richardson Greenshields
of Canada Limited

Dean Witter Reynolds
(Canada) Inc.
   
Deacon Barclays de Zoete Wedd
Limited
   
First Boston Canada
Limited

First Marathon Securities
Limited
   
Lévesque Beaubien Geoffrion
Inc.
   
Peters & Co.
Limited

### 5,750,000 Common Shares

This portion of the offering is being managed in the United States by the undersigned.

Morgan Stanley & Co.
Incorporated

Goldman, Sachs & Co.

Salomon Brothers Inc

June 1991

in importance from top left to lower right. The simultaneous offering in both countries and the participation of foreign-owned firms are recent developments that reflect the increasing internationalization of the securities business (discussed in more detail in Chapter Eleven).

While underwriting is the traditional method of selling securities in the primary market, more than half of the new issues are now either "bought deals" or private placements. In a private placement, the securities pass directly from the borrower to a small number of institutional lenders. This will be arranged by an investment dealer, but with a lower margin for his efforts because of the reduced risk. Since the purchasers are institutions and presumed to be informed buyers, the borrowers may be excused from providing a prospectus, and this saving, along with the lower margin for the dealer, makes the private placement a less expensive way of raising money if the size of the issue and the reputation of the borrower make it a possibility.

The "bought deal" has been a very important and innovative development in recent years. In this case, a single investment dealer, or a small group of dealers, simply buys the complete issue of securities from a borrower, probably in conjunction with a prompt offering prospectus, and accepts the risk of reselling it. This has cut the cost of floating new issues and greatly heightened competition in the primary bond market in Canada. One of the consequences of this development is the need for the security firms themselves to attract capital, since additional equity is required to elicit the loans necessary to provide the capital to finance these acquisitions. The need for increased capital and the consequences for the ownership of investment firms are also discussed further in Chapter Eleven.

# Further References

Freedman, C. "Aspects of Securitization." *Bank of Canada Review*, January, 1987. pp. 5-16.

Fullerton, D.H. *The Bond Market in Canada*. Toronto: Carswell, 1962.

Government of Canada. *1964 Report of the Royal Commission on Banking and Finance*. Ottawa: Queen's Printer, 1964. Chapter 16.

"Some Developments in Financing and Capitalization of Non-Financial Business in Canada." *Bank of Canada Review*, December, 1986. pp. 3-23.

66

## CHAPTER FIVE

# the money market

WHILE THE TERM "MONEY MARKET" IS SOMETIMES USED BY CASUAL observers to refer to the whole capital market, within the capital market the use of the term refers specifically to the short term end of the market for fixed income securities. It might be defined as the market for government bills and bonds up to three years to maturity and other fixed income securities with terms up to one year, but it is centred on securities with terms of less than one year.

The Bank of Canada is a central institution in the money market. After it was established in 1935 it traded with the chartered banks in Treasury Bills, which had been sold at tender by the Government of Canada for the first time in 1934. However secondary trading in these securities was very limited, with few transactions between the chartered banks, and investment dealers only buying Treasury Bills very occasionally on orders from their customers.

The money market really only developed in Canada after 1953-4 as a result of certain institutional changes initiated by the Bank of Canada. A number of investment dealers were authorized by the central bank to be eligible for lender of last resort facilities at the Bank of Canada, in order to encourage them to hold inventories and trade in money market securities. At the same time the chartered banks instituted a new type of loan called a day-to-day loan, or simply day loan, which was available only to these authorized money market dealers, or jobbers, to finance their inventories of securities in the ordinary course of business. The dealers could borrow from the banks against certain specified money market securities up to the limits of their lines of credit at the central bank, and these loans could be terminated by either party by noon on any business day for repayment by three o'clock that same afternoon. The loans were impersonal, and termination of them by the banks did not indicate that the banks considered the dealers unworthy of credit. Rather the banks would call the loans in order to bolster their cash reserves if they were near or below the statutory minimum required under the Bank Act. Since these loans could be called for payment the same day, with the cheque being cleared the next day and being added to the bank's cash reserves at the Bank of Canada, day-to-day loans were only 24 hours away from cash, and the most liquid of the banks' assets next to cash reserves themselves. Consequently, the banks were prepared to charge a rate of interest on day-to-day loans which was slightly below that on the marginally less liquid Treasury Bills, which by convention were at that time paid for the first day after sale, with the cheque being cleared the second day and increasing cash reserves for the selling bank 48 hours later. The jobbers, in turn, had to be able to borrow money to finance inventories at a rate lower than the rate of interest on the securities held in order to make the operation profitable.

If an authorized money market dealer had his day-to-day loan called by a bank, and could not receive accommodation at any other bank, he could turn to the Bank of Canada under their lender of last resort facilities. Since the Bank is not authorized to lend to such firms under its charter, the loan would take the form of a purchase and resale agreement (PRA), whereby the jobber would sell certain authorized securities to the Bank of Canada and then buy them back at a somewhat higher price at a later date, perhaps a few days hence. The difference between the selling and buying prices is the rate of interest, which is equal to the Bank Rate, or the rate of interest which the Bank charges on loans to the chartered banks. This rate used to be set by the Bank of Canada and changed periodically to reflect market conditions, or to indicate a change in the stance of the central bank with regard to monetary policy. Now it is set automatically each week at 25 basis points, or ¼%, above the average yield on 91-day Treasury Bills at the weekly tender. The margin is to ensure that the Bank Rate is in fact a penalty rate, so that banks and jobbers will only borrow from the Bank of Canada as a last resort. If borrowers must pay more for such accommodation than they are making on the securities given for collateral, it will be costing them money and so discourage them from borrowing. They will borrow from the Bank only when this is preferable to selling the securities and forcing down their prices.

The institution of day-to-day loans and purchase and resale agreements enabled the authorized money market dealers to hold inventories of money market securities and to trade in them, which was fundamental to the development of a money market. It also was fundamental to the development of a more sensitive response to monetary policy, wherein the chartered banks kept their cash reserves much closer to the statutory minimum, and when under pressure called in day-to-day loans, thereby forcing the money market dealers to borrow at the central bank. This extension of lender of last resort facilities to investment dealers by the central bank, and indirect adjustment through forcing the dealers into borrowing from the central bank, copied the method employed in England over many years.

There are now twelve major investment dealers who are authorized money market dealers with access to the Bank of Canada's lender of last resort facilities through purchase and resale agreements.[1] The value of trade in money market securities far oustrips that in either stocks or bonds. Figures from the Investment Dealers Association for 1990 put total money market trading for that year in Canada at $1,217 billion, or in excess of one trillion dollars. However, this figure includes some primary issues as well as trading in outstanding securities, and is consequently not entirely comparable with the figures given in Chapter Four for trading in stocks and bonds which measure only trade in outstanding securities.

The keystone of the money market is the Treasury Bill. Treasury Bills are short term obligations of the Government of Canada which are sold each week, normally on Thursdays, at public auction. All of the institutions and dealers on the Bank of Canada's list of primary distributors for Government of Canada securities are eligible to submit sealed tenders for bills, in accordance with the conditions outlined by the Bank of Canada. The amounts of the bills to be tendered and the maturities are announced by the Bank the preceding week when it announces the results of that week's auction. 91-day and 182-day maturities as well as one year maturities are available each week. Of course previously-issued bills are maturing each week, so that the Government is only adding to its debt if the amount of new bills offered exceeds the amount being redeemed. The Bank of Canada will also submit bids on its own account, either to replace its own holdings of maturing issues or to alter the cash reserves of the banking system. As well, the Bank submits a reserve bid in order to ensure that all the bills are in fact taken up at a reasonable price, although the Minister of Finance has the right to refuse any bids and leave the bills unsold, and did in fact do this once in 1959. Since the Bank can set the minimum price accepted through its reserve bid, it can keep the rate of interest paid below whatever level it deems appropriate. Moreover, it also affects bids by its own actions in the marketplace, both by indicating its view as to the correct rate of interest through its own trading in the days preceding the auction, and by the effect of its purchases and sales on the cash reserves of the banking system, and consequently on the amount of liquidity in the system.

The bills are available in denominations of $1,000, $5,000, $25,000, $100,000 and $1,000,000, and bids are submitted in multiples of $1,000 par value with the bid price in terms of 100 expressed to not more than three decimal places. The bills are sold at a discount, with the difference between the purchase price and the value at maturity being the interest. Thus a bid of, say, 97.500 on a 91 day bill would represent interest of:

$$\frac{100.000 - 97.500}{97.500} \times \frac{365}{91} \times 100 = 10.28\%$$

The bids are arranged in order and the highest bids accepted in sequence until the total amount of each maturity is taken up. If the number of bids at the lowest successful price exceeds the amount available, the remainder is divided *pro rata* among those submitting bids at that level. The bids have to be submitted by noon on Thursday, except in weeks where the markets are closed on Friday, in which case the auctions are held on the day before the last day on which the markets are open. At 2:00 p.m., the successful bidders are informed, and the average successful bid is announced along with the corresponding yield, as well as the high and low bids and their equivalent yields. The average yield on successful bids for 91-day bills becomes the basis for the Bank Rate for the ensuing week.

The average yield on 91-day Treasury Bills is, then, set by the forces of supply and demand in the money market, albeit with these forces very much affected by the actions of the Bank of Canada. We have seen why the rate on day-to-day loans would normally be below this rate, while the Bank Rate is set 25 basis points, or 1/4%, above the Treasury Bill rate in order to ensure that it is, in fact, a penalty rate. The prime rate of the chartered banks, that is the rate that they charge on loans to their most creditworthy customers, is also affected by the rate on Treasury Bills, since the prime rate is usually kept about 3/4% to 1 1/2% above the Bank Rate, which is in turn tied to the Treasury Bill rate. The prime rate is affected both by the demand for loans and by the competition between the banks for customers, but it will always be above the rate at which the banks can borrow from the central bank. The banks seldom do borrow in this fashion, but the Bank Rate reflects interest rates in the money market, and particularly the Treasury Bill rate; of course banks require a higher return on loans to customers, which are illiquid and on which there is a risk of non-payment, than they can get on default-free liquid assets such as Treasury Bills. When the prime rate changes the rates on all commercial loans change accordingly, since loans to less creditworthy customers are made at prime rate plus a fraction, for example at prime rate plus one per cent. Consequently, the Treasury Bill rate is the key rate upon which other rates depend, and when it changes the ripples move out to the farthest reaches of the capital pool.

This constitutes the central core of the money market which developed out of the changes instituted in 1953-4, but the market has grown greatly and seen the establishment of many new instruments and participants since then, particularly in years when inflation risk shortened severely the term of fixed income securities, and lenders and borrowers both turned increasingly to the money market in the face of extreme interest rate volatility.

A very important instrument is bankers' acceptances. The market for these was slow to develop after their introduction in 1962, but they are now a major constituent of the money market. A bankers' acceptance is an order for payment drawn up by a business to finance some self-liquidating transaction connected with the production or marketing of goods. It will be for $100,000 or some multiple thereof and have a term of 180 days or less. The company makes the bill payable to itself and then takes it to the bank to have it accepted, which means that the bank guarantees payment. The company then endorses the bill so that it becomes payable to the bearer, and sells, or discounts, it in the money market, probably to a money market jobber. When it finally matures and is presented for payment at the accepting bank, the bank expects the original drawer to have made available sufficient funds for payment, but in any case the bank is obliged to redeem the acceptance. The effective rate of interest on it will be only slightly higher than the current rate on Treasury Bills, reflecting the high quality of an instrument based not only on the credit of the company but also on that of the bank. The bank charges a fee for accepting the bill, so that the total cost to the borrower is the combination of this fee and the rate of interest determined by the discount at which it is sold.

In the early years of bankers' acceptances, when interest rates were relatively low and the banks charged a fee of 1 1/4% for accepting the bill, the total cost was not very competitive with straight borrowing from the banks, but later on the banks reduced their fees to as little as 1/4% and the market began to develop. The foreign Schedule B banks reduced their "stamping" charge in order to compete for business in this area. A sufficiently low fee can make borrowing by this route attractive. Just how attractive will depend on how the fee plus the rate of interest just above the Treasury Bill rate compares to the prime rate. There was remarkable growth in the market for bankers' acceptances beginning late in 1978, and by the end of 1990 the outstanding amount was in excess of $44 billion. There have been substantial fluctuations in this figure, however, reflecting changes in the cost relationship between acceptances and regular bank loans. Bankers' acceptances were acceptable as security for day-to-day loans from the banks and for purchase and resale agreements at the Bank of Canada from 1962 until 1980, but with the growth of the market this special support was unnecessary, and now only a very small proportion could possibly be financed by day loans or PRAs in any event. Consequently these provisions were terminated with the 1980 revision of the Bank Act.

New instruments have also been introduced to assist the banks in adjusting their cash reserves. In 1967, a special call loan was introduced under which banks lend money to investment dealers on conditions similar to those for day-to-day loans but against the security of money market instruments not necessarily meeting the collateral requirements for day-to-day loans. They provide the banks with an additional tool for flexible and rapid cash management. By the mid-1980s the day-to-day loan had all but disappeared and been replaced by special call loans.

An inter-bank deposit market was established in 1973. Deposits in this market are clearing house funds that offer the alternative of adjusting reserves through direct transactions between banks at rates negotiated between them, rather than the more indirect flow of reserves through investment dealers as a result of calling loans. Originally the transactions had to be denominated in Canadian currency and have a maximum term of one day, but these limitations were removed in July, 1982. At the same time the minimum denomination was lowered from $500,000 to $100,000. These changes were of particular benefit to the smaller banks and foreign-owned banks, and had a significant impact on market activity as the amount of interbank deposits rose from about $500 million at the beginning of 1981 to over $2.5 billion by the end of 1985. The activity of foreign-owned banks accounts for about half of the total, and reserve management by means of inter-bank deposits is now a widely-used alternative to adjustment by means of other liquid assets.

The chartered banks also raise funds in the money market through a variety of instruments. Bearer deposit notes are issued in minimum amounts of $100,000, run for terms from 30 days to one year, and are transferable but not redeemable before maturity. They also issue instruments variously called certificates of deposit, term deposit receipts, or term notes, which are in smaller denominations from $5,000 to $100,000 with terms ranging from one day to five or six years and which are not transferable or negotiable. Trust and mortgage loan companies issue similar instruments bearing such names as deposit receipts, short-term guaranteed trust certificates, guaranteed investment certificates and guaranteed investment receipts. Term deposits range from one day to one year with a minimum size of $5,000, while certificates or receipts have terms from one to five years with a minimum size of $500, but neither instrument is transferable or redeemable.

Finance paper is notes issued by sales finance and consumer loan companies as a way of borrowing funds in the money market. It is offered in minimum amounts of $50,000 and has a term from 30 to 365 days. It may be secured in the case of Canadian finance companies by a pledge of the instalment obligations due to the company, but in the case of subsidiaries of foreign-owned companies operating in Canada the general credit standing of the parent may suffice. While finance paper is negotiable, it is customarily held to maturity. The rate of interest is just slightly above the Treasury Bill rate. Sales finance companies were the first big issuers of private paper in the Canadian money market, and this was promoted in part by measures taken by the Bank of Canada to limit their lines of credit at the chartered banks. By the end of 1964, finance paper was by far the most important private instrument in the money market, with more than $1 billion outstanding. However, the failure of Atlantic Acceptance in 1965 shattered investor confidence and led to a shrinkage in finance paper outstanding. Although growth eventually resumed it has remained moderate, as the competition from chartered banks has cut into the business of consumer loan companies in particular.

Commercial paper is issued in Canada by commercial and industrial corporations, both financial and non-financial. Financial corporations borrow to finance investment and lending activities, while non-financial corporations use the funds to offset seasonal cash outflows, finance inventories or extend trade credit. The borrowers need a standby line of credit from a bank or guarantee from a parent or affiliate as security. There is really very little difference between commercial paper and finance paper, and in the United States the term commercial paper encompasses both. The minimum amount issued is $50,000 with terms from one day to one year, but typically three months or less. While there is a limited secondary market for commercial paper, it often carries provision for payment on 24-hour notice from the lender. Yields on commercial paper are slightly above those on finance paper. The market for commercial paper is another area where foreign-owned banks have been competing very vigorously to make loans to Canadian corporations, and it was reported in 1988 that the banks were promoting the issuing of commercial paper, which they had been allowed to underwrite as of June 1987, by raising their stamping fees on the bankers' acceptances which form the principal competition.

There are a number of other borrowers which issue money market instruments. Many of the provinces issue Treasury Bills and all of them borrow funds in the money market. Provincial securities with terms of less than three years are considered part of this market as well, and these of course include issues nearing maturity as well as new issues. Large municipalities like Toronto and Montreal may sell short term obligations at competitive tender, and other municipal governments issue short term paper in the money market. These obligations are in denominations of $100,000 or multiples thereof with terms up to one year, but usually less than three months. Still others who borrow money in the money market are real estate investment trusts, mortgage investment companies, caisses populaires, credit unions and closed end investment companies.

A complete listing of all money market securities is difficult to arrive at, particularly when consideration is given to the market's international dimension, but a partial listing of some selected money market assets at December 31, 1990 is given in the table below.

| *Selected Money Market Assets at December 31, 1990* | |
|---|---|
| | (millions of Canadian dollars) |
| Government of Canada: | |
|   Treasury Bills | 135,400 |
|   Bonds under 3 years | 42,216 |
| Corporate short-term paper: | |
|   Finance company paper: | |
|     Canadian dollars | 7,906 |
|     Other currencies | 1,098 |
|   Other commercial paper: | |
|     Canadian dollars | 15,526 |
|     Other currencies | 5,808 |
| Canadian dollar bankers' acceptances | 44,109 |
| Provincial and municipal government treasury bills and other short-term paper | 13,954 |
| Chartered banks bearer term notes | 7,050 |
| Chartered banks non-personal fixed term deposits | 35,450 |
| Trust and mortgage loan companies term deposits and guaranteed investment certificates under 1 year | 21,600 |
| Source: *Bank of Canada Review*, April, 1991. Tables C2,D1,F3,G6 | |

On the lending side in the money market we have already discussed the role of banks, but there are many other sources of funds. Given the large sums involved, institutions have always predominated, but wealthy individuals also participate. One of the most interesting developments in recent years has been the opening up of the money market to smaller investors through the device of money market funds, particularly in the United States, and the retail sale of Treasury Bills to individuals in Canada. While the standard trading unit in Treasury Bills in the over-the-counter market in Canada is $250,000, we saw that the bills are available in denominations as small as $1,000, and investment firms have been actively selling them to retail investors as an alternative to Canada Savings Bonds.

Another source of funds in the money market is sometimes referred to as the "country banks." These are non-bank institutions willing to buy specified money market securities from a dealer, at the same time agreeing to sell them back later at a higher price. The difference between the buying price and the selling price is the rate of interest on the loan, which is referred to as a repurchase agreement, or "buy-back." It was this type of arrangement that went awry in December, 1987 and led to the failure of Osler Inc., a long-established investment dealer in Toronto. The Canadian Co-operative Credit Society, a credit union central, had entered into buy-backs with Osler, but the investment firm had not recorded these on its balance sheet, thereby apparently meeting its capital requirements, and when it came time to buy back the securities it did not have sufficient funds. While formal bankruptcy was avoided, and the investment firm's clients protected, part of the retail business was sold to another dealer and the firm put in receivership.

There are also "offstreet" lenders that provide overnight financing to money market dealers on essentially the same call and collateral terms as special call loans from the banks. The main offstreet lenders are the largest non-bank financial institutions, major industrial corporations and major provincial and municipal agencies.

The foregoing description of the market ignores its very important international dimension. For example, banks offer swapped deposits where a lender deposits funds at the bank, which are converted into foreign currency at the spot exchange rate, held on deposit in the foreign currency for a specified term and then changed back into Canadian currency at the forward exchange rate. The net return is composed not only of the interest on the deposit but also of the difference between the spot and forward rates of exchange, and is quoted by the bank as an "all-in" yield. These swaps are an example of the process of covered interest arbitrage which is described below in Chapter Nine. It is also frequently encountered in the Euromarkets

THE MONEY MARKET

described in Chapter Ten. The international extension of the money market not only involves additional opportunities for investors, but also supplies additional sources of short term funds for Canadian borrowers and consequently provides competition for the Canadian market, a topic to which we return in Chapter Eleven.

The money market has developed rapidly since its inception in 1953-4, but not without setbacks. Perhaps the most notable of these was the 1965 failure of Atlantic Acceptance, which dried up the flow of U.S. money into Canadian finance paper and which necessitated extraordinary support measures from the Bank of Canada. However, the market has grown enormously in recent years and many of the institutional innovations introduced in 1953-4 to foster its development have been phased out. Day-to-day loans are almost extinct and Treasury Bills are now settled on the same day. The amount of Government of Canada Treasury Bills outstanding grew from $6 billion in 1975 to $135 billion in 1990, a statistic that illustrates most vividly the market's growth. Some of this has undoubtedly been  spurred by inflation and the resulting high and volatile interest rates, which have driven lenders and borrowers away from longer term alternatives. Even with inflation abated, continued development and increasing internationalization of the money market seem safe predictions for the future.

# Note

1   The twelve authorized money market jobbers, or "B" dealers, as of August, 1991, were: Burns Fry; Deacon Barclays de Zoete Wedd; Gordon Capital; Lévesque, Beaubien, Geoffrion; Loewen, Ondaatje, McCutcheon; McLean, McCarthy; Midland Walwyn; Nesbitt Thomson Deacon; RBC Dominion Securities; Richardson Greenshields; Scotia McLeod; and Wood Gundy.

# Further References

Fullerton, D.H. *The Bond Market in Canada*. Toronto: Carswell, 1962. Chapter 11.

Government of Canada. *1964..Report of the Royal Commission on Banking and Finance*. Ottawa: Queen's Printer, 1964. Chapter 16, pp. 318-22.

Hossfield, T. "The Interbank Deposit Market in Canada." *Bank of Canada Review*, February, 1986. pp. 3-12.

Merrett, D. "The Evolution of Bankers' Acceptances in Canada." *Bank of Canada Review*, October, 1981. pp. 3-12.

"Overnight Financing in Canada: Special Call Loans." *Bank of Canada Review*, May, 1983. pp. 3-11.

Sarpkaya, S. *The Money Market in Canada*. Second Edition. Toronto: Butterworths, 1980.

"The Corporate Short-term Paper Market." *Bank of Canada Review*, September, 1976. pp. 3-16.

"The Market for Government of Canada Treasury Bills." *Bank of Canada Review*, December, 1987. pp. 3-14.

Watts, G.S. "The Bank of Canada in 1953 and 1954: A Further Stage in the Evolution of Central Banking in Canada." *Bank of Canada Review*, January, 1976. pp. 3-14.

Wilson, J.S.G. "The Canadian Money Market Experiment." *Banca Nazionale del Lavoro Quarterly Review*. March, 1958. Reprinted as Chapter 11 of Wilson, J.S.G. *Monetary Policy and the Development of Money Markets*. London: Allen and Unwin, 1966.

## CHAPTER SIX

# the mortgage market

ORTGAGES PLAY A VERY IMPORTANT ROLE IN CANADIAN FINANCIAL markets. At the end of 1990, financial institutions had more than $230 billion outstanding in residential mortgages alone. Before the distortions of the 1980s brought on by high inflation, mortgage financing accounted for more than half of all long-term financing. Mortgages are the main source of housing funds and play an important role in long-term farm finance. Borrowers can also raise money through mortgages against real estate and use the funds for purposes other than buying real estate, and there are indications that borrowing in this way to purchase nonhousing assets is not uncommon.

Mortgages are debt instruments secured against real estate. They can be defined more formally as "contracts in which a lender advances a sum of money to a borrower who promises to discharge the debt over a predetermined period of time and who pledges real property as security." The mortgage is really the conveyance of interest in real property as security for a loan. Mortgages in Canada which are insured by the federal government under the National Housing Act are referred to as NHA mortgages, while those from institutional investors with no government involvement are termed conventional mortgages.

Mortgages in Canada are usually amortized over a period of time, which means that repayments of the principal plus interest are combined into equal instalments, normally monthly, which if maintained over the full amortization period would discharge the loan. However, the amortization period used to calculate the payments may or may not coincide with the term of the loan, which is the actual time by which the loan is to be repaid.

In the 1950s and 1960s, the term of the loan and the amortization period of the mortgage were usually identical, particularly for NHA mortgages, and typically they were for 20, 25 or 30 years. However, in more recent years the terms have been drastically shortened, with five years normally a maximum and terms as short as six months. This is a consequence of efforts by lenders to protect themselves from losses suffered from unanticipated inflation, and represents a shifting of the burden of risk from inflation and rising interest rates to the borrower. Some might consider it an evening up process, since borrowers, who were not joint stock companies, have always had the legal right to repay conventional mortgages after five years, and to repay NHA mortgages after three years, thereby giving them the opportunity to benefit from refinancing in periods of falling interest rates. The average amortization period, on the other hand, has not decreased and perhaps has even increased, so that monthly payments based on this period do not discharge the debt by the end of the term, and the large balance owing, or "balloon payment," normally has to be refinanced at the interest rates current when the term is up. Consequently, borrowers are not really contracting a long term loan against a long term asset, but rather a short term loan that has to be continually rolled over.

The ratio of the money lent to the market value of the supporting real property reflects the equity of the owner in his house or farm, and is called the loan-to-value (LTV) ratio. This ratio has tended to rise over the years. Inflation usually increases the value of the underlying property, and as a result the lender's risk of loss through default is reduced. Consequently, lenders have required a smaller proportion of the total value for a down payment, although the absolute amount of this smaller proportion may well be higher. The LTV ratio for NHA loans has risen from 80% in the 1950s and 1960s to 90% in the 1970s and 1980s, while the ratio for conventional loans over the same period has gone from a range of 40-45% to 65-75%. This trend is not without its dangers, however, since if real estate prices do, in fact, decline, the mortgage can easily exceed the value of the underlying property and there is then some incentive for the borrower to simply walk away.

One more important variable is the ratio of the monthly payment to the before-tax income of the borrower. This ratio is referred to as the gross debt service (GDS) ratio. For this purpose, the monthly payment usually includes payments for property taxes. This ratio has been rising in recent years, although 30% is normally an upper limit.

Second mortgages are debt instruments secured against real property in the same manner as first mortgages, except that the lender's rights to the property in the event of default come only after all the claims of the first mortgage holders have been settled. Since the security is weaker, the loan is riskier and will carry a higher rate of interest. Third mortgages carry the process one step further. With the increase in the LTV ratio in recent times, second and third mortgages are now less common.

Mortgage lenders may be individuals, financial institutions such as banks, trust companies, mortgage loan companies, life insurance companies, credit unions and caisses populaires, or government agencies. Federal government involvement has been very important in the evolution of the Canadian mortgage market. In more recent years the activities of provincial government agencies have to some extent supplanted those of the federal government.

There is a very small secondary market for mortgages because of the key role of institutional lenders, the differing size and terms of the instruments, and the legal difficulties of transferring ownership. There were some auctions of blocks of mortgages by the CMHC in the 1960s, and some private dealings in blocks of mortgages have occurred in more recent years. While shorter terms have made mortgages somewhat more liquid, they must still be considered an illiquid and unmarketable asset.

A new innovation in Canada introduced at the start of 1987 is mortgage-backed securities, modelled on the Ginnie Mae (Government National Housing Association) mortgage-backed bonds in the United States. Bonds backed by pools of National Housing Act mortgages are issued in units of $5,000. These pools are put together by institutions such as chartered banks and have a minimum size of $2 million and a minimum term of 4 1/2 years, the individual mortgages carrying similar amortization periods and rates of interest. Since the NHA mortgages are backed by the Canada Mortgage and Housing Corporation, in effect they carry a government guarantee, and are identical to regular federal bond issues in quality. However, the blended payments of capital and interest that are paid monthly run up to 1/2% above the yield on similarly dated Government of Canada issues. By the end of 1990 there were $6 billion of mortgage-backed securities outstanding, but there was little institutional interest and the bulk was held by some some 40,000 individuals. This is another example of the process of securitization, inaugurated by the CIBC in January, 1987.

There are, of course, other real estate related investment possibilities, including the purchase of units in a mortgage fund. This provides the security of diversification over a number of different properties as well as the convenience of buying units of the desired size, along with enhanced liquidity resulting from the provisions for redeeming the units. However, such funds do not always allow for capturing the capital gains which are often the prime motivation for investing in real estate in an inflationary climate. To accomplish this, investors may turn to limited partnership arrangements, titled condominium units or co-ownership arrangements.

## The Evolution of the Market

The mortgage market in Canada has developed to a significant degree as a result of government initiatives. The original rationale for this intervention was to overcome market imperfections, specifically, gaps in the supply of mortgage funds available to borrowers.

Government involvement began in 1935 with the Dominion Housing Act. Mortgages up to then had usually not provided more than 60% of the value of the property and had had terms of ten years or less. Under the Dominion Housing Act the federal government provided approved lenders with 20% of the value of the property at an interest rate of 3%, so that these approved lenders could make mortgage loans to borrowers for up to 80% of the value and for a term of 20 years at an interest rate of 5%. In 1938 the National Housing Act (NHA) replaced the Dominion Housing Act and provided for direct loans to borrowers in small and remote communities. However, housing construction remained at low levels in the later 1930s and during World War II; at the end of the war the stock of housing was both low and in bad shape. Consequently, the Central Mortgage and Housing Corporation—later renamed Canada Mortgage and Housing

Corporation (CMHC)—was set up in 1945 to make loans for housing out of public funds when private financing was not available.

The Government attempted to change the nature of its involvement in 1954 with the introduction of mortgage insurance under the NHA and the revision of the Bank Act to allow banks to make NHA-insured mortgage loans. When mortgages were insured under the NHA, the rate on them was fixed by the Government, and they applied only to new houses. Sometimes this fixed rate proved unattractive to institutions in comparison with rates on conventional mortgages, and then the CMHC was forced to extend its role as residual lender.

The CMHC gradually shifted its emphasis to the provision of "social housing," and in the 1970s programmes such as the Assisted Home Ownership Programme (AHOP) and Assisted Rental Programme (ARP) were introduced. The role of Government intervention changed its focus from one of overcoming market deficiencies to one of income redistribution. The Economic Council, for one, feels that the Government has been less successful in this role, and that income redistribution would be better achieved if it were based on direct grants rather than loan subsidies. Assistance provided through loan programmes appears to have reached only a small proportion of the disadvantaged, without the benefits being related to their relative income or to the quality of their previous accommodation.

As well, the CMHC began to lend more to lower levels of government through shared cost programmes. In response to this development came a proliferation of new provincial government organizations providing loans and loan guarantees to the housing sector. Since 1978, CMHC has been trying to retrench and the federal government has been attempting to disengage itself from previous arrangements.

Recent government involvement in the mortgage market has focused more on questions of accessibility to house ownership and stabilization of the construction industry. To this end, the federal government in the 1981 budget provided for assistance to mortgage holders who would be paying, upon renewal of their mortgages, more than 30% of their incomes for monthly payments of principal, interest and taxes. Subsidies of this type are inherently inequitable, both over time and among various groups in the economy, especially if the beneficiaries of the plans get to keep any subsequent capital gain in the value of the house. In fact, not many people qualified for the programme. The federal government also gave grants and the Ontario government offered interest free loans to assist people buying houses in an effort to stabilize the construction industry. Once again the equity of such grants can be questioned. Moreover, studies have shown that direct government lending for house construction has to a large extent merely replaced funds that would have been available from the private sector and thus has not had much real additional impact on housing demand, except perhaps to alter its timing.

The 1967 revision of the Bank Act allowed banks to make loans against conventional mortgages as well as NHA-insured ones, and also removed the ceilings on interest rates charged. In 1963, private mortgage insurance was established, and since 1970 regulated financial institutions have been able to accept this private coverage. These changes have meant that, for normal mortgages, greater reliance has been placed on the private market, in which the most obvious institutional change has been the greater role played by the chartered banks. With the removal of restrictions and the shortening of terms, the banks, with their extensive branch systems, have been well placed to gain a larger share of the market. By 1984, it was reported that they had become the largest provider of new loans for residential housing, supplanting the trust companies who had traditionally been the pre-eminent lenders. In 1990 the banks' share of a depressed market was 53.5%, with trust companies at 29.6%.

## Inflation and the Mortgage Market

Under conditions of price stability, a person borrowing to purchase a house by means of a standard mortgage faces a long stream of monthly payments which are fixed in amount. In the early years most of these payments are for interest and relatively little goes toward principal, but over time equity rises, and if income is also rising the monthly payments will take up a smaller proportion of income.

These characteristics are illustrated in the left hand part of the table on the following page. The basic model is of a house costing $60,000 against which a mortgage for $51,000 is issued. In other words the LTV ratio is 85%. The mortgage has a term of 25 years and is amortized over the same period. It can be seen that with this standard mortgage constant monthly payments of $441 over the full

Comparison of Standard and Indexed Residential Mortgages[1]

| | Standard mortgage | | | | | | | | Fully indexed mortgage: 7% interest on capital indexed at 10% | | | | |
| | No inflation; 7% interest | | | | 10% inflation; 17.7% interest | | | | | | | | |
| Year | PIT | GDS | Loan balance | Equity | PIT | GDS | Loan balance | Equity | PIT | GDS | Loan balance | House value | Equity |
| | (Dollars) | (Per cent) | (Dollars) | (Per cent) | (Dollars) | (Per cent) | (Dollars) | (Per cent) | (Dollars) | (Per cent) | (Dollars) | (Dollars) | (Per cent) |
|---|---|---|---|---|---|---|---|---|---|---|---|---|---|
| 1 | 441 | 20.7 | 50,208 | 16.3 | 828 | 35.4 | 50,862 | 22.9 | 449 | 19.2 | 55,229 | 66,000 | 16.3 |
| 2 | 441 | 20.3 | 49,359 | 17.7 | 837 | 31.9 | 50,699 | 30.2 | 494 | 18.8 | 59,724 | 72,600 | 17.7 |
| 3 | 441 | 19.9 | 48,450 | 19.3 | 847 | 28.8 | 50,506 | 36.8 | 543 | 18.5 | 64,487 | 79,860 | 19.3 |
| 4 | 441 | 19.5 | 47,476 | 20.9 | 859 | 26.0 | 50,276 | 42.8 | 597 | 18.1 | 69,510 | 87,846 | 20.9 |
| 5 | 441 | 19.2 | 46,433 | 22.6 | 871 | 23.5 | 50,005 | 48.3 | 657 | 17.7 | 74,780 | 96,631 | 22.6 |
| 6 | 441 | 18.8 | 45,315 | 24.5 | 884 | 21.3 | 49,683 | 53.3 | 723 | 17.4 | 80,279 | 106,294 | 24.5 |
| 7 | 441 | 18.4 | 44,118 | 26.5 | 899 | 19.3 | 49,302 | 57.8 | 795 | 17.1 | 85,974 | 116,923 | 26.5 |
| 8 | 441 | 18.0 | 42,836 | 28.6 | 915 | 17.5 | 48,850 | 62.0 | 875 | 16.7 | 91,822 | 128,615 | 28.6 |
| 9 | 441 | 17.7 | 41,462 | 30.9 | 933 | 15.9 | 48,315 | 65.8 | 962 | 16.4 | 97,765 | 141,477 | 30.9 |
| 10 | 441 | 17.3 | 39,990 | 33.3 | 953 | 14.5 | 47,681 | 69.4 | 1,058 | 16.1 | 103,724 | 155,625 | 33.3 |
| 11 | 441 | 17.0 | 38,414 | 36.0 | 974 | 13.2 | 46,930 | 72.6 | 1,164 | 15.8 | 109,000 | 171,187 | 36.0 |
| 12 | 441 | 16.7 | 36,725 | 38.8 | 998 | 12.0 | 46,040 | 75.6 | 1,281 | 15.4 | 115,259 | 188,306 | 38.8 |
| 13 | 441 | 16.3 | 34,916 | 41.8 | 1,024 | 11.0 | 44,985 | 78.3 | 1,409 | 15.1 | 120,540 | 207,136 | 41.8 |
| 14 | 441 | 16.0 | 32,978 | 45.0 | 1,053 | 10.1 | 43,735 | 80.8 | 1,550 | 14.8 | 125,235 | 227,850 | 45.0 |
| 15 | 441 | 15.7 | 30,902 | 48.5 | 1,085 | 9.3 | 42,255 | 83.1 | 1,705 | 14.6 | 129,087 | 250,635 | 48.5 |
| 16 | 441 | 15.4 | 28,679 | 52.2 | 1,119 | 8.5 | 40,501 | 85.3 | 1,875 | 14.3 | 131,777 | 275,698 | 52.2 |
| 17 | 441 | 15.1 | 26,297 | 56.2 | 1,158 | 7.9 | 38,422 | 87.3 | 2,063 | 14.0 | 132,915 | 303,268 | 56.2 |
| 18 | 441 | 14.8 | 23,745 | 60.4 | 1,200 | 7.3 | 35,959 | 89.2 | 2,269 | 13.7 | 132,019 | 333,595 | 60.4 |
| 19 | 441 | 14.5 | 21,011 | 65.0 | 1,246 | 6.7 | 33,042 | 91.0 | 2,496 | 13.4 | 128,502 | 366,955 | 65.0 |
| 20 | 441 | 14.2 | 18,083 | 69.9 | 1,297 | 6.2 | 29,565 | 92.7 | 2,745 | 13.2 | 121,653 | 403,650 | 69.9 |
| 21 | 441 | 14.0 | 14,946 | 75.1 | 1,353 | 5.8 | 25,489 | 94.3 | 3,020 | 12.9 | 110,605 | 444,015 | 75.1 |
| 22 | 441 | 13.7 | 11,586 | 80.7 | 1,415 | 5.4 | 20,635 | 95.8 | 3,322 | 12.7 | 94,313 | 488,417 | 80.7 |
| 23 | 441 | 13.4 | 7,987 | 86.7 | 1,483 | 5.0 | 14,885 | 97.2 | 3,654 | 12.4 | 71,513 | 537,258 | 86.7 |
| 24 | 441 | 13.1 | 4,131 | 93.1 | 1,557 | 4.7 | 8,072 | 98.6 | 4,019 | 12.2 | 40,685 | 590,984 | 93.1 |
| 25 | 441 | 12.9 | - | 100.0 | 1,639 | 4.4 | - | 100.0 | 4,421 | 11.9 | - | 650,083 | 100.0 |

[1] PIT is the monthly payment for principal, interest, and property taxes; GDS is the gross debt service ratio. These figures are based on the following assumptions: purchase price, $60,000; loan amount, $51,000; borrower's initial income, $25,000 per year; annual rate of real income growth, 2 per cent; initial property taxes, $1,000.

Source: Economic Council of Canada, Intervention and Efficiency. Ottawa: Minister of Supply and Services, 1982. Appendix F, p.165. Reprinted with permission.

term are sufficient to discharge the debt by the end of the period. In the first year, payments of $5292 cause the loan balance to fall by a little less than $800, as almost all of the money goes toward the payment of interest. However, as time goes on more and more of the payments are directed toward reducing the principal amount outstanding, and towards the end of the term equity rises quickly until it finally reaches 100%. As the person's income is assumed to rise by 2% per year in line with the general increase in productivity in the economy, the GDS falls from 20.7% in the first year to 12.9% in the final year. This is referred to as the "tilting effect." It is manageable in periods of stable prices, and indeed felt desirable by many borrowers who are prepared to make a greater sacrifice in the early years in order to become houseowners, and who wish to have more of their income available in later years for refurbishing their house, educating their children, or whatever.

If prices start to rise, lenders under existing mortgage contracts lose while borrowers gain. Lenders lose if inflation is not anticipated, since the money that they receive back from their loan has decreased in real terms. If nominal interest rates also rise to reflect expectations of rising prices, the value of their existing mortgages will fall. Borrowers, on the other hand, gain because the money they pay back has less value in real terms, if inflation is not anticipated and nominal interest rates adjusted accordingly. If the values of their houses rise, their equity rises even more quickly than originally anticipated, and if their incomes rise, their monthly payments becomes less onerous as the GDS ratio falls dramatically.

As prices rise, however, nominal interest rates can also be expected to rise in line with expected inflation. For example, if the expected rate of inflation rises to 10%, the nominal rate of interest in the preceding example would rise to 17.7%, 7% for the real rate of interest, plus 10% for expected inflation and .7% for depreciation of the interest payment (see note 1 to Chapter Three).

If it were possible to obtain a standard mortgage amortized over 25 years and with a term of 25 years at a 17.7% rate of interest, the results would be as shown in the middle columns of the preceding table. The monthly payments almost double compared to the earlier situation as a result of the much higher interest rate, and they increase moderately over the years because of the increase in taxes which are assumed to rise at 10% per annum. Equity rises much more quickly than in the previous case because of the rapidly increasing value of the house, while the GDS ratio falls dramatically from over 35% to less than 5% as income rises at 12% per annum, 10% to keep up with inflation plus 2% to reflect rising productivity.

However, there is a limit to the extent to which housebuyers can manage to make these higher payments, or from the lender's point of view, a maximum ratio of debt service to income that they are willing to accept. The normal limit is 30%, and we can see that in the previous example the GDS ratio exceeds this level. Moreover, the cost of houses will be rising, perhaps by more than the rate of inflation. The combination of rising prices and rising interest rates can make it impossible for many people to buy houses. One estimate for the period 1965-75 was that the fraction of a new housebuyer's income necessary to meet monthly mortgage payments rose by 55%, and the situation undoubtedly worsened thereafter, particularly when the mortgage interest rate peaked at 21 1/2% in September, 1981.

The other effect on mortgages that we have already noted is that the terms have been shortened. The case of the 17.7% mortgage with a term of 25 years is only given for illustrative purposes, since it is no longer possible to obtain funds for such long terms. It became impossible after 1979 to obtain NHA mortgages with a term longer than five years, and terms as short as six months were introduced. Shortening the term reduces the lender's risk from unanticipated inflation and from inflation risk and shifts it to the borrower. The shorter terms also mean that the problems of mortgage financing are not restricted only to new buyers, since existing borrowers are faced with refinancing their mortgages at the new higher interest rates. This will greatly increase the size of their monthly payments. While their houses may have increased in value in the period since they took out their first mortgage, this gain is only on paper and not in the form of the cash required to service the debt.

In theory, the adjustment of the nominal interest rate in line with expected inflation leaves lenders and borrowers in exactly the same position as they would be if prices were stable and the nominal and real rates of interest were the same. However, higher nominal interest rates in the face of inflation have the effect of shortening the true maturity of a loan. Some of the money paid as interest is really a payment to make up the loss in purchasing power of the principal, so that the real value of the principal outstanding is falling more rapidly than the nominal value. Thus the debt will become rapidly less onerous in real terms as income rises. Even in nominal terms, the monthly payments quickly decline as a proportion of rising income, and as we have seen the "tilt" of the GDS in such circumstances becomes very extreme, much more so than with a standard level payment mortgage in periods of stable prices.

Given the nature of the standard mortgage contract, rising nominal interest rates so exaggerate the "tilting effect" that home ownership becomes inaccessible to many people. They simply cannot overcome the cash-flow problems associated with a high initial debt service ratio. It is not surprising, then, that high interest rates have a pronounced negative effect on housing demand, particularly in conjunction with the taxation system (as demonstrated on page 41 of Chapter Three). One estimate is that a 1% rise in anticipated inflation, and consequently nominal interest rates, decreases housing demand by 4-5%. Moreover, many people may find it impossible to keep their houses when it comes time to refinance existing mortgages at sharply higher nominal interest rates.

When the "tilting effect" becomes so severe as to make houses simply unaffordable, there are various possible remedies. Extending the amortization period can provide some relief, but this is very limited when interest rates become very high and amortization periods are already very long. As we also noted earlier, the LTV ratio has risen in recent years, and this change can assist houseowners insofar as the down payment required for a given house is reduced; but to the extent that it increases the debt it only exacerbates the problem of managing the carrying costs of that debt.

Accelerating inflation and the rising interest rates that accompany it essentially pose a cash flow problem for those who wish to borrow by means of mortgages. While inflation will mean a rapidly increasing equity and a rapidly decreasing real burden for those who can manage a very high initial debt service ratio, it will make it impossible for many others to take out a mortgage. The solution to the problem lies in the houseowner surrendering a portion of the paper profit that will accrue on his property in exchange for assistance in meeting the high initial mortgage payments. The question is what the best mechanism is for doing this.

Perhaps the best solution to the problem is the one endorsed by the Economic Council of Canada—the introduction of the indexed mortgage. Here lenders and borrowers agree on a real rate of interest for the mortgage, and monthly payments are computed at this rate in accordance with the amortization period. However, the initial price is periodically written up by the amount of inflation, so that the principal outstanding changes by this amount less that part of the monthly payments that goes to retirement of principal. Payments on the new outstanding principal are then recomputed over the remaining portion of the amortization period at the agreed real rate of interest. Payments rise throughout the period of the mortgage, but are stable in real terms. Moreover, they fall gradually as a proportion of income, if income increases more quickly than inflation in line with gains in productivity. As a result, the stream of payments of the borrower in real terms, as well as the increase in his equity, approximate that which would have occurred under stable prices and a market rate of interest equal to the agreed real rate.

This is illustrated in the final columns of the preceding table on page 84, which show the case of a fully indexed mortgage of $51,000 amortized over a twenty-five year period at a real interest rate of 7%, while inflation is running at 10%. The GDS ratio is comparable to that for the standard mortgage of 7% under stable prices shown in the left hand columns, while the equity figures are identical for the two cases.

Of course, the outstanding principal rises for much of the period; it can be seen that in this case it would do so for the first seventeen years, and indeed would only come back below the original principal outstanding in the twenty-fourth year. This raises the question of whether the owner's original equity could be erased if house prices did not rise as quickly as prices in general. In the event of negative equity, there is a risk that the owner will default rather than keep up payments. Since this greatly increases the lender's risk of loss from default, it would seem imperative that loan to value ratios would have to decline to more traditional levels if indexed mortgages were to be adopted.

The other risk is that the borrower's income would not rise in line with inflation, so that increasing monthly payments in nominal terms would also mean an increased burden in real terms. A prospective borrower looking down the table to find eventual monthly payments of over $4,000 might well question the wisdom of taking on such a commitment. Concern with these dangers led the Lortie Committee, which was formed by the Government to comment upon various proposals for offsetting the effects of inflation in the capital market, to recommend only partially indexed mortgages, with one quarter of the inflationary gain in value added to the outstanding principal at regular intervals.

It should also be realized that the above example is only for illustrative purposes, and that inflation in the real world is unlikely to progress at the same rate for 25 years. With indexed mortgages, the outstanding principal and consequently the monthly payments rise only in line with the actual inflation experienced. This is one of the great merits of this solution compared with ones based in some fashion on market rates of interest, which incorporate a measure of expected inflation. The indexed mortgage comes closest to reproducing the conditions which would exist for borrowers under stable prices, and it would allow them to once again match a long term liability with a long term asset.

However, there are practical difficulties in introducing indexed mortgages. A problem facing lenders under indexed mortgages would be that their obligations might not be similarly indexed to inflation. Consequently, it would be necessary to offer a corresponding type of indexed deposit in order to match the assets and liablilities of lenders. One variant of the indexed mortgage has been labelled PLAM for price level adjusted mortgage. Its advocates propose the introduction of the price level adjusted deposit, or PLAD, at the same time. Another problem concerns whether the increase in the balance outstanding, which is really a contingent asset, will be treated as income or as a capital gain for tax purposes. The Economic Council's recommendation to circumvent this problem was to have the mortgages offered by tax-exempt financial institutions such as registered pension funds and RRSPs. Still another technical problem to be solved is the choice of index for writing up the values, since borrowers will want one tied to incomes or house prices, while depositors who provide the funds for lenders will want one such as the Consumer Price Index which is tied more generally to the purchasing power of money. Whether because of the practical difficulties or because of reluctance on the part of both borrowers and lenders to try such a radical solution, indexed mortgages have not, in fact, been seen to any extent in Canada. Now that mortgage rates have moved below those that prevailed in the early 1980s, even though well above those of earlier times, the pressure to introduce such an instrument seems to have eased.

One solution that has arisen in the private market in Canada is the variable rate mortgage (VRM). This is a kind of deferred mortgage where the lender sets a certain reference interest rate that may fluctuate with market conditions. When the mortgage is taken out, payments are computed at the reference rate over the complete amortization period. If market rates are above the reference rate at the beginning of any month, then payments are made in accordance with the original computation, but at the end of the period the difference between this payment and that which would have been required at the going rate is added to the principal outstanding. Consequently, if market rates consistently run ahead of the reference rate, the equity at the end of the period will be less than it would have been if the reference rate had been the going rate. This may be offset, however, by a rise in the market value of the property if the higher interest rates reflect inflation, which also affects house prices. As long as the reference rate is not too far below the market rate the danger of a decrease in equity should not be too great, but then the assistance provided by such a scheme is correspondingly limited.

In 1978 the Canada Mortgage and Housing Corporation introduced a Graduated Payment Mortgage (GPM) which was also offered as a new NHA-insured mortgage formula. Monthly payments on a GPM begin at a level which is $2.25 per $1,000 of loan less than on a comparable level payment mortgage, and then increase by 5% each year until they eventually reach a level, which, when maintained for the rest of the amortization period, will discharge the debt. These eventual payments are higher than they would be under a level payment mortgage, and are subject to alteration in accordance with market interest rates at the time for renewal of the mortgage. The outstanding balance under a GPM rises for about six years, and it takes nearly eleven years before the outstanding balance falls below the initial loan, assuming an amortization period of twenty-five years. There is thus a partial deferral of interest payments in the early years, with the amount deferred added to the principal outstanding to be amortized and paid off with interest in future years.

While both the VRM and GPM were used in Canada, their adoption was not widespread, probably because the amount of relief they provided in times of very high interest rates was not great.

Moreover, they were based on changes in nominal rates of interest which reflected an allowance for expected inflation, rather than on actual rates of inflation experienced, so that they did not eliminate the risk from unanticipated inflation, whether positive or negative. Under the VRM, a fall in the market rate of interest to the reference rate would mean that no interest would be deferred and added to the oustanding balance at the end of the period, while under the GPM, payments would increase until the next renewal date regardless of the course of market interest rates.

A more widespread response in the marketplace in 1981 and 1982 was the vendor take-back or buy-down. Here the seller of the house offered a mortgage at lower than market rates of interest in exchange for an increased price for the house. In the case of a take-back, the cost of the reduction of initial mortgage payments can be added to the price of the house and the amount of the loan, while in the case of a buy-down, the vendor pays the lender upfront for reducing the mortgage rate.

For example,[1] if a purchaser needs a mortgage for $50,000 and the going rate of interest is 17%, the monthly payments, based on a twenty-five year amortization period, would be $696.26. However, if the vendor were prepared to offer a three year mortgage for $59,106.09 at 10%, amortized over twenty-five years, the monthly payment would be $528.70. The purchaser can thereby significantly reduce the size of his monthly payments by increasing the price offered for the property by $9,106.09. In the case of the mortgage for $50,000 at 17% the balance due after three years would be $49,456.44, and in the second case of the 10% mortgage, the balance due after three years would be $57,185.69. The additional principal amount due after three years, when added to the 10% interest on the loan, provides the vendor with a return of 17% on $50,000, so he is not making any real financial sacrifice. Moreover, if the vendor holds the mortgage until the end of three years, the capital gain of $9,106.09 is normally tax free. Both parties gain, and once again the solution involves the houseowner giving up a portion of the paper profit that accrues on his property in exchange for assistance in meeting the high initial mortgage payments.

Another way of achieving the same result involves a more direct sharing in the appreciation of the value of the property by the lender, through some agreement for payment of a portion of the gain in the value of the property at the end of the mortgage period by the borrower to the lender. Such participation mortgages are found with commercial property in Canada, but not normally with residential property. However, in the United States, a company in Florida introduced shared appreciation mortgages (SAM) in 1981, whereby mortgages were contracted at 10% when market interest rates were at 15% in return for a payment by the borrower of one third of the appraised gain in value at the end of ten years. The popularity of this particular arrangement may have resided in the fact that a large proportion of the borrowers did not expect to be around in ten years when the gain in value was to be paid, whether or not it was actually realized.

We have seen that over the years the Government has played a key role in the development of the mortgage market in Canada. Early programmes introduced the long term standard mortgage, while the introduction of government mortgage insurance greatly facilitated the participation of private lenders, and subsequently the establishment of private mortgage insurance. Along with the removal of restrictions on the operations of private institutions, these developments helped to remove much of the original justification for government involvement, which had been focused on filling gaps in the supply of mortgage funds. Subsequent government initiatives were really designed to redistribute income, but assistance under these programmes reached only a small proportion of the truly disadvantaged, while the effectiveness of more recent programmes to stabilize the construction industry and improve accessibility to house ownership is also questionable. However, if interest rates rise again in the wake of inflation, the Government may have a role to play in both increasing affordability and introducing new instruments to the market by championing the indexed mortgage.

# Note

1   This example is taken from Appendix F (p. 163) in *Intervention and Efficiency*, the Economic Council of Canada's study on government credit and credit guarantees to the private sector.

# Further References

Economic Council of Canada. *Intervention and Efficiency*. Ottawa: Minister of Supply and Services, 1982. Chapter 5 and Appendix F.

Fallis, G. "Governments and the Residential Mortgage Market—Part I: A Normative Analysis; Part II: Programs and Evaluation." Economic Council of Canada Discussion Papers No. 239 and No. 240. Ottawa: Economic Council of Canada, 1983.

Government of Canada. *1964 Report of the Royal Commission on Banking and Finance*. Ottawa: Queen's Printer, 1964. Chapter 14.

Hatch, J.E. *The Canadian Mortgage Market*. Toronto: Ministry of Treasury, Economics and Intergovernmental Affairs, Province of Ontario, 1975.

Kesselman, J.R. "Mortgage Policies for Financial Relief in Inflationary Periods." *Canadian Public Policy*, Winter, 1981.

Pesando, J.E. *The Impact of Inflation on Financial Markets in Canada*. Montreal: C.D. Howe Research Institute, 1977. Chapter 4, pp. 45-63.

Pesando, J.E. and Smith, L.B. *Government in Canadian Capital Markets: Selected Cases*. Montreal: C.D. Howe Research Institute, 1978. Chapter 2.

Ryba, A., Damus, S., and Carriere, J. "Practical Issues in Mortgage Finance with Applications to the Standard and Indexed Mortgages." Economic Council of Canada Discussion Paper No. 228. Ottawa: Economic Council of Canada, 1983.

**CHAPTER SEVEN**

# the stock market

T HE JOINT STOCK COMPANY IS, ARGUABLY, IN A LEAGUE WITH THE WHEEL as one of humanity's greatest inventions. It has allowed the accumulation of capital well beyond the resources of individuals or partnerships, while at the same time limiting the liability of the several shareholders to the amount of capital that they have subscribed. The joint stock company dates back to the early seventeenth century. An early Canadian example was "The Governor and Company of Adventurers Trading into Hudson's Bay," the company that today is known simply as the Hudson's Bay Company, or as it likes to style itself, the Bay.

The capital stock of the company represents the money which the owners have invested in the business. The owners receive votes on the basis of one vote for each share of voting stock, and share in the profits of the business if it is successful by receiving dividends and by appreciation in the value of their stock. The value of the capital stock combined with that part of the profits that has been retained rather than distributed as dividends comprise the owners' equity in the business. There are two basic types of capital stock, common and preferred shares, with a further classification of restricted shares sometimes added to distinguish common shares without voting privileges, or with subordinated voting rights.

## Common Shares

The common shareholders are the basic owners of the company and control its operation through their power to elect the Board of Directors. The Board of Directors, in turn, appoints the management and is responsible to the shareholders for the running of the company.

More than half a century ago, it was suggested by Adolf Berle and Gardiner Means in *The Modern Corporation and Private Property* that control had been effectively divorced from ownership in the modern corporation. Ownership had become widely dispersed in many cases, and management was able to perpetuate itself through its influence on the Board of Directors where managers held many of the important positions, and through the use of the proxy. A proxy is a written authorization given by a shareholder to someone else, who does not need to be a shareholder, to represent him and vote his shares at a shareholders' meeting. Management regularly solicits proxies from the shareholders, and normally these votes along with those of the Board are more than enough to carry any motions at the meetings.

On occasion, dissident shareholders will also try to solicit proxies, and while they have access to the list of shareholders, they are disadvantaged in such a "proxy battle" because they have to finance their efforts out of their own resources, while management is able to rely on company coffers. Consequently, these battles are infrequent, though often very colourful, and seldom result in victory for the dissidents. The attempt by the Mesa Petroleum group headed by T. Boone Pickens Jr. to wrest control of Gulf Corporation is a famous recent example, which, while unsuccessful, did precipitate the takeover of Gulf by Standard Oil of California, and did result in substantial profits for the dissident group; as a result of the takeover, they were able to sell their shares for considerably more than they paid for them. When shares are acquired in a hostile unsuccessful takeover bid and are subsequently sold back to the company at a higher price, the process is known as "greenmail."

It is certainly the case that most large corporations can be effectively controlled by a person or group that holds much less than 50% of the voting shares. The working tactic of the original Argus Coporation set up by E.P. Taylor was to control major Canadian companies through holdings that were in the range of only 10% to

20% of the outstanding shares, and to have a large percentage of the holding company's own capital in the form of preferred shares without voting privileges. Some large utilities may not have any dominant shareholder; it was said that before it was broken up, American Telephone and Telegraph in the United States, or Ma Bell, had no single shareholder with as much as 1% of the stock.

In more recent years, ownership of some large corporations has become concentrated in the hands of institutional investors such as trust companies and pension plans, and while these groups do not usually intervene in the management of companies, their relatively large holdings raise the possibility of their doing so at any time. The Caisse de Dépôt et Placement du Québec, which invests the funds of the Quebec Pension Plan, is an outstanding Canadian example; the federal government introduced legislation to limit the Caisse's holdings in Canadian Pacific to less than 10% of the voting stock. While this development is a source of worry to some, other commentators have pointed out that common shareholders are supposed to control the company, and this indirect manner of achieving control is a kind of "pension fund socialism." Indeed, there have been a number of cases recently where investment counsellors and money managers have opposed management tactics and attempted to champion the rights of minority shareholders.

Almost all common stock outstanding today has no par value. The number of shares authorized by the company's charter is often very large—indeed it may be unlimited—and normally only a portion of the authorized shares will actually have been issued. The number of shares outstanding is the same as the number issued, unless the company has bought back some of its shares and retired them, in which case shares outstanding will be less than shares issued, which in turn will be less than shares authorized. Some of the shares which have not been issued may be held in reserve for issue in conjunction with warrants, convertible debentures or stock option plans for employees.

The difference between "A" shares and "B" shares depends upon the particular case. It used to be common for A shares to receive cash dividends while B shares received stock dividends. However, changes in the tax treatment of stock dividends has pretty well eliminated this type of B share. In other cases, class A shares are non-voting, while class B shares are voting; Canadian Utilities is an example of this difference. The difference can be even more extreme. For example, class B shares of Magna International are entitled to 500 votes each, thereby enabling the chairman, Frank Stronach, to have 52% of the votes with only 2.5% of the shares. In still other cases, class A shares are a special type of preferred share with different characteristics from other outstanding preferred shares of the same company. Dofasco's class A preferred shares exemplify this.

The declaration of dividends is one means by which stockholders share in profits made by the company. Dividends are paid out of profits after taxes have been paid, and preferred shareholders receive dividends before holders of common stock. The Directors decide what proportion, if any, of profits will be paid as dividends, and that proportion can vary widely between companies. Utilities generally pay out a relatively high proportion of profits, since their earnings are usually relatively stable. Growth companies pay out a relatively low proportion, or none at all, preferring to reinvest profits in the company to help finance expansion, and in this case shareholders may be rewarded by an increase in the value of their shares. Established companies cherish stability in their dividend record, and not entirely without reason, since regulations governing some institutional investors may restrict their investment in common stocks to companies that have paid dividends regularly for a given period. Companies may continue to pay dividends even when they are experiencing losses. This could be possible since companies may have a positive cash flow even with losses recorded in the financial statements, because entries like depreciation, depletion and deferred income taxes do not actually require cash outlays. Indeed, the company could borrow money in order to continue paying dividends.

Dividends are normally paid quarterly to those on the shareholders' register as of the date of record, and companies may also declare an "extra" dividend. This extra usually comes at the end of the fiscal year and is distributed in this fashion rather than as an increase in the regular dividend, so that shareholders will know that it may not come every year.

If a stock dividend is paid, the shareholder receives additional stock in the company. Of course, issuing more stock for which no money is received does not in itself increase the value of the company, so that the same value is divided into smaller parts. While the shareholder has more of these parts, the value of each part is diluted. For example, a 100% stock dividend would be the same thing as splitting the stock 2 for 1. However, this type of dividend has the benefit from the company's point of view of conserving cash, at least until the payment of any subsequent cash dividends. In Canada, until the 1985 budget, it had the advantage from the shareholder's point of view that the stock dividend was not subject to tax until such time as the shares were sold, in which case the price received would be subject to tax as a capital gain. Since May 23, 1985, stock dividends have been taxable at the same rate as ordinary dividends.

Some companies also have a dividend reinvestment plan whereby dividends are automatically used to buy additional shares. In some cases, shares may be bought on the open market with the dividend money by a trustee, in which case the company does not conserve cash. In other cases, the shares are issued from the company's treasury, possibly at a slight discount to the market price, with a consequent increase in the number of shares outstanding and a conservation of cash. If the latter alternative were followed, the company might make a "normal course issuer bid" to buy its own shares on the open market to offset some of the dilution involved in the dividend reinvestment plan. Dividends under such plans are taxable to the shareholder as ordinary cash dividends.

The yield on stock is normally computed by expressing the indicated annual dividend as a percentage of the market price. As we have seen earlier, the dividend tax credit reduces the effective rate of taxation on this form of income and tends to reduce relative pre-tax yields. Moreover, this way of computing yield ignores any capital gains, which are part of the return anticipated by most shareholders and which, if realized, are taxed at partial rates, or not taxed at all if the shareholder has not exhausted his capital gains exemption. The outcome of all this is that the quoted pre-tax yields on stocks are usually lower than those on fixed income securities, although stocks carry a higher risk.

The Directors may decide to split the common stock if its price has risen to the point where they think this could be a barrier to purchasing it. The idea is to widen the market for the shares and thereby increase demand for them, and this may explain why news of a stock split often causes the price of the stock to rise, since a straight stock split simply subdivides the existing shares into smaller units and reduces the dividend correspondingly, and in itself provides no rationale for any increase in value. The reverse process, or a stock consolidation, would combine a number of outstanding shares into a single share, and might occur with a very low priced stock if the company wished to issue additional shares and wanted them to have a reasonable value. However, neither stock splits nor stock consolidations in themselves provide any additional capital for the company.

A rights issue, on the other hand, does provide additional equity, while at the same time constituting a type of additional dividend for the shareholder. Existing shareholders are given the opportunity to add to their holdings when the company sells additional shares in recognition of a kind of pre-emptive right not to have their share of ownership in the company diluted. Shareholders are given the right to buy new shares in proportion to their existing holdings, and to do so at a price which is normally below the going market price. Usually they are given one right for each share owned, and it takes a certain number of these rights to buy one additional share. For example, it might take ten rights plus a certain amount of money to buy one new share, in which case the number of shares outstanding would increase by ten per cent if the rights issue were fully subscribed.

Rights are traded in the stock markets just like shares, and normally they have a life of no more than a few weeks. Their value reflects the difference between the price of the share on the market and the lower price obtained through using the rights, in conjunction with the number of rights required to purchase one additional share. If, for example, it takes ten rights plus $20 to buy one new share, and the shares are selling on the market at $25.50, then each right should be worth one tenth of the difference between the market price and the subscription price, or:

$$\frac{\$25.50 - \$20.00}{10} = \frac{\$5.50}{10} = .55$$

This assumes that the shares are selling in the market after the rights have been issued, that is, they are selling "ex rights."

However, if people purchased the shares in time to have their names on the shareholders' register on the date of record for the rights issue, they would buy the shares "cum rights," and the calculation of the intrinsic value of the right would be slightly different. Suppose now that a person were to buy ten shares of the company at the going price of $25.50, for a total price of $255. They would also receive ten rights with which they could buy an additional share for $20, so that for a total outlay of $275 they would have 11 shares of the company. The average cost would then be 275/11 = $25, and thus each right is worth 50 cents, or the difference in the cost per share by acquiring them this way rather than buying them all at the market price. An alternative method of arriving at this theoretical value of the right during the "cum rights" period would be to divide the difference between the market price and the subscription price by the number of rights required plus one, or:

$$\frac{\$25.50 - \$20.00}{11} = \frac{\$5.50}{11} = .50$$

Rights are sometimes confused with warrants, but they are really quite different. Warrants are usually attached to a new issue of securities as an added inducement to the purchaser. If the warrants confer the right to purchase shares, they normally enable the holder to buy one share per warrant. Warrants are usually exercisable over a period of years and therefore have a time value, but when they are issued they have no intrinsic value since the purchase price of the share with the warrant is above the going market price. Rights, on the other hand, are issued to existing shareholders, and it normally takes a number of rights to purchase one additional share. They usually last for a relatively short period of a few weeks and thus have no real time value. However, they do have an intrinsic value since they enable the holder to purchase additional shares at less than the market price as soon as they are issued. Rights and warrants are similar insofar as they both can be sold separately on the market, and because they both possess substantial leverage they have considerable speculative appeal. They also both raise additional capital for the company.

## Preferred Shares

Straight preferred shares lie somewhere between debt and equity. They are like bonds insofar as the return on them is usually fixed, and like equity in that there will only be a return if profits are made and the dividends are declared by the Directors. The preference that such shares possess refers to two things: the right to assets ahead of common shareholders in the event of liquidation of the company, and the right to dividends before the common shareholders get any. If a company goes into bankruptcy and is liquidated, there will not likely be any money for any of the shareholders, but if it is liquidated as a result of other circumstances such as a decision to terminate operations, preferred shareholders would be entitled to a share of the assets remaining after the creditors had been paid and before the common shareholders got anything. This portion would usually be related to the par value of the preferred shares plus any dividend accrued but unpaid. In the case of dividends, preferred shareholders usually get their dividends in full before the common shareholders receive any, subject to some possible qualifications noted later. The voting privileges for preferred shares vary, but as a general rule, preferred shareholders only have the right to vote when their dividends are in arrears.

The dividend on straight preferred shares is usually fixed and there is normally no maturity date for such shares, so that the yield on preferred shares which are regularly paying their dividends is computed by dividing the dividend by the current market price. This is similar to the treatment for a perpetual bond. When the going rate of dividends on new issues of comparable preferred shares goes up, prices on outstanding preferred shares fall in order to bring their yields into line. Just as bond prices move inversely to interest rates, prices of preferred shares vary inversely with dividend rates, and of course these dividend rates move more or less in line with the interest rates with which they must be competitive.

Generally, yields on preferred shares are above those on common stock but below those on bonds. They are above the yields on common stock because the prospect for capital gain is limited to whatever upward price movement is warranted by falling interest rates. The yield is below that on bonds, at least in Canada, because the dividends on preferred shares are eligible for the dividend tax credit, and thus the after-tax yield on preferreds may be higher than the after-tax yield on bonds for investors with high marginal tax rates. Moreover, companies do not pay tax on dividends from other Canadian companies and therefore are attracted to investment in preferreds even though their yields are lower than those on bonds, the interest from which is taxable. The ranking, then, in decreasing order of quoted yields, is bonds, preferred shares and common shares. At first glance this may seem strange, since risk would seem to be increasing and one would expect yield to vary directly with risk. The explanation for this paradox lies in the differing prospects for capital gain, the exclusion of capital gains on stocks from the computation of yield and the differing tax treatment of the returns.

These generalizations about preferred shares and the yield on them may be complicated by any number of special features which may be attached to the preferred shares. They may be, and usually are, cumulative, which means that if dividends are not paid in any period, then these dividends as well as those for current periods must be paid before any dividends are paid to the common shareholders. This protection for dividends in arrears is obviously an advantageous feature for holders of the shares. The preferred shares might be participating, in which case preferred shareholders may get their stated dividends, and then after the common shareholders get a dividend of a specified amount, both preferred and common share-holders may participate in any further distribution of profits according to some stated formula. Once again this would be a favourable situation for investors, which should argue for a slightly lower yield on the shares. If such additional dividends were in fact paid, the computation of the yield would be altered.

A common feature of many preferred share issues in the first half of the 1980s was retractability, a provision which was advantageous for investors and which was necessary to sell preferred shares in times of volatile interest rates and increased investor concerns over inflation protection. Just as with retractable bonds, the option for redemption lies with the holder, or lender, and there will be a date set for exercising this privilege. Preferred shares might also be callable or redeemable at the option of the issuer which would, of course, be an advantage to the borrower. If preferred shares are both retractable and redeemable at a specified date, then one of these options is likely to be exercised, since if market rates have risen above the specified dividend rate the lender will want to reinvest, and if market rates have fallen below the specified rate the borrower will want to refinance. Consequently, such preferred shares really have a maturity date and are more like debt than equity, and are so treated by financial analysts. There may also be sinking fund or purchase fund arrangements.

Preferred shares might also be convertible into common shares of the company, and this would provide the investor with an opportunity to participate in the growth of the company along with the security of a more stable dividend. This two-way option may cause the preferred share to sell at a premium in comparison with otherwise comparable issues, particularly as the price of the common stock approaches the conversion price. The investor would convert as soon as the dividend on the common stock equalled or exceeded that on the preferred stock, and conversion could be forced if the issuing company exercised a call or redemption feature. Preferred shares could also come with warrants attached, an extra potential benefit to the investor, designed to make the issue more attractive.

A given issue of preferred shares might combine any number of these features. For example, a 1982 issue of series E 14.5% preferred shares issued by Stelco was cumulative, redeemable, retractable and possibly convertible near the retraction date into a further issue of preferred shares. The issue price was $25.00 and the annual dividend was $3.625 per share. As interest rates in the market fell after the issue, the price of these shares rose accordingly, in line with the observations made earlier in discussing yield. However, the price did not rise sufficiently to bring the yield into line with comparable preferreds because the provisions for retraction or redemption in 1988 put an effective maturity date on the issue.

New wrinkles are constantly being devised. In the mid-1980s there were a number of new issues of floating rate preferreds, where the dividend rate changed in line with interest rates. A common formula tied the dividend to some percentage, normally in the range of 70-75%, of the prime rate charged by the chartered banks. There are really two distinct markets for preferred shares, one for individual investors and one for corporate investors, and these floating-rate issues were designed primarily for corporations who found them attractive in comparison with bonds carrying higher nominal rates, since bond interest was subject to corporate taxation but dividends from other Canadian companies were not. The provision for non-taxation of inter-corporate dividends led to inequities when the corporation paying the dividend had not itself paid taxes as a result of accelerated deductions and/or tax credits. Tax reforms plugged this loophole and in the process diminished the supply of new preferred shares designed for corporate investors.

## Stock Trading

The primary market is where companies originally issue common and preferred shares. This might be done privately, as with private limited companies in which there are not more than fifty shareholders and the company is not required to make its financial statements public, since it is not appealing to the public for funds. Such companies may not necessarily be small, however. The T. Eaton Company and General Motors of Canada are examples, the latter being a wholly-owned subsidiary of General Motors of the the United States and thus having only one shareholder. Public companies, on the other hand, may have a new issue of shares underwritten and publish the required prospectus. There is also provision for selling new shares of junior companies, particularly mining and oil companies, through the stock exchanges, accompanied by a statement of material facts which is a less stringent requirement than a prospectus. Other alternatives would be private placements of new issues with institutions, which would not require a prospectus even though the issuing company might be a public company, or "bought deals" where an individual investment dealer or dealers will purchase the complete issue of securities from the company for resale to the public, probably in conjunction with a prompt offering prospectus. In all of these cases, the proceeds from the primary distribution of shares go to the issuing company, except for the underwriting spread.

Trade in outstanding shares, on the other hand, does not bring in capital to the company and takes place in secondary markets. This may be in over-the-counter (OTC) markets which operate through a telecommunications network similar to the bond market, or it may be in centralized locations called stock exchanges. The over-the-counter market deals mainly in unlisted stocks, while stock exchanges provide facilities for trading in the stocks listed on them. The clear distinction between OTC markets and the exchanges is rapidly disappearing, however, as electronic trading via computer screens in "upstairs" markets replaces face-to-face contact on the trading floors.

Generally speaking, in stock trading brokers act as agents in bringing together buyers and sellers, and charge a commission for their services, in contrast to bond trading where dealers act as principals and actually own the securities which they buy from and sell to customers. However, trading in stocks by dealers who make markets and act as principals is becoming more important.

While trade outside the exchanges is increasingly important, the more highly visible trade on the stock exchanges customarily attracts more attention. The exchanges are private organizations whose facilities are open only to member firms. Companies whose stocks are listed for trading have to meet certain minimum requirements, and must make regular financial reports to the exchanges as well as give notice of any material changes in their operations in order to maintain their listing. Some stocks are interlisted on more than one exchange and in more than one country, thus setting up competition between the exchanges to obtain the business of trading in these stocks.

There are four stock exchanges in Canada, located in Montreal, Toronto, Calgary and Vancouver. The Toronto Stock Exchange is now the dominant one, accounting for about half of the total volume of shares traded in Canada, and about three quarters of the value of trade. Vancouver is particularly identified with trade in more speculative junior mining and oil issues, and has replaced Toronto as the centre of this activity to a large extent. Montreal was once the leading exchange, and in recent years has made strenuous efforts to regain some of its lost share, capitalizing on the new issues under the Quebec Stock Savings Plan and aggressively pursuing trade in financial futures and options. The Alberta Stock Exchange in Calgary is very much smaller and deals mainly in provincially-based companies.

The following table gives the preliminary figures for the value and volume of trade in 1990 on the four Canadian exchanges as reported in the *Globe and Mail Report on Business* on January 9, 1991:

|  | Dollar volume (millions) | Share volume (millions) |
|---|---|---|
| Toronto | $64,009 | 5,660 |
| Montreal | 15,590 | 1,370 |
| Vancouver | 4,063 | 4,128 |
| Alberta | 621 | 663 |
| **Total** | $84,100 | 11,817 |

The 1990 figures show a decline of 22.6% in value and 8.4% in volume from 1989, and are down 35.7% in value and 21% in volume compared to 1987. As can be seen from the figures, share volume in Vancouver was relatively high, but the average value of each share traded was under $1.

There are, of course, stock exchanges all around the world. London, New York and Tokyo dominate trading in their respective time zones, and provide virtually around-the-clock trading facilities. In 1991, the New York Stock Exchange (NYSE) was experimenting with extended trading hours to avoid losing business while the NYSE was closed. The other North American exchanges were considering matching the NYSE's hours in order not to lose business to the "Big Board." The NYSE is usually considered the most important with the highest value of trading, but with the appreciation of the yen and the high prices on the Tokyo exchange, the capitalization of companies listed there had, by 1987, become the highest in the world. The Midwest Exchange in Chicago and the American Stock Exchange (AMEX) in New York are other important exchanges located in the United States, and NASDAQ is a rapidly-growing American computerized network for over-the-counter trading. The Toronto Stock Exchange in 1990 was the third largest exchange in North America after the NYSE and Midwest in terms of value of trade, and second in terms of volume after the NYSE, but only accounted for 3.4% of the total value and 9.3% of total volume of trade in North America. Moreover, this excludes NASDAQ which is a trading system rather than an exchange, but which ranked second behind the NYSE in 1990 in both categories.

These exchanges are linked to each other in various ways and competitive with one another. Investment firms may be members of more than one exchange, and many Canadian firms are members of all the Canadian exchanges, as well as in some cases of exchanges in other countries. Stocks may be listed for trade on more than one exchange. Well over 100 Canadian-based stocks are listed for trade in the United States on the NYSE, AMEX and NASDAQ, while about 50 US-based stocks are listed for trade on Canadian exchanges. Further afield, BCE and the Royal Bank are Canadian stocks listed for trade in Tokyo. In the opposite direction, the Montreal Exchange has attempted to obtain listings of European stocks, but with limited success. There is competition between the exchanges for trade in interlisted stocks, and mounting evidence that Canadian exchanges are losing a growing proportion of the trade in interlisted stocks to American exchanges. One of the reasons for this is the greater liquidity in American markets, which ensures customers of being able to make large trades at quoted prices. As a result, the Canadian exchanges sought trading links with the American exchanges so that they could at least share in this trading. For example, the Montreal Exchange has hooked up with the exchange in Boston, and for a while the Toronto Stock Exchange combined with AMEX and Midwest for trading in some interlisted stocks. The latter experiment was abandoned in 1988, since TSE member firms had their own direct order-routing systems to the U.S. and American traders had also failed to use these facilities.

At the end of 1990, the Toronto Stock Exchange had 71 member firms who held between them 121 seats. Obviously some member firms held more than one seat, and each seat entitles the member firms to have six traders on the floor, up to a maximum of twenty-four. The seats trade at prices set by supply and demand. Until 1987, the highest price ever paid for a seat on the Toronto Stock Exchange was $200,000 in 1929, but in 1987 a new record of $370,000 was set and the TSE sold five treasury seats to foreign firms for $361,000 in 1988. The TSE had 1,193 companies and 1,593 issues listed for trading at the end of 1990.

If you place an order to buy or sell a stock with your broker, and this trade is made on the floor of the TSE, the process starts with the broker calling the clerk at his seat on the exchange with the necessary information. The clerk in turn communicates it to the firm's trader on the floor, and this trader then goes to the post where that particular stock is traded and where all the bid and ask prices for the stock are posted. If the highest unsatisfied offer (bid) posted were 12, the lowest unsatisfied asking price (ask) were 12 1/4 and the trader was trying to buy the stock, he might cry out a bid of 12 1/8, and if another trader was prepared to sell at that price, the trade would be agreed on. In that case a three part floor ticket would be initialled, one part going to the exchange to be recorded and each of the other parts going to the brokers involved. Alternatively, the trader might have to pay 12 1/4, in which case the first broker on the list of ask prices would make the sale for his client. Block trading has been developed to reduce the impact of large volume trading on stock prices. When a large block of shares is ordered or offered, the brokerage firm will shop around "the street" looking for another institutional investor to take the other side of the trade at a specific price. If successful, the deal is consumated and "crossed" on the floor of the exchange. If unsuccessful, the firm may take the offsetting position itself, in which case it will be on both sides of the block order crossed on the floor.

As an alternative to the trade being negotiated on the floor of the exchange, it might be arranged through the Computer Assisted Trading System (CATS). Orders are executed directly from the office by computers without the use of floor traders. CATS is used to trade more than half of the listed stocks on the TSE, but the more heavily-traded issues are still done by auction on the trading floor. The CATS software has been licensed for use in Paris and elsewhere, and a system patterned on the TSE's CATS is used in Tokyo to trade the majority of listed stocks. Early in 1986, a new system for trading unlisted stocks was introduced called COATS, or Canadian Over-the-Counter Automated Trading System. It was initially operated by the Ontario Securities Commission using computer facilities provided by the TSE, but the TSE took over the operation early in 1991 and renamed it the Canadian Dealing Network.

There is a great deal of controversy about how the system should evolve, as some say there is no need any more for trading floors while the traders naturally resist a diminution of their role. The trading floors have been deserted in London and Vancouver, and electronic trading through such systems as Instinet is making inroads in the United States. The TSE was going to test the more heavily-traded issues on CATS, but decided instead on new procedures early in 1990 which created an electronic order book and made provision for computer trading off the floor in co-existence with the traditional floor trading. The objective was to make trading fairer, more visible and more accessible.

The transaction described earlier involving the purchase of shares on the floor of the exchange would be an example of a market order, or a trade made at the best price available in the market, but there are many other kinds of orders that could be placed. One might wish to specify that a stock only be bought at a certain price or lower, in which case that would be a limit order, which is normally left open for a specified period, or until it is filled or withdrawn. Another common type of order is a stop loss order, where a client specifies that a stock is to be sold if the price falls to a certain level, perhaps to ensure that a certain paper profit is actually realized. Once the stock sells at that price, the order becomes a market order, and the stock is sold for the best price that can be realized, which may, however, be below the specified limit price. Still other possibilities would be switch orders, which involve selling one stock and using the proceeds to buy another stock, or contingent orders to buy one stock and simultaneously sell another, the order being contingent upon both stocks being at the same price or at some specified maximum or minimum spread between the prices.

Trading takes place in standardized amounts, or board lots, the amount varying according to the price of the share and the rules of the particular exchange. On the TSE, the board lot for shares selling under 10 cents is 1,000; for shares between 10 cents and one dollar it is 500; for shares selling from $1 to $100 it is 100; and for shares sellling over $100 it is 10. There are very few shares selling at more than $100, and one notable one that is, IBM, is an exception to the above rule as it has a board lot of 100, since it is interlisted with New York. Consequently, in the majority of cases on the TSE the board lot is 100, and in this case an odd lot is anything from 10 to 99 shares, and a broken lot is anything from 1 to 9 shares. The exchange also prescribes the minimum quotation spreads, and on the TSE it is half a cent for shares selling under 50 cents each; one cent for shares selling at 50 cents and under $3.00; 5 cents for shares selling at $3.00 and under $5.00; and 12 1/2 cents for shares selling at $5.00 and over. Thus, 26 1/2 cents, $2.81, $4.45 and $5 1/8 are all possible selling prices.

For many years, the exchanges fixed the commissions to be charged by brokers, but since April 1, 1983 rates have been negotiated, or set competitively, in Canada. When commissions were fixed, they were not fixed percentages, but percentages which varied with the value of the shares and were combined with fixed amounts, so that larger trades were charged less in percentage terms, reflecting the economies of scale that were obviously present. On the basis of experience to date with negotiated rates in Canada, it appears that commissions have gone down for large institutional investors, while commissions have increased for smaller individual investors. The Canadian exchanges were forced to move to negotiated rates to compete with the United States, where negotiated rates have been in

effect since May 1, 1975. This change gave rise in the United States
to discount brokers who simply execute trades and offer no advice or
analysis, and the same development occurred in Canada when fixed
commissions were abolished. For small investors, commissions at
full-service brokers may amount to 2% or more, whereas the commissions at discount brokers are about 1%.

The "no-frills" brokers were slow to gain acceptance in both
countries, but by 1985 they had achieved a market share of 20% in
the United States, and an estimated 40% of new accounts being
opened. In Canada, some of the early entrants into the discount
brokerage business disappeared as investors showed limited enthusiasm for this new development, but there now are signs of greater
acceptance and all of the big five chartered banks had entered the fray
by 1991. Originally the banks arranged for the execution of orders
for their customers by discount brokers, but the Toronto-Dominion
bought a seat on the Toronto Stock Exchange in March, 1987, and by
acquiring controlling interests in investment dealers the other major
banks now also have direct access to trading facilities.

Full-service brokers are considering moving to a fee-based system. The fee would be a fixed percentage of the client's assets, the
percentage decreasing with the size of the portfolio. Such a system
would overcome the problem of churning, or trading that is not in the
interests of the clients but designed only to generate commissions for
brokers. While churning is outlawed, brokers can still feel uncom-
fortable recommending trades if it perceived by the client that they
are doing so to increase activity in the account.

The normal settlement for stock trades is on the fifth business day
following the trade, which in most cases means one week later. The
seller must deliver stocks in acceptable form to his broker, and the
buyer must come up with the money for his broker. Since it takes five
business days to arrange the transfer of the names on the shareholders'
register, purchasers must have bought shares at least five days in
advance of the date of record to receive dividends or rights offerings.
Consequently, shares are said to sell "ex dividend" or "ex rights,"
that is, without the dividend or rights, four business days before the
date of record. A certificate may be registered in the owner's name,
or it may be in "street" form, in which case it is registered in the name
of an investment dealer or stock broker who keeps the certificate for
the client and arranges for payments of dividends to him. Street

certificates are more easily negotiable, and ultimately the system may evolve into a computerized book of record. That is the goal of the Canadian Depository for Securities, which presently provides the clearing services for listed and unlisted institutional transactions, and facilitating settlement is fundamental to the growth of international transactions in interlisted stocks.

There are many other important aspects of the stock exchanges and its many regulations. Registered traders, or "pros" on the TSE and specialist traders on the ME and NYSE help to make markets in particular stocks. They arrange for trades in odd and broken lots in accordance with rules that ensure that these take place within a prescribed margin in relation to posted prices, they provide liquidity by ensuring that orders up to a certain size will be filled at posted prices, and they may act as principals in trades. Arrangements exist to ensure that client orders are filled at the best possible prices available, where stocks are interlisted on more than one exchange. There are special rules governing the dispersal of control blocks of shares and for takeover bids which take place through public offers on the exchange. As we have already noted, the exchanges are primarily engaged in trading in outstanding shares, but there is provision for primary distribution of shares of junior companies. As sanctions against companies that do not regularly submit financial statements or give notification of material changes in their affairs, the exchanges may suspend trading in their stocks, or in more serious cases delist their stocks. However, if the stocks are interlisted or traded over-the-counter it may be hard to make such sanctions effective, and competition between the exchanges for business may limit the willingness of a single exchange to discipline an offending company. All these, and many other provisions, make a thorough examination of the stock exchanges a very complex undertaking, and a more detailed examination will not be attempted in this overview.

## Information

Information on stock trading is plentiful. All trades are recorded on the exchange's stock ticker as soon as they take place, and at the end of the day's trading, highest, lowest and closing prices, the change in the closing price from the previous day and the volume of shares traded are all recorded. This information is readily available in the financial press, and is usually given in the following form:

| 52 Week High | Low | Stock | Div | High | Low | Close | Change | Vol |
|---|---|---|---|---|---|---|---|---|
| 43¾ | 34¾ | BCE | 2.56 | $43 | 42⅝ | 42⅞ | +⅜ | 343004 |

This summarizes the information for trading on the TSE in the stock of BCE, formerly Bell Canada Enterprises, for July 9, 1991. The figures on the left give the highest and lowest prices that a board lot of BCE has sold for during the past 52 weeks. BCE is the ticker symbol and $2.56 is the current annual dividend rate. On this day the highest price at which a board lot was traded was $43, while the lowest price was $42 5/8. The closing price was $42 7/8, up 3/8 from the previous day's closing price. 343,004 shares of Bell were traded on the TSE during the day. Weekly, monthly and yearly summaries of trading are also published in both the financial press and the exchange's own publications, which in the case of the TSE is the monthly *Review*. During normal trading hours, from 9:30 a.m. to 4:00 p.m. EST in the case of North American exchanges, information on current bid and asked prices is available from brokers, while information on the trades occurring is carried by the ticker.

The overall trend of prices is given by the indexes. The TSE 300 Composite Index is a weighted index with a base year of 1975 set equal to 1000. The index is further subdivided into 14 groups and 46 subgroups. It was introduced in January, 1977 to replace the old TSE industrial index based on 151 stocks that had been in existence since 1934. The value of the index is computed every fifteen minutes during the trading day and recorded on the ticker, and summaries of its value throughout the day as well as the closing value are available in the financial press. The TSE 300 Index closed at an all-time high of 4112.86 in August of 1987, and at the end of trade on July 9, 1991 stood at 3497.39. The BCE stock that we looked at earlier accounts for nearly 8% of the TSE 300 Index and is the largest single component. The weights assigned to the various companies are based on the market value of the shares outstanding, less any control blocks of shares. The index is based on the 300 most widely traded stocks, although this represents less than 300 companies, since some of them have more than one class of stock included. The list of companies making up the index is reviewed annually, less actively-traded shares are dropped and more actively traded ones are added.

As well as the values of the index, a chart illustrating its history is also given in the financial press. A vertical line is drawn joining the low points and the high points for the day, with a small horizontal bar at right angles to the vertical line to indicate the closing level. The volume is indicated by bar charts at the bottom of the chart. The Montreal Exchange and the Vancouver Stock Exchange also have indexes, and similar information and charts are available for them.

In May of 1987 the TSE launched a new 35 Index which had a very high correlation with the 300 Index, but was designed to facilitate trading in derivative products such as index options and index futures, which will be discussed in the following chapter. The 35 stocks are of large companies, over half of which are interlisted on other exchanges and in which there is an active market, but a ceiling of 10% has been placed on any one stock's share. The index is calculated by multiplying the price of each of the 35 stocks by a set number of shares and then dividing the total by a base value, equal to 5019.02 in July, 1991.

Another widely-used indicator of a stock's performance is the price/earnings ratio. This is computed by dividing the current price by the company's earnings in the most recent twelve month fiscal period. This may be the latest fiscal year, or the most recent four quarters for which figures are available, perhaps spanning more than one fiscal year. The earnings are expressed as earnings per share, that is, earnings after taxes and preferred share dividends but before extraordinary items, divided by the total number of common shares outstanding. The P/E ratio for any particular stock may vary widely, but provides one indication of the confidence of investors in the company. A high price relative to earnings usually indicates an expectation that earnings will continue to grow. Lower P/E ratios are typical of more stable companies such as banks and utilities, or of more speculative stocks that investors have lost confidence in. The P/E ratio for the 300 stocks combined in the TSE Index is also published, and on July 9, 1991 it stood at 24.88. We have already discussed the measurement of yield on stocks, and this too is a widely-quoted number. The dividend yield on the TSE 300 Index as of the same date was 3.38%. Some of these stocks would not be paying any dividends, however, and this, of course, would depress the average yield.

Yields tend to move in the opposite direction to the P/E ratio, since when the price of a stock rises, the P/E ratio rises, everything else being equal, but the yield falls, since it is the dividend divided by the price. This is very apparent in the accompanying chart which

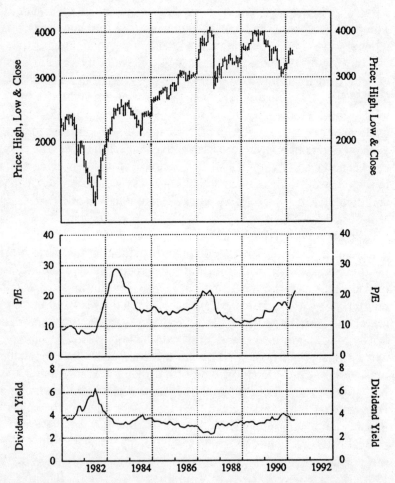

Source: Toronto Stock Exchange, *TSE Review*, 1991. Reprinted with permission.

shows the TSE 300 Index as well as the P/E ratios and yields based on it for the period from 1981. However, the sharp rise in the P/E ratio starting in the second half of 1982, which is pretty well mirrored by a fall in the yield, is better explained by a sharp decline in earnings and an accompanying reduction in dividends than by changes in prices. A similar, though not as dramatic, trend is evident in 1991. The chart for the index is drawn on semi-logarithmic graph paper in order that equal distances up or down indicate equal percentage changes. The TSE 300 Index is plotted on a monthly high, low and close basis, while other values are plotted on a month-end basis.

The most famous stock market indicator of all is the Dow Jones average. Originally conceived by Charles Dow as an aid to technical analysis, it is simply an arithmetic average of the prices of a number of stocks, originally 14 (12 railway stocks and 2 industrials) and presently 30 industrials. Unlike an index, it does not have a base period value, but it has been computed for more than a century now beginning in 1885. The Dow Jones Industrial Average reached an all-time high to that date of 2722 in August of 1987, and the most often-quoted statistic for the Crash of October 19, 1987 is that the Dow fell a record-setting 508 points on that one day.

While the divisor of the Dow Jones average has been adjusted many times to make allowance for stock splits and changes in the composition of the average, and in 1991 stood at 0.559, the indicator remains a simple average, so that higher value stocks are effectively given greater importance. It has also been criticized because it is only based on blue chip stocks, and is therefore not held to be representative of the overall market. Nevertheless, it is the most widely quoted of all indicators even though there are other indexes of market activity in New York, such as the Standard and Poor's 500 composite index. When somebody asks his broker, "How's New York to-day?," he invariably is given the latest figure for the Dow Jones Industrial Average, or even more likely, the change in the average from the previous day.

All this information, and much more, is used by analysts in trying to make recommendations, and the analysts can be more or less grouped in three schools. Technical analysis, for which the Dow Jones average was constructed, is a method of analysis of stock price behaviour based on the proposition that the future trend of prices can be predicted on the basis of patterns from past history. The raw materials for such analysis are records of stock prices and trading volume, while the most frequently used tools are graphs and charts. Charles Dow was one of the first of a long line of technical analysts that runs through to Joe Granville of more recent fame.

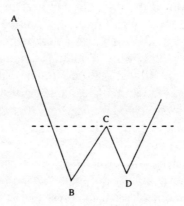

As a simplified example of technical analysis we can look at the famous Dow buy signal, as roughly illustrated above. The industrial average declines in a bear market from A to B, but then recovers about one third to one half of this loss in moving back from B to C. The market declines again to D, but D is somewhat above B, and if the average moves back up past the level at C we have a new bull market starting, as long as the Dow Jones transportation average confirms the trend. Bull markets are, of course, ones where prices are on average rising, while bear markets display falling prices. Another definition might be that bull markets occur when all news, good or bad, is interpreted favourably, while in bear markets all news, no matter how good, is interpreted unfavourably.

The same type of analysis can be applied to price movements of an individual stock in order to select a suitable investment, since knowledge of the overall market trend still does not select a particular security for purchase or sale. In sharp contrast to technical analysis, fundamental analysis focuses on a thorough knowledge and understanding of any industry and of the individual companies in that industry as a guide for the selection of stocks. Fundamental analysts comb through financial results and look carefully at management as well as the general state of the economy and the prospects for particular sectors.

The third and most recent school might be called the random walkers, or supporters of the Capital Assets Pricing Model (CAPM). This group holds that capital markets are efficient in the sense that they reflect all available information, so that it is impossible to make money by buying undervalued stocks and selling overvalued stocks. A strong version would hold that this is true even of information that is not publicly available, while weaker versions would admit that it may be possible to profit from the possession of inside information.

Moreover, it is impossible to predict price movements because they basically follow a random walk. The notion of a random walk is perhaps best grasped by envisaging a completely drunken man in the middle of a large field and trying to guess in which direction his next step will lead him. As empirical support for these contentions, the random walkers point to the record of analysts in trying to predict price movements in the markets, and show that such simple hypotheses as that all stocks will rise by 4% per annum, in line with the average growth of the economy, give better results than those of the analysts when compared after the fact. Indeed, picking stocks by throwing darts at the quotations has tested favourably compared to following the specific recommendations of analysts.

It does not follow, however, that there is no such thing as an investment strategy for stocks. The Capital Assets Pricing Model defines two types of risk, systematic and unsystematic. Unsystematic risk refers to the fortunes of particular companies or industries and can be eliminated through diversification. Systematic risk is the risk affecting all stocks as the market in general goes up and down with the swings of the economy. A particular stock may have more or less systematic risk, depending upon whether its price movements are more or less extreme than the market in general. Beta is the measurement of the degree of systematic risk that a stock possesses, and a beta of 1.25, for example, would indicate that this particular stock is 1 1/4 times as volatile as the market in general. Return in CAPM is determined by the risk free rate of return on government securities, plus the product of the difference between the risk free rate and the return on the market in general, times the beta of the particular security. Thus the market rewards risk, but only systematic risk. The greater the systematic risk taken on, the greater the reward. Consequently, the strategy to be followed is first to decide on the amount of risk that the person wants to undertake and then to buy stocks that have this degree of risk. Of course, it is necessary to diversify in order to eliminate unsystematic risk, since this goes unrewarded by the market. A relatively small number of stocks, perhaps 15 to 20, can eliminate most of nonsystem risk, but if this is beyond the resources of the individual, then recourse can be had to a mutual fund embodying the correct amount of systematic risk.

Mutual funds sell shares to individuals and invest the funds collected in a portfolio of securities. Mutual funds may be closed end, in which case the shares are limited to a predetermined number and they sell in the secondary market according to supply and demand, but typically at a discount to the market value of the fund's investments. On the other hand, an open end fund can issue new shares to shareholders and invest the additional funds. The market value of the fund's investments is regularly calculated to determine the value of each share in an open-end fund both for new purchases and for redemption. There may be an additional charge for buying shares, in which case the fund has a "front-end load," or there may be a charge on redemption, or "rear-end load." Alternatively, the managers of the fund may take a percentage of the value of the assets under management as a commission for their services.

There are an almost infinite number of different funds, and the choice is proliferating steadily. The funds may invest in bonds, stocks, mortgages, money market instruments, or some combination of them, and may also employ strategies involving the use of derivative instruments such as options and futures (discussed in the following chapter). Within the stock category there are funds with different investment and geographical emphases. For example, funds may be invested in growth stocks where the expectation is for capital gain, or in blue chips where the return is principally in the form of a steady stream of dividends. The fund may invest primarily in Canadian securities, or it may be based on Japanese stocks or even in stocks issued by companies in a newly-industrialized country like South Korea. Other possibilities are funds composed of stocks of companies that meet some kind of criteria for ethical behaviour, or a labour-sponsored venture capital fund.

A new instrument introduced in March of 1990 called Toronto Index Participation units or TIPs allows investors to buy part of a basket of stocks mirroring the Toronto 35 Index. The value of the shares is one tenth of the TSE 35 Index. TIPs pay quarterly dividends, and short sellers are required to make up these dividends. TIPs are convertible into the underlying securities, and these shares are held by a trustee. TIPs allow an investor to get the diversification of a mutual fund and performance which corresponds to the market average with no load charges beyond normal brokerage commissions.

The strategy that follows from the Capital Assets Pricing Model is one of holding on to the securities, except for weeding out obvious losers, since it is not possible to outguess the markets by trading. The random walk school, with its negative view of traditional analysis and consequent recommendation not to trade actively is not particularly welcome in the investment community. However, the degree of acceptance of the efficient markets hypothesis is reflected in the fact that there now are many index funds that simply invest in stocks in the same proportions in which they are contained in the market indexes, in effect operating on the presumption that you cannot do better than match the average market performance. Indeed, many funds would have done better had they simply equalled the performance of the indexes, and growing investment in mutual funds is matched by increasingly close scrutiny of their performance.

A slightly different tack, but one that is at least consistent with the weak efficient markets hypothesis, is to follow the trading activity of insiders, the senior officers and major shareholders in a corporation. Insiders are not meant to trade on the basis of prior knowledge of material changes in the affairs of the company, but they are presumably in the best position to form a general opinion on the company's prospects, and their trading activity in the shares of their own companies should reflect this opinion. Information on their trading has to be divulged on a regular basis to the regulatory authorities, and there are analysts who study this data. Buying may be a more reliable signal than selling, however, since insiders may have to liquidate holdings to meet pressing financial needs, just like anyone else.

## Buying On Margin and Selling Short

One of the major motivations in buying securities, and particularly stocks, lies in the hope that they will go up in value and that a profit in the form of capital gains can be realized. Buying on margin is a strategy which attempts to increase this profit by using leverage. Instead of employing only your own money to finance a purchase, you use borrowed funds in addition, and as long as the securities increase in value more quickly in percentage terms than the cost of borrowing the money, your profit will be enhanced. The rates for such borrowing are usually one or two percentage points above the prime rate at the banks, and minimum margin requirements are specified by the stock exchanges and regulatory authorities. In the case of stocks the required margin for shares selling at $2.00 and over is 50%, while stocks selling between $1.50 and $2.00 require higher margins, and stocks selling below $1.50 per share cannot be carried on margin at all. Margin requirements for bonds and debentures are lower, reflecting the smaller volatility in their prices.

Suppose that you have selected a stock which you think is soon going to rise in value and which is presently priced at $10 per share. If you wanted to invest $1,000, you could buy 100 shares of the stock, not including commissions. Alternatively, you could buy 200 shares by putting up the $1,000 as margin and borrowing an additional $1,000 from your broker. If the stock rose to $12, in the case of a straight purchase you would make a profit of $200, again not including commissions. By contrast, if you had bought 200 shares on margin they would now be worth $2,400, and after selling the shares and repaying the loan you would have $400 profit, less the costs of interest on the loan and of commissions. In the first case you make 20% on your outlay before costs, while in the second case you make 40%. While costs are greater in the second case because of interest on the loan as well as somewhat higher commissions, you would still be ahead as long as the increase in the value of the stocks in percentage terms is greater than the rate of interest on the loan. In the above example, let us suppose that the rise in the price of the stock took place over two months and that the rate of interest on the margin loan was 12%. The cost of the loan over the period of the transaction would be roughly 2%, while the rate of increase in the value of the stock over the same period would be 20%. Buying on margin increases the gross rate of return to 40%, while the net rate of return would be about 38%, before commissions.

Leverage is what is at work here, increasing profits by using borrowed money. However, leverage can work both ways. Suppose the stock in the above example had fallen to $8. Since the market value of the shares bought on margin has fallen to $1,600 but you still have a debt of $1,000, your equity is now only $600, but you need to keep a margin of at least 50% of market value, or $800. Consequently, you will receive a margin call from your broker for an additional $200. Should you wish to sell out to prevent any further loss, your proceeds would be $1,600, and after repayment of the margin loan you would end up with $600 before the payment of interest costs and commissions. In this case, your loss of $400 represents a 40% decrease in the amount originally put up, or 42% after allowing for interest, compared with a loss of only 20% if you had simply bought 100 shares at $10 and sold them at $8.

Buying on margin is a higher risk strategy, as was dramatically illustrated in the Great Crash of 1929 when the practice was widespread. With the collapse of market prices, margin positions were quickly erased. When clients did not or could not put up extra cash, their shares were sold, thereby adding further downward pressure to the plummeting market. In some cases brokers did not have time to get in touch with clients, and sold them out before jumping out the windows themselves. Today margin requirements are higher and more strictly enforced, but the 1929 scenario was still repeated to a smaller extent in the break of October 1987.

Selling short is a method of profiting from the fall in value of a security. The technique can be applied to any security, but we will look at it in relation to stocks. If a stock rises in price one can make a profit by buying at a low price and selling at a higher price. It is still possible to make money when the stock falls in price by reversing the order of the transactions—that is, sell first at the higher price and then buy later at the lower price. Since you are selling something that you don't yet own, you have to borrow it. This can be arranged through a broker, and if he does not have the stock to lend, he may arrange to borrow it from someone else through the clearing facilities of the stock exchange. People are prepared to lend securities because they can get the use of the cash proceeds of the sale in the interim, as well as credit for any dividends or rights issued. Anyone selling short must declare that he is doing so, and is required to keep a certain margin in cash with the broker over and above the proceeds of the sale. On the TSE, the margin requirement is that the total credit balance must be 150% of market value for stocks selling over $2.00 per share, and proportionately more for stocks selling at lower prices.

Suppose, for example, that a stock were selling at $10 and you thought that it would soon fall in value. You could arrange to sell short 100 shares of the stock, for which the proceeds would be $1,000 before commissions. You must declare that it is a short sale, and you would have to deposit a further $500 with your broker in order to have the minimum required credit balance of $1500. If the stock subsequently fell in price to $8, and you decided to realize your profit, you would buy the stock for $800 and give it back to the lender. The credit balance in the short account before the purchase was $1,500, so that after paying for the shares there would be $700 left. Since you originally put up $500, the profit on the transaction is $200, the same amount that would have been realized if the stock were rising in value and you bought it at $8 and sold it at $10. However, this return of $200 would be realized on an outlay of only $500, for a percentage return of 40%. Thus selling short under these conditions is the obverse of buying on margin, except for the interest charges on the money borrowed in the case of buying on margin.

Of course, the stock could go up in value rather than down. If the stock in the above example had risen to $12, say, further margin would have had to be put up. Since it would cost $1,200 to buy back the stock to discharge the loan, you would need a credit balance of $1,800 to have the necessary margin of 150%. However, your credit balance is only $1,500— the $1,000 from the proceeds of the short sale plus the additional $500 deposited. Consequently, there would be a margin call from your broker for a further $300. Should you decide to buy in to limit any further losses, the cost of the shares to repay the loan would be $1,200, leaving you with a credit balance of only $300 compared to the initial outlay of $500, so that the loss is $200, before commissions, or 40% in percentage terms. Except for interest charges, this would be the same as if you had bought the stock on margin at $10 and it subsequently fell to $8.

The New York Stock Exchange has a rule that short selling can take place only on an uptick, that is at a price higher than the previously recorded sale, and this has the effect of inhibiting short sales in a declining market. On the Toronto Stock Exchange a short sale can be made as long as the price is the same as the previous trade.

There could be difficulties in borrowing a sufficient quantity of the security to be sold short, either originally or in the event that the owner calls the stock back for some reason. Short sellers are responsible for any dividends or other benefits to the shareholder over the period during which the stocks are borrowed. If there are a lot of short sales in a particular security, the price could move up sharply if a number of sellers try to cover their short sales at the same time. Moreover, it is difficult to obtain up-to-date information on the extent of short sales since they are not reported on a daily basis by the exchanges, and not at all for unlisted stocks. There is no limit in theory to the possible losses with short sales, since there is no limit to how much the stock could rise in value, and the short seller must maintain adequate margin by putting up additional funds, or else the broker will buy in the stock to close out the position.

Obviously, short sellers are speculating on a price fall, while those who buy on margin are speculating on a price rise. In both cases the time horizon is short, and unlike long term investors, the speculators are not very concerned with any return on the investment in the form of dividends. However, as shown above, the profit from a successful short sale is similar to that from buying a rising stock on margin, and if there are equal probabilities of either a price rise or fall, it is not inherently more risky to sell short, beyond the possible difficulties mentioned above. Nevertheless, short selling is widely perceived as a high-risk highly speculative activity. It remains true, of course, that both buying on margin and short selling are riskier than straight purchases.

# Further References

Galbraith, J.K. *The Great Crash, 1929*. Second Edition. Boston: Houghton Mifflin, 1961.

Government of Canada. *1964. Report of the Royal Commission on Banking and Finance*. Ottawa: Queen's Printer, 1964. Chapter 17, pp. 331-44.

Malkiel, B.K. *A Random Walk Down Wall Street*. Fourth Edition. New York: Norton, 1985.

Ross, A. *The Traders: Inside Canada's Stock Markets*. Toronto: Collins, 1984.

# CHAPTER EIGHT

# futures and options markets

FUTURES AND OPTIONS MARKETS PROVIDE A VENUE FOR HIGHLY LEVERED speculative activity, but at the same time provide an important mechanism for hedging against risk. In recent years there has been much greater volatility in interest rates, in exchange rates, and in the prices of securities and commodities. The increased risks which this situation presents help to explain the dramatic growth in demand for ways of offsetting these risks. The strategies behind offsetting risks through the use of futures and options have been used for a long time, but organized markets provide increased access to these strategies as well as increased liquidity for those who employ them. Moreover, new instruments have been introduced, particularly in the financial area. As a result, futures and options markets have been two of the most rapidly growing sectors of the capital market. Unlike the financial markets that have been discussed up to this point, futures markets and options markets do not in themselves serve to transfer funds from surplus units to deficit units, and are thus sometimes said to deal in derivative instruments; but in doing this, they may increase the efficiency of the financial markets that do transfer funds.

## Futures

A futures contract is a legal obligation to take or make delivery of a stipulated amount of a commodity or financial instrument at a specified delivery period in the future. Someone buying such a contract has an obligation to take delivery of the commodity or instrument and is said to be in a long position, while someone selling such a contract has to make delivery of the commodity or instrument and is said to be going short. However, buyers and sellers of futures contracts in most cases do not really take or make delivery of the commodity or instrument, but instead close out their positions by making a sale or purchase of futures contracts equal and opposite to their original transaction.

Traditionally, futures contracts were based on physical commo- *developt* dities such as agricultural products and, later, precious metals. In recent years, however, the list of commodities covered has expanded, and new contracts based on debt instruments, stock indexes and currencies have been introduced. The markets where these contracts are traded are run like stock markets, with a physical location, member firms, traders, etc. The trading is done by open outcry in trading pits, perhaps the most colourful and raucous of any trading arrangements anywhere. The best known centre for trading in futures is in Chicago, where the Chicago Board of Trade and the Chicago Mercantile Exchange are located. In Canada, trading in commodity futures developed first in Winnipeg, and in January of 1984, the Toronto Futures Exchange began operations as a separate institution specializing in financial futures at the same physical location as the Toronto Stock Exchange. Financial futures contracts are also traded on the Montreal Exchange.

Let us look at an example of a particular commodity futures contract. A grain for which Canada is particularly renowned is rapeseed, or canola, and the most active market for rapeseed futures is in Winnipeg. The contracts are for 20 metric tonnes; the contract price is in dollars per tonne with a minimum price fluctuation of 10 cents per tonne or $2.00 per contract; the maximum daily fluctuation is $10.00 per tonne or $200 per contract; and the delivery months are March, June, September, November and January. The figures on the following page summarize the trading in these contracts in Winnipeg for July 11, 1991.

These figures give the opening, high, low and closing prices for each of the five possible delivery months. For example, the contract for delivery in November, 1991 closed at $251.80, up $1.20 from the close on the previous day. Each contract was worth $5,036.00 at the close, since each is for 5,000 bushels or 20 metric tonnes, and this

| Season | | | | | | | | Open |
|---|---|---|---|---|---|---|---|---|
| High | Low | Mth. | Open | High | Low | Settle | Change | Interest |
| 339.00 | 250.00 | Sep | 254.00 | 255.00 | 253.80 | 254.40 | +1.40 | 7,245 |
| 325.20 | 248.10 | Nov | 252.00 | 252.00 | 251.00 | 251.80 | +1.20 | 13,451 |
| 317.50 | 255.00 | Jan | 257.40 | 258.00 | 256.70 | 257.90 | +1.50 | 5,542 |
| 319.80 | 261.30 | Mar | 262.60 | 263.70 | 262.69 | 263.40 | +1.50 | 1,325 |
| 288.00 | 267.00 | Jun | 271.00 | 271.60 | 271.00 | 271.50 | +1.50 | 440 |

Sales: 4,358

Total open interest: 28,003, up 115

represented a gain of $24.00 per contract from the preceding day. The previous high and low prices for this contract since its inception are given, along with the number of contracts outstanding at the end of the day's trading, in this case 13,451. Outstanding contracts are "marked to market" at the end of each day using the closing or settlement price. This means that each client's position is evaluated on the assumption that the position was closed out at the settlement price, and the client pays or receives the "variation margin."

Someone wishing to buy such a contract would not pay $5,036 but only a margin deposit equal to somewhat less than 10% of the value of the contract. The margin is not a down payment, but rather a good faith deposit or performance bond. The broker charges a commission for making the purchase on behalf of the client, but the commission is not charged until the transaction is reversed and the position closed out. Commissions are lower as a percentage of the value of the trade than they are on stocks, and as has also developed recently with stock brokerage, there are discount commodity brokers.

The purchaser is, of course, entitled to take delivery of the rapeseed should he wish to do so, in which case he must come up with the full value of the contract and will receive in return a warehouse receipt. The grade of the commodity acceptable in fulfillment of the contract is carefully specified, but the actual grades deliverable may differ from these specifications, subject to premiums or discounts. Consequently, the buyer could not be certain of meeting specialized requirements, and moreover the location specified for delivery may not be convenient. Actually taking delivery is thus usually impractical, except for merchants or dealers. Similarly, a seller of a futures contract has to be prepared to make delivery of acceptable grades of rapeseed to a warehouse licensed by the exchange, if he does not close out his position.

The price at any time of the contract for future delivery of a commodity is a function of supply and demand, just as the price for the commodity in the marketplace at the present time is a function of supply and demand. However, the price in the spot market reflects primarily the current forces of supply and demand, while the price in the futures market reflects as well the expectations of forces affecting supply and demand in the future, and there is no reason why these prices will be the same. For example, in the case of canola, just before this date prices had fallen to new lows as U.S. government and weather forecasts had indicated record crops of soybeans this fall, and soybeans are a competing source of protein. New fears of drought were reversing these expectations.

Almost any event in the world can affect prices of futures contracts, from a frost in Brazil to a war in the Middle East. Futures prices usually move in a parallel manner to the prices of the corresponding commodity in the spot market, but they are seldom equal or move in exactly the same amounts. The difference between the price of the commodity in the spot market and the price of the nearby futures contract is called basis. For example, the price of canola in store in Vancouver was reported as $247.70 on the same day as the above quotations. While futures markets allow people to hedge against price fluctuations, they do not eliminate basis or the risk that basis will change. Of course, the closer the futures contract gets to its maturity date, the closer the value of the futures contract will be to the value of the corresponding commodity in the marketplace.

Who are the people who lie behind the demand for and supply of futures contracts? There are two basic types of participants in the futures markets: hedgers and speculators. Hedgers are people who are involved in a business which uses or produces the commodity involved in the futures contract, and who wish to protect themselves against the risk of adverse price movements in the commodity. For example, a farmer producing rapeseed may wish to hedge against the risk of a fall in the price of his produce when it is ready for sale. Suppose that he has already got his crop for the current season planted, is afraid of prices falling in the face of record crops, but knows that he can survive as long as he receives $250 a tonne when he sells his crop after harvest. He sees that November futures for rapeseed are selling at $251.80 in Winnipeg, as given in the above quotations. He can then arrange with a commodities broker to sell the number of November contracts that more or less equals his expected crop. When his rapeseed is actually harvested, the contracts will be approaching maturity and their value should be nearly equal to that of the commodity in the spot market. The farmer then buys an equal number of November rapeseed contracts to close out his position with his commodities broker. If the price of the contract has fallen he will be able to do this at a profit, since he will be buying the contracts for less than he sold them for, and he profits in a manner that is exactly analagous to short selling. However, when he actually sells his rapeseed on the spot market, this price will be about the same as the price of the futures contract, which will be lower than the price he needs to survive, or $250. The shortfall when he sells his actual crop will be offset by the profit he made on the futures contracts, and he ends up receiving in total $251.80 per tonne less commissions. This, then, would be a short hedge, which effectively locks in the price of $251.80 for the farmer.

To illustrate the above process, suppose that the farmer anticipates a crop of 100 tonnes. He would sell five November futures, hopefully at $251.80, and receive a credit at his broker for $25,180. If he buys back in at, say, $200, he would have to pay only $20,000, and would realize a profit of $5,180 before commissions. However, when he sells his rapeseed he would receive only $20,000 for it, since the going price should be about the same as that for the maturing futures contract, or $200 a tonne. This is $5,000 short of the amount that he figured he needed to survive. However, the profit that he made on the futures contract makes up this shortfall; he has received in total the equivalent of $251.80 per tonne for his rapeseed, before paying commissions.

Of course, the price of rapeseed might well rise above $251.80 per tonne by November, if, for example, growing conditions for other sources of protein are adverse in other parts of the world. Then the November futures contract would go up in price to reflect the price in the marketplace as it approached its maturity date, and the farmer would have to close out his futures position with his broker at a loss since it would cost him more to buy the contracts back than he sold them for. However, when he sells his crop he also gets a higher price than $251.80, so that this offsets the loss. Suppose, for example, that the price of rapeseed was $300 per tonne in November. It would cost him $30,000 to buy back the five futures contracts, and he would have lost $4,820 before commissions on the futures contracts; but he would be able to sell his crop for $30,000, which is $5,000 more than he needed to get by.

We see, then, that a producer can sell futures contracts short to hedge himself against the risk of a fall in the price of the commodity that he produces. He is able to lock in the price at which he sells the futures contracts and avoid any loss resulting from a price in the marketplace lower than this. Of course, he also foregoes any profit if the price in the marketplace should rise above this.

A producer hedges by going short, but a business which uses this commodity as an input can hedge against an adverse price change by going long. For example, a milling company that crushes rapeseed to produce oil may have long term contracts at fixed prices, and it may estimate that it needs to be able to buy rapeseed for no more than $252 a tonne in order to meet its commitments and still make money. It would buy the number of futures contracts corresponding to its needs. To continue with the above example, if it needed one thousand tonnes of rapeseed in November, it would buy 50 November contracts, hopefully at $251.80 or better, which would cost it $251,800. In November, it would close out its position by selling the contracts, and would buy the rapeseed it needed in the marketplace. If the price had risen to $300 in the interim, it would sell the contracts for $300,000 and would make $48,200 on the futures transactions. Then, when it went to buy its supplies in the marketplace, it would find that they cost $300,000, which would be $48,000 more than it had budgeted. However, the profit on the futures transactions would more or less offset this higher cost, and it would have protected itself against the adverse price change in its input.

On the other hand, the price of rapeseed could fall in the interim, and then the company would have to sell its futures contracts at a loss. For example, if the price fell to $200 per tonne, it would receive only $200,000 for its contracts, and it would lose $51,800 on the transaction, before commissions. Of course, it would be able to buy the rapeseed it needed on the marketplace for $200 per tonne, or $200,000, which is a saving of $52,000 from the amount budgeted, and this would offset the loss. A business engaging in a long hedge, then, is able to protect itself against any rise in price above what it pays for the futures contract, but it also foregoes any gain which might result from a fall in price below that level.

The other major force in the futures market is provided by speculators who buy and sell in expectation of making money from changing prices. Obviously, someone who thinks prices are going to rise should be long and should buy futures contracts so that he is able to sell them later at a higher price, while those who feel that prices are going to fall would sell contracts, or go short, and make money by buying back those contracts in the future at a lower price, just as in selling stock short. The speculators may in this way take up the risk which the hedgers are trying to protect against. Alternatively, the other half of the speculator's contract could equally well be taken by another speculator with a contrary opinion of the future, in the same way as long and short hedgers in the same commodity may to some extent offset each other's positions, as in the above example involving rapeseed futures.

## Financial Futures

The preceding description of hedging and speculation has been couched in terms of commodities, and this is the traditional kind of futures contract. In Canada, commodity futures have been traded in Winnipeg for nearly a century, with the great majority of the trade in grains. While new commodities have been introduced in recent years in futures markets around the world, the really dramatic growth has been in financial futures. The Toronto Stock Exchange and the Montreal Exchange began trading such contracts in 1980 and Winnipeg started to do so in 1981. In 1984, the Toronto Futures Exchange (TFE) started trading financial futures as a separate institution, using a part of the trading floor of the Toronto Stock Exchange.

Interest rate futures are the most important type of financial futures. Futures contracts in fixed income securities allow investors to hedge against changes in short-term and long-term interest rates that would adversely affect their portfolios. Reference was made earlier to inflation risk—the danger that rising inflation rates, even if correctly anticipated in terms of nominal interest rates, would bring higher interest rates and lower bond prices, and decrease the value of existing portfolios. A portfolio manager trying to guard against this risk could sell bond futures. If interest rates did in fact go up, the manager would be able to buy back these contracts for future delivery at lower prices, since bond prices fall when interest rates rise, and in this way the profit on the futures transaction would offset the decrease in the value of his or her portfolio. This method of hedging avoids the necessity of selling the securities themselves and putting further downward pressure on prices, while also enabling interest payments to be maintained.

The Toronto Futures Exchange was unsuccessful in establishing futures trading in Government of Canada bonds in 1984, and in 1989 the Montreal Exchange introduced futures contracts in government bonds. The contracts are for $100,000 worth of 10-year bonds. Similarly, a Treasury Bill futures contract introduced on the TFE never caught on and was abandoned, but there is a futures contract for $1 million in bankers' acceptances traded on the Montreal Exchange that provides an instrument to hedge short term interest rates.

A short term borrower who knows that she will need funds in a few months but is afraid that interest rates will rise in the interim could use a short hedge in bankers' acceptance futures to overcome this risk. She would sell bankers' acceptance futures, and if the anticipated rise in interest rates did occur, buy them back at a lower price, since when the rate of interest rises the discount on bankers' acceptances increases and their price falls. The profit on the futures transaction could be used to offset the increased cost of short term borrowing.

Of course, there are also speculators who might buy or sell futures contracts as a way of gambling on interest rate changes. Someone who felt that interest rates were going to fall rather than rise would buy futures, and if he were right would be able to sell back these future contracts at a later date at a higher price, since when interest rates fall the price of bonds and bankers' acceptances rises. Someone who felt that interest rates were going to rise would sell futures.

Investors in the stock market face different kinds of risk. The particular company chosen may perform badly relative to others in the same industry and this would be known as company risk; the industry in which the company is operating may fare poorly relative to other industries, which is industry risk; or the whole stock market may be depressed, which is called market risk. In outlining the Capital Assets Pricing Model earlier, the first two types of risk were lumped together as unsystematic risk, while the latter type of risk was called systematic risk. The market or systematic risk can be offset by hedging through the use of stock market index futures.

On the Toronto Futures Exchange contracts are traded based on the TSE Index. The TSE 35 Index has replaced the 300 Index as the basic futures contract, and indeed it was specifically introduced to facilitate such strategies as portfolio insurance and index arbitrage, which will be explained below. An investor trying to guard against a decline in the value of his portfolio resulting from an overall market decline could engage in a short hedge by selling TSE 35 Index futures, and if the decline did in fact occur, buy them back at a lower price so that he would make a profit on the futures transactions that would offset the decline in the value of his stock portfolio.

The futures contract on the TSE 35 Index traded on the TFE is for $500 times the value of the index, quoted to two decimal places, so that if the Index were at 192.50, for example, the contract would be worth $96,250. The minimum price variation is .02, or $10 a contract, and the daily limitation on price changes is $9.00, or $4,500 a contract. The contracts are for the three consecutive near months, and settlement is only in cash and not in the underlying securities. The contracts come due on the third Friday of the contract month and trading terminates at the close of business the preceding Thursday.

Suppose, then, that an investor fears a market decline in the next month and decides to hedge against this by selling futures. If his portfolio were worth, say, $500,000 and the TSE 35 Index were at 192.50, he could sell five futures contracts, which at the current value of the TSE 35 Index would be worth $481,250 (5 x $96,250). Of course, the price of the futures contract would not normally be the same as the current value of the 35 Index, but reflect the supply and demand for futures, and if there were a large number of investors with similar fears who were also hedging, this selling pressure might lead to a quoted futures price below the current value. If, for example, the one month's future price were at 190.00, the hedger would receive a credit of $475,000 for the sale of five futures contracts. If, in fact, the market went down by, say, 10% to 173.25 (.9 x 192.50) in the following month, and he closed out his position by buying five contracts at this price, just prior to the close of trading in the contract (when its price should be the same as the market value of the Index), he would have to pay $433,125. This would leave him with a profit of $48,125 (481,250-433,125) in his account with his broker, before paying commissions. This profit would more or less offset the loss of $50,000 or 10% of the value of his $500,000 portfolio. Of course, if the market went up by 10% to 211.75 he would have to buy back the futures for $529,375, and would lose $48,125 (529,375-481,250) on the transaction before commissions, although his portfolio would now be worth 10% more to offset this loss. In effect, he locks in a value of about $500,000 for the portfolio by engaging in a short hedge.

The change in the value of his portfolio would depend upon its average beta, or amount of systematic risk compared to the market average. If the beta were greater than one the change would be more than $50,000, and conversely less than $50,000 if it were less than one. He could buy a larger or smaller number of contracts to reflect the beta factor, and in our example five contracts would allow for a beta slightly less than 1.

A speculator gambling that the stock market will rise in the next month would, of course, go long and buy futures, and he might be the other party to the hedger's contract in the above example. If he is correct, he will be able to sell the future contracts closer to their maturity date for a higher price and realize a profit. It used to be said that "you can't trade in the averages," meaning that even if you can predict in which direction the market in general is going to move you still need to pick a stock. However, with futures contracts on the overall market index, and with the TIPs described in the preceding chapter, this is no longer true.

Portfolio insurance is a strategy designed to allow institutional investors to participate in a rising market, yet protect their portfolios if the market falls. Using computer-based models, portfolio insurance programmes compute optimal stock-to-cash ratios at various stock market price levels, but rather than buying and selling stock as the market moves, the stock-to-cash ratio is adjusted by trading index futures. In a rising market index futures are purchased, and in a falling market index futures are sold.

Index arbitrage, on the other hand, is a strategy designed to take account of discrepancies in the prices of the index futures and of the prices of the stocks which underly them. Basically, the arbitrager profits by buying in the lower-priced market and selling in the higher-priced market. If, for example, it is less expensive to buy the basket of stocks on the futures market than it would be to buy them on the stock market, one can profit by selling the stocks on the stock market and buying a futures contract for the same stocks on the futures market. Of course, account has to be taken of commissions, the dividends foregone in the interim and interest earned on the money derived from the sale less the margin required for the futures contracts. More precisely, the theoretical value of the index futures is a function of the value of the index, the time remaining to expiration, the relative carrying costs for stocks and futures, and the dividends to be paid on the stocks in the index until expiration. At theoretical fair value, the spread between the value of the index and the price of the index future equals the difference between the rate of return on Treasury Bills and the dividend yield of the stocks comprising the index.

If the futures index is at a discount in excess of theoretical fair value, arbitragers would buy futures and sell stock, and conversely when the futures index is at a premium in excess of theoretical fair value they would sell futures and buy stock. In this way, any pressure in the futures market is transmitted to the cash market. For example, selling pressure in the futures market from speculators expecting a decline or investors fearing a fall in the value of their portfolios, will cause the value of futures contracts to move to a discount, and if this exceeds theoretical fair value, arbitragers will buy futures and sell stock in the cash market, so that the prices of the stocks underlying the index will move down in tandem with the price of the index futures. The buying or selling of the actual stocks underlying the index requires portfolios normally only held by institutions such as pension funds or dealers who hold inventories. Selling the stock short is constrained in a falling market, at least in New York, by the requirement that short sales must take place on an uptick. Arbitrage is obviously easier the fewer stocks that are involved, and this explains why the TFE 35 Index was devised to track closely the broad market movements as given by the TSE 300 Index, while at the same time facilitating trading strategies in derivative instruments.

People or companies that have future obligations denominated in foreign currencies can guard against a rise in the price of these currencies by buying currency futures. If the foreign currency does go up, they will make a profit when they close out their positions, which will offset the higher costs they face when buying the currency. Conversely, people receiving foreign currency in the future who fear that it will decline in value could engage in a short hedge by selling futures. If the foreign currency does in fact fall, they will be able to buy back the contracts to close out their position at a profit, which will offset the lower value they will get when they sell their foreign currency. Speculators can also gamble on the direction of the exchange rate in this market, going short if they expect the foreign currency to fall and going long if they think it will rise.

The expansion of futures markets and the introduction of new commodity and financial futures is a world wide phenomenon, with exchanges in London, Paris, Sao Paulo, New Zealand, Sydney, Tokyo, Osaka, Hong Kong and Singapore, and contracts in all kinds of bonds and mortgages, currencies and indexes of stock markets, both broadly based and based on special subsectors such as oil and gas stocks. Perhaps the most synthetic futures contract yet devised is a new one proposed in July 1991 based on pollution rights. Since 1984, financial futures have accounted for a higher proportion of futures contracts than agricultural commodities. Competition between the exchanges for business is intense. The exchange which introduces new contracts usually has an advantage, and this explains the scramble to obtain regulatory approval to introduce new contracts. The important thing for those using the markets is liquidity, which assures that positions can be reversed without greatly affecting prices. Canadian markets have to develop greater liquidity by attracting traders willing to make markets on their own account.

Accompanying the growth of futures markets has been a growth in research concerning their operations. Much of this suggests that while a futures market composed only of or predominantly of hedgers is not viable, a strong involvement by hedgers is important for the success of any futures market. Thus both hedgers and speculators are needed to make futures markets work. Some people fear that futures trading, and the speculation encouraged by it, will aggravate fluctuations in commodity prices, but the evidence does not support this fear; if anything, it points in the opposite direction. Still another question is whether futures prices are good predictors of actual prices in the future, and it seems that when there is no unusual volatility of prices, futures prices often provide better forecasts of the future than econometric models.[1]

## Options

An option is an agreement between two parties in which one party grants the other the right to buy or sell an asset under specified conditions, while the counterparty assumes an obligation to sell or buy that asset. The person who must decide whether or not to exercise the option is the buyer, and he pays a premium for this right. The person who grants the right and assumes the obligation is the seller, or option writer, and he receives the premium. A call option gives the buyer the right to purchase or "call away" the underlying asset from the writer, while a put option gives the buyer the right to sell or "put" the underlying asset to the writer. An American option can be exercised before the expiration date, while a European option can only be exercised on the expiration date.

In the case of options on stock, puts and calls have been available in the over-the-counter market for many years. However, this market has now been formalized at the exchanges, a development which provides added liquidity for the holders of options should they decide to alter their strategies. Trading in listed stock options began in Chicago in 1973, on the Montreal Exchange in 1975 and on the Toronto Stock Exchange in 1976. At the present time Trans Canada Options combines option trading in the shares of over 60 companies on the Montreal, Toronto and Vancouver Exchanges. The Trans Canada Options contracts are in standard units of 100 shares with expiry dates three, six and nine months away when introduced.

Thus a contract conferring the right to buy 100 shares of BCE for $42.50 until next August is a BCE Ag 42 1/2 call option. On July 9, 1991 it closed at a premium of $1.30 per share, or $130 per contract. Someone buying this call option would have the right to purchase or call away 100 shares of Bell at $42.50 from the writer any time on or before the third Friday of August, 1991, and would do so if the price of the shares on the market were above $42.50. Alternatively, the buyer could resell the contract on the options market. If the price were not above $42.50 at the expiry date the option would expire unused.

The key variables are the striking price, in this case $42.50, and the time until expiry. As we saw in the last chapter, the price of the underlying BCE stock on the market was $42 7/8 on July 9, 1991. Consequently, this call option was "in-the-money," since it conferred the right to buy shares for $42.50 which were selling on the market for $42 7/8. When the option is "in-the-money" it has an intrinsic value, in this case $0.375 per share. The rest of the per share premium, or $.925, is the option's time value, since the right was exercisable any time on or before August 16, 1991, which on July 9 represented a period of more than five weeks. The longer the time period the greater the time value should be, and the time value will decrease as the contract approaches its expiry date. If the option is not "in-the-money" when it matures it will have neither time value nor intrinsic value, and it will simply expire without being exercised.

A put option has instrinsic value when the striking price is above the market price, since this allows the holder to sell shares for more than they are worth on the market. On July 9, 1991 a put option to sell 100 shares of Bell Canada Enterprises at $42.50, exercisable on or before the third Friday of August 1991, sold for 50 cents per share, or $50 per contract. As the price of Bell shares on the market was $42 7/8, the put option had no intrinsic value, since nobody would sell shares for $42.50 that were worth $42 7/8; but the guarantee that one could do this at any time until August 16, 1991 had some time value, in this case $.50 per share. One could even argue that this option really had a negative intrinsic value of 37.5 cents and consequently a time value of $ .875. As with call options, the time value will disappear as the expiry date is reached, and if Bell shares continued to sell above $42.50, the contract would simply expire without being exercised.

In summary, call options are "in-the-money," or have an intrinsic value, when the striking price is below the market price, while put options are "in-the-money" or have intrinsic value when the striking price is above the market price. The difference between the intrinsic value of the option and the premium paid for it represents the time value, which will decrease as the contract approaches maturity.

The quotations on the following page summarize trading on July 9, 1991 for the options described above. The two options listed both have striking prices of 42 1/2, and August expiry dates. The second one is the put option, as indicated by the P after the striking price. The volume column gives the number of contracts traded during the day, while the open interest is the number of such contracts outstanding. The column headed "Last" gives the last premium paid, or closing price, for such a contract on that day, while the bid and ask prices are

| Option | | | Bid | Ask | Last | Option Volume | Open Interest |
|---|---|---|---|---|---|---|---|
| BCE Inc | Ag | 42½ | 110 | 130 | 130 | 46 | 1,712 |
| | Ag | 42½P | 40 | 65 | 50 | 25 | 176 |
| | C 42⅞ | | Opt Vol 170 | | | | |

the highest unsatisfied offer and lowest unsatisfied asking price at the close of trading. C refers to the closing price of the underlying stock, while Opt Vol gives the total number of BCE options traded during the day, there being other expiry dates and striking prices available. If the market price of the stock moves sufficiently, new contracts at new striking prices will be introduced.

Trans Canada Options issues and guarantees the options contracts that are traded on the Canadian exchanges. This includes guaranteeing delivery of the underlying shares upon exercise of the contract, and consequently the risk of default is negligible. If the buyer or writer of an option wishes to close out his position prior to the expiry of the contract, he can do so by reselling or buying back the identical contract. In so doing he closes out his position with the clearing corporation, and cancels any further rights or obligations. Buyers and sellers of options pay commissions to brokers to execute the trades. While these are not as large as the commissions that would be paid on the purchase and sale of the corresponding number of underlying shares, they are higher as a proportion of the value of the transaction.

The buyer of a stock option can lose his entire outlay if the price of the underlying stock does not rise above the striking price in the case of a call option, or fall below the striking price in the case of a put option. On the other hand, the losses are limited to the original premium paid. The writer of the call option runs the risk of having shares called away from him for less than the going market price, while the writer of put options runs the risk of having to buy shares at more than the going market price. When would it make sense to buy options, and when would it be a good strategy to write options?

Speculators buy call options if they believe the underlying stock is going to rise in price. For them one of the appeals of options is the leverage which they provide. Using the price of BCE options given above, assume we have a person who believes that BCE shares are going to go up sharply. She could either buy BCE shares directly, or buy a call option on BCE shares. In the case of the Ag 42 1/2 call options, the premium was $1.30 a share and the stock sold last at $42 7/8. If the stock rose to $45 before the expiry date of the option, a person buying BCE shares at $42 7/8 would make $2.125 on an outlay of $42.875, or about 5% before commissions. On the other hand, the option would be worth at least its intrinsic value, and this would be $2.50 if the stock were selling for $45. Consequently, the options bought at $1.30 a share would have almost doubled in value, for a gain of 92% before commissions. The difference in percentage return is dramatic, illustrating leverage at work.

The returns, of course, are very sensitive to the number chosen for the future value of the share. If BCE stock rose only to $43.50, the person who bought stock directly would have made $.625 a share on an outlay of $42.875, or about 1.5% before commissions, while the option buyer would not break even if she receives the option's intrinsic value of $1.00, losing 30 cents a share, or 23%, before commissions. Another possible attraction for the speculator is that unsystematic risk could be offset by diversification through buying a number of different stock options with the same outlay that would be required to buy 100 shares of any one of the underlying stocks.

People might also buy call options as a way of hedging. Someone who expects to have cash available for purchasing BCE stock in August might be worried that the market will rise sharply in the interim, but if he can afford to buy options now he could ensure that the maximum price he pays for the stock is no more than the striking price plus the cost of the option.

The writer of the call option is agreeing to sell his shares for a certain price within a specified period of time. Why would he do this and limit his potential profits? First of all, the writer receives the premium as additional income. If the stock does not rise in price above the striking price, the option will not be exercised and the writer simply keeps the premium. If the stock does rise in price, the writer receives a net price equal to the exercise price plus the premium, and he may be content with this return. Should the price of the stock fall on the market, the premium he receives for writing the option provides added downside protection, since the writer will only begin to suffer a paper loss when the price of the shares on the market falls below the price he paid less the premium received. In a bear market, then, writing call options effectively reduces the cost price of the writer's shares.

A speculative buyer of put options is obviously hoping that the price of the underlying stock will fall on the market. If it does she can buy the stock in the market at the lower price and then sell it at the higher striking price stipulated in the contract. Alternatively, she could resell the put option at a profit. In most cases it would be better to do this, since the commission on the option transaction will be less than that on the stock transaction. This is an alternative strategy to selling short which possesses greater leverage. On the other hand, an investor might buy a put option to protect a paper profit on stock he already holds, since it will give him the right to sell the shares at a stipulated price and in this way insure against the possibility of a decline in the price of the stock on the market. The premium is the cost of the insurance.

People who write put options do so to gain additional income, but of course they may end up buying stock at more than the going price, so that they should be wanting to buy this stock in any event. Alternatively, an investor might wish to buy a certain stock but feel that the current market price is too high. If he writes a put option at the current price, he may end up buying the stock at that price if the current market price falls, but his net cost will be reduced by the amount of the premium, and if the price does not fall he will still get the premium.

Options, like futures, provide opportunities for both hedging and speculation. However, options represent a right rather than an obligation. The potential for different strategies using options is almost limitless, and moreover they can be used in conjunction with futures. Strategies in these markets have been likened to chess, in contrast with the snakes and ladders of ordinary purchases and sales of securities. For example, someone who expects the price of a stock to move a long way in one direction or the other, but is uncertain of the direction, might buy both a call option and a put option at the same striking price close to the current market price. This is known as a "straddle." If the stock price did in fact change markedly it could be very profitable in spite of the double premium required. Volatility is what makes options attractive to speculators and what hedgers are trying to avoid. Consequently, stocks like Alcan that display wider price movements typically attract the most action in the options market. Another possible use of options is to affect the timing of gains or losses for tax purposes. A very speculative strategy is to write call options without owning the underlying security, in which case the writer is said to be writing a naked option.

Options are also available on debt instruments. For example, an option contract on $25,000 Government of Canada 9 1/2% bonds maturing on October 1, 2001 is traded on the Montreal Exchange. An institution wishing to hedge against a decline in the value of its portfolio due to interest rate increases could use such a contract. For example, if in July 1991 a money manager anticipated a rise in interest rates by September of that year he could buy an September put option on bonds. If the '01 bond were selling at 96 1/2 and the portfolio to be hedged were worth $1 million, the manager could buy 40 September 97 1/2 put options at, say, the closing price of $1.55 on July 9, 1991. The premium would be $387.50 per contract, since premiums are given in terms of fluctuations of $100 face value and need to be multiplied by 250 to get the value per contract. If interest rates did rise, and consequently bond prices fell, the put option would be worth more. Suppose the price of the underlying bond fell to 95 and the put option was sold at its intrinsic value of $2.50 close to its expiry date. Each contract would be worth $625, and if the money manager sold all his contracts he would make a profit of $237.50 on each contract, or $9,500 on the 40 contracts, before commissions. The corresponding decrease in the value of the bond portfolio would depend upon how closely its composition matched the characteristics of the underlying bond; but given a 1 1/2 point drop in the price of the underlying bond from 96 1/2 to 95, a drop of about 1 1/2% in the value of the bond portfolio would mean a loss of $15,000 on a total value of $1 million, which exceeds the profit on the options hedge. In this case, the premium for the put option has both intrinsic value and time value, and the erosion of the time value eats up some of the increase in intrinsic value and limits the profit.

Some of the most interesting option contracts to appear in recent years are based on the stock indexes. The most popular one, OEX, is based on Standard and Poor's 100 Index. Hundreds of thousands of these contracts are traded daily on the Chicago Board Options Exchange. The Toronto Stock Exchange trades option contracts on the TSE 35 Index where each contract represents $100 times the value of the Index. Thus if the Index is at 192.5, each contract represents a value of $19,250. Someone anticipating an overall rise in prices on the TSE could buy a call option with a striking price of, say, 195. On July 9, 1991, the Index closed at 192.38 and an August 195 call option sold for $2, or $200 per contract. If the index subsequently rose to 200, the 195 call would have an intrinsic value of $5, or $500 for the 100 units represented, and the person selling at this value would realize a profit of $300 per contract. Settlement is in cash only on the day after the last trading day. Of course, the contract can be be resold in the market at any time until then. This is another way that people can "trade in the averages," or speculate on the general direction of the market. Bulls buy call options and bears buy put options.

At the same time, the TSE 35 Index option provides investors with a way of hedging against risk. To insure against the market or systematic risk of decline in a portfolio suggests a strategy of buying put options. If the market does go down, the option position can be closed out at a profit which will offset the decline in the value of the portfolio. Writers of such put options earn additional income, but lose money if the index declines below the striking price by more than the amount of the premium. Writers of options on the TSE 35 Index have to settle in cash and not by buying or supplying the underlying securities. This may be beneficial, particularly for call option writers, insofar as the securities in a portfolio are not subject to call as they would be in a normal covered writing position.

Currency options are still another type of option that provide opportunities for both speculators and those wishing to hedge against risk. For example, a business that had submitted a bid to sell goods in the United States might wish to insure against the risk that the American dollar would go down in value in the interim. Since this would be the same as a rise in the value of the Canadian dollar, the strategy would be to buy a call option on the Canadian dollar. If the bid were successful and the U.S. dollar did decline, the business could still buy Canadian dollars with the American currency proceeds at the striking price, which would be below the current market price. Alternately, someone speculating that the Canadian dollar would decline in relation to the U.S. dollar might buy a put option. If the Canadian dollar did in fact decline, he would be able to buy it at the striking price and then sell it at the higher market price.

Currency options were first seen in the Netherlands in 1978. They were introduced in 1982 on the Montreal Exchange, and later on the

Vancouver Stock Exchange. These were contracts which allowed the buyer to purchase (call) or sell (put) certain standard amounts of currencies at a stipulated price in terms of U.S. dollars within a specified period of time. The options were cleared through the International Options Clearing Corporation (IOCC) in Amsterdam. The Canadian exchanges found it difficult to develop this market and abandoned it, while Philadelphia has become the most prominent centre for trading currency options.

There are four possible markets for a financial asset: a cash market, a futures market, an option on the cash market, and an option on the futures market. The option on the cash market and the option on the futures market serve similar risk-transferring functions and operate in similar manners.

For example, both futures and options on futures in Canadian dollars are traded in Chicago. A person fearing a decline in the value of the Canadian dollar would sell futures, or buy a put futures option, while someone hedging against or speculating on a rise in the Canadian dollar would buy futures, or buy a call futures option. The futures option contract confers the right to buy or sell a futures contract, as opposed to the currency itself. The options expire before the futures contracts come due. The greater liquidity of the market in Chicago was what caused the failure of the futures contract on the U.S. dollar introduced on the Toronto Futures Exchange. A contract for U.S. dollars denominated in Canadian dollars is, of course, just the obverse of the contract for Canadian dollars denominated in U.S. funds which is traded in Chicago.

There are also options on futures in bonds. An option on Canadian bond futures is traded on the Montreal Exchange, so that one can buy options, futures, or options on futures in Canadian government bonds on that exchange. In the case of bonds, options on futures would appear to have an advantage over straight options, since options based on the actual bonds involve buyers of calls and writers of puts in payments for accrued interest when exercise occurs. As well there is a danger of a price squeeze that could raise the price of any particular bond that is limited in amount if large purchases of it were required to fulfil contracts. In the United States there are also options on futures in stock indexes, and in this case the options on the indexes appear to be more popular than those on index futures.

We saw earlier that there have been a great many new futures contracts introduced in recent years, particularly on financial instruments. Similarly there has been a proliferation of option contracts, particularly on such financial assets as currencies, debt instruments, stock indexes, and gold, as well as options on futures. Just as futures are no longer limited to commodities, options are no longer limited to stocks. These developments have taken place since 1982 as exchanges in different countries scramble for regulatory approval for new contracts. Regulatory approval is required for trading on the exchanges, and standardized contracts on organized exchanges overcome the risk of default by providing a clearinghouse for contracts. In the United States, the Commodity Futures Trading Commission regulates trade in both commodity and financial futures, but there is no corresponding body in Canada.

As noted earlier, the development of liquidity is essential for the success of the markets, and the first exchange to provide the market has a distinct advantage in developing this required liquidity. While individual investors may trade in these derivative instruments, and indeed tend to dominate trading in the stock index options, the role of institutions is fundamental to these markets. They engage in programme trading, using sophisticated computer programmes to buy and sell large amounts of stocks, or of the derivative instruments—options and futures. The machine itself works out when orders should be triggered, and the transactions are facilitated by automated execution systems provided by the exchanges, such as the Designated Order Turnaround (DOT) system of the New York Stock Exchange.

Perhaps the ultimate manifestation of the changed order comes four times a year on the third Friday of March, June, September and December at the "triple witching hour" when stock index futures, stock index options and options on the underlying stocks expire simultaneously. As traders unwind their positions, inter-market arbitrage orders for millions of shares, to be executed at the exchange's closing price, come into effect. The resulting price movements, in both the indexes and the underlying stocks, can be both dramatic and unpredictable.

By now the complexity of the futures and options markets should be apparent. They both provide opportunities for hedging and for speculation. Given the greater volatility of commodity prices, interest rates, and exchange rates, it is logical that increased demand for methods of offsetting the risk inherent in this variability would give rise to new instruments; but many fear that the new contracts and markets simply meet the increased desire for speculation, and thus divert savings from true investment. In any event, new contracts keep on appearing as the exchanges vie for business; the competition is not only between exchanges within each country but also between exchanges in different countries. The Canadian exchanges are trying to build liquidity by encouraging more independent market makers to participate, while at the same time trying to educate Canadian investors and to introduce new contracts particularly suited to Canadian needs. However, institutional use of these markets in Canada has been limited, partly as a result of legislation which prevents pension funds, insurance companies and mutual funds from participating in such markets. Foreign banks and investment dealers operating in Canada make great use of these instruments, but tend to use markets in other countries in many cases. Many Canadian corporations use forward contracts in both interest rates and foreign exchange to offset risk. (Forward rate agreements will be explained in subsequent chapters.) The consequence of all this is that options and futures markets in Canada are relatively underdeveloped.

## Note

1  See Yamey, B. "The Economic Performance of Futures Trading." *The Three Banks Review*, No. 141 (March, 1984).

## Further References

Economic Council of Canada. *Globalization and Canada's Financial Markets*. Ottawa: Minister of Supply and Services, 1989. Chapter 3, pp. 40-50.

Friedberg Mercantile Group. *Understanding the Commodity Futures Market*. New York: Commodity Research Publications, 1981.

Goodman, L.S. "New Options Markets." *Federal Reserve Board of New York Quarterly Review*, Vol. 8, No. 3 (Autumn, 1983).

Yamey, B. "The Economic Performance of Futures Trading." *The Three Banks Review*, No. 141 (March, 1984).

## CHAPTER NINE

# foreign exchange markets

I NTERNATIONAL TRADE AND INVESTMENT NECESSITATE TRANSACTIONS TO change one currency into another, and foreign exchange markets exist to perform this function. They do not in themselves serve to transfer funds from surplus units to deficit units, but by facilitating such transfers on an international basis they may increase the efficiency of those financial markets that do so. The increasing integration of international capital markets has caused an enormous increase in trading in foreign exchange, and figures for April 1989 estimated the daily volume in London, New York and Tokyo alone at $431 billion U.S. While this figure may include some double counting, the total world market surely exceeds $500 billion daily. However, most of the trading is between the dealers themselves, and less than ten per cent of this total may be accounted for by international trade and investment. The most important market is in London, followed by New York and Tokyo.

Far and away the most important foreign currency in Canada, and indeed in most countries, is the U.S. dollar. In Canada the principal foreign exchange market is the market for the American dollar and the exchange rate in this market, then, is the price of the U.S. dollar in Canada, say, $1.15. However, there is also a market for Canadian dollars in New York and elsewhere which performs the same function of changing American currency for Canadian currency. In both markets the demand for U.S. dollars is the same thing as the supply of Canadian dollars, while the supply of U.S. dollars is the same thing as the demand for Canadian dollars. In the world market, the exchange rate is the price of the Canadian dollar in terms of the U.S. dollar, or in our example, about 87 cents American. \$1 U.S. = \$1.1500 Canadian, and \$1 Canadian = \$0.8696 U.S. tell the same story; the equation is simply solved for a different unknown in each case. The price must be the same in both markets, or traders with ready access to both markets could profit by arbitrage, buying in the market where the currency is cheap and selling at the same time in the market where the currency is more expensive.

The main Canadian market for U.S. dollars is in Toronto. The daily volume in it in April 1989 was estimated at \$15 billion U.S., an amount roughly equivalent to the country's foreign exchange reserves. It is not in a specific location like the stock exchange or the futures market, but rather is like the bond market, consisting of a network of communications via telephones, computers and video screens. It is a wholesale market, where the minimum order is for \$1,000,000 U.S. What is bought and sold is access to bank deposits held in branches abroad or with correspondent banks, and transfer is effected by telex or SWIFT (Society for Worldwide Interbank Financial Telecommunications).

An interbank market originated in 1950 when the Bank of Canada's monopoly on foreign exchange dealings arising from wartime controls was terminated, in conjunction with the decision to let the value of the Canadian dollar float rather than be fixed. A market responding to the forces of supply and demand was organized over the weekend, the job being greatly facilitated by the small number of banks involved at the time. Brokers, employed by the Canadian Bankers' Association and located in Toronto and Montreal, communicated bids and offers to the participants while maintaining the anonymity of the other party to the potential transaction. They were paid salaries rather than being principals surviving on the difference between their bid and asked prices. The arrival of the foreign banks and the increasing international integration of the market caused the demise of the brokered interbank market which was accounting for a smaller and smaller part of the trade. The wholesale market in Canada is now integrated into a worldwide market that operates 24 hours a day.

This is the inner hub of the foreign exchange market; the outer rim of the wheel is the retail market, where individual customers deal with the banks or other outlets at rates which reflect those in the wholesale market. The foreign exchange trading department of a bank is located at the head office, and based on its contact with the wholesale market it communicates a rate for buying and selling foreign exchange to the bank's branches. This rate will be higher than that in the wholesale market, of course, reflecting the smaller scale of orders, and there will be a margin between the prices at which the bank or dealer buys and sells foreign exchange in order to make the operation profitable. Large orders may be relayed directly to the foreign exchange trading department at the head office and receive more favourable rates. The trading department at head office must react to these orders as well as to all the buying and selling done at the branches in order to keep the bank's overall position in balance.

The Canadian market for other foreign currencies is not so highly developed, while very active markets for these other currencies are located in London, New York and elsewhere. Consequently, the rates for other currencies in Canada are cross rates derived from the price of the U.S. dollar in Canada times the price of the foreign currency in New York or London. For example, if the U.S. dollar is priced at $1.15 in Canada while the British pound sterling is quoted at $1.65 U.S. in New York, then the pound sterling will be quoted in Canada at $1.8975 (1.15 x 1.65).

If these rates for other currencies were not consistent, (a situation referred to as disorderly cross rates), profitable opportunities for three point arbitrage would be presented. Taking the above example, if for some reason the British pound were quoted at $1.85 in Canada it would be underpriced, and arbitragers could make money by simultaneously transferring funds from Canadian currency into British sterling, from British sterling into U.S. dollars, and from U.S. dollars into Canadian dollars. The three separate transactions involving three different currencies would take place at the same time. Suppose, for instance, that a trader in Canada bought one million pounds for $1,850,000 Canadian. He could at the same time use the million pounds sterling to buy $1,650,000 U.S., and then simultaneously sell the $1,650,000 U.S. for $1,897,500 in Canada. A profit of $47,500 would be realized immediately at a cost of three simultaneous telephone calls.

If such a situation really did exist, the forces of supply and demand resulting from such arbitrage would soon push the rates back into line. The sterling demand for the U.S. dollar would push up the price of the dollar, and consequently the $1.65 price of sterling in U.S. dollars would fall. The U.S. dollar demand for Canadian dollars would push up the price of the Canadian dollar, and consequently the $1.15 price of the U.S. dollar would fall. It follows that the cross rate, which is the product of these two rates, would also fall from $1.8975. Meanwhile the increased demand for pounds sterling in Canada would push up the $1.85 price quoted there, and eventually the two rates would come together and eliminate any possibility of profit from three point arbitrage. In this case, the $1.85 rate is in a thinner market and is out of line, or disorderly, with respect to the much more active markets, so that one would expect it to do most of the moving. In any case, such profitable opportunities simply will not arise in well organized markets today, since modern communications give all traders access to prices in all the relevant markets, and they will post prices which are consistent with orderly cross rates, in the absence of exchange control or other restrictions.

## The Forward Exchange Market

The foreign exchange market that has been described up to this point is the spot market for immediate delivery, with transactions normally settled two days later. However, it is also possible to buy foreign exchange for delivery at a future date but with the price set now; this is known as forward exchange. There are really three distinct groups of participants in the forward exchange market:

(a) hedgers

(b) covered interest arbitragers

(c) speculators

Any international transaction which involves changing one currency into another at some future date involves the risk that the rate of exchange may change in the meantime, and that such a change will affect the buyer or seller adversely. Even when exchange rates were fixed this risk was not entirely absent, since devaluations and revaluations did sometimes occur; but since the formal abandoning of fixed rates in 1973 the risk has been greater as the rates of exchange between most of the industrialized countries have been freer to move in response to market forces. For example, a Canadian supplier shipping goods to the United States in the future at a price in U.S. dollars that is set now runs the risk that the U.S. dollar might decline in value in relation to the Canadian dollar in the interim, and that as a result the proceeds of the sale will not be worth as much when converted into Canadian currency. Conversely, a company borrowing money in the United States at the present time and converting the funds into Canadian dollars runs the risk that the American dollar might increase in value in relation to the Canadian dollar, and consequently the costs in Canadian funds of repaying the loan will rise.

These risks can be overcome to some extent by buying forward exchange. Thus, the Canadian supplier would sell U.S. dollars forward, while the Canadian borrower would buy U.S. dollars forward. The length of the forward contract would correspond as closely as possible to the date when receipts or payments were due, and contracts for 1, 2, 3, and 6 months as well as one year are standard. Maturities beyond one year are possible, but not common, so that forward exchange is not a common way of hedging against risk in the long run. Banks try to "marry" their purchase and sale commitments in the forward exchange market, either internally or in the wholesale market, but offset any remaining long or short position in the spot market rather than accept all the risk that hedgers are trying to offset. While there are minimum amounts required for trading in the forward market, at the retail level these are not large (for example £5,000), and the contracts can be tailored in size to the requirements of the buyer. There is a broad and active market for forward U.S. dollars in Canada, and a less well developed forward market for some other currencies. The rates in the forward exchange market are not necessarily the same as the spot rate, so that hedgers cannot always protect themselves from all changes from the present spot rate.

A second important group using the forward exchange market are covered interest arbitragers who move money internationally to maximize their total returns by taking into account both differences in interest rates between countries and differences between the spot and forward exchange rates. Covered interest arbitrage includes a swap of foreign exchange, which is a simultaneous spot purchase and forward sale, or spot sale and forward purchase, so that there is no foreign exchange risk involved—hence the term covered. Since forward cover normally only exists for up to one year, covered interest arbitrage involves short term flows which really constitute an international extension of the money market.

The process of covered interest arbitrage is perhaps best illustrated by means of an example. Suppose that the following exchange rates and interest rates on three month certificates of deposit were in existence:

| | |
|---|---|
| spot exchange rate | $.8700 U.S. = $1.00 Canadian |
| 3 month forward exchange rate | $.8625 U.S. = $1.00 Canadian |
| 3 month deposit rate (U.S.) | 6.00 % per annum |
| 3 month deposit rate (Canada) | 8.50 % per annum |

A person or institution in Canada with a substantial amount of money to invest for a short period of time, perhaps a company with funds that will be required for an interest or dividend payment in three months time, would wish to maximize the return from these funds in the intervening period. They could buy a three month certificate of deposit in Canada that would yield approximately 2.125% over that time (1/4 of the per annum rate of 8.50%). If, for example, they had $1,000,000 to invest, they would have $1,021,250 at the end of the period. Alternatively, they could buy U.S. dollars, invest the money in the United States in a certificate of deposit, and arrange now to convert the proceeds back to Canadian dollars at the prevailing forward rate. The $1,000,000 Canadian would buy $870,000 U.S. at the spot rate, and this would be worth $883,050 U.S. (870,000 x 1.06 x 1/4) at the end of three months. Converting these proceeds back into Canadian currency at the forward rate of .8625 yields $1,023,826.09 Canadian. Consequently, investing the funds in the U.S. on a covered basis would increase returns by $2,576.09 (1,023,826.09 - 1,021,250.00) compared with investing in a Canadian certificate of deposit. Covered interest arbitrage in this example would give rise to an outflow of funds from Canada, in spite of the fact that interest rates are higher in Canada than in the United States.

The process of covered interest arbitrage would cause demand and supply pressures that would change the variables and eliminate the profitable opportunities. The purchase of U.S. dollars would put downward pressure on the spot rate of $.8700, and the sale of forward U.S. dollars would put upward pressure on the forward rate of $.8625. While these are the rates that would most likely change, it is at least theoretically possible that the increased supply of funds in the United States would cause interest rates to fall there, while the decreased supply of funds in Canada would cause interest rates here to rise. The narrowing of the differential between the spot and forward rates, and possibly the widening of the differential between the interest rates would bring to an end the possibility of profiting from covered interest arbitrage. This is best understood in terms of the covered interest parity condition.

In the above example, it is more profitable to invest in short term funds in the United States even though it is the jurisdiction with the lower interest rates. This is because the gain which arises from the fact that the U.S. dollar is worth more in the forward market than it is in the spot market outweighs in percentage terms the difference in the interest rates between the two countries. The difference between the spot exchange rate and the forward exchange rate is three-quarters of a cent U.S. and is realizable after three months. Expressed as a percentage per annum return on the spot rate of 87 cents this is 3.4%, which exceeds the negative interest rate differential of 2.5%. When the difference between the spot and the forward exchange rate, expressed in percentage per annum, is just equal and opposite to the difference between the interest rates in the two countries, there will be no incentive for covered interest arbitrage. This is known as the covered interest parity condition. In terms of the above example, if the differential between the spot and forward rates exceeded the differential between the interest rates, a narrowing of the exchange rate differential and a widening of the interest rate differential would bring about covered interest parity, and bring to an end covered interest arbitrage.

It follows that, as long as covered interest parity obtains, the country with the lower interest rates will have a premium on its forward currency, and the country with the higher interest rates will have a discount on its forward currency. The latter is the usual situation in Canada, where short term interest rates are normally above those in the United States, and the Canadian forward dollar is normally at a discount. Covered interest parity does not exist in the above example of how covered interest arbitrage operates, but in fact the covered interest parity condition normally holds, thereby preventing the flow of short term funds on a covered basis.

The third group that operates in the forward exchange market is ~Speculators~
the speculators. They were referred to by British Prime Minister
Harold Wilson as the "gnomes of Zurich," and one is tempted to think
of them as faceless individuals operating out of numbered bank
accounts. Such individual speculators undoubtedly exist, but speculation in the forward exchange market is more frequently done by
corporations with liquid assets located in a number of different
countries. Such corporations are trying to suffer as little damage as
possible from anticipated changes in foreign exchange rates. If a
company has dealings in a country whose currency is expected to fall
in value, it will try to minimize its holdings of that currency. It will
do this by leading payments out of the country, for example for
imported inputs, and lagging payments into the country, for example
for finished exports. Such leads and lags increase the supply of the
weak currency and decrease the demand for it, thereby adding to the
downward pressure on it, and helping to bring about the very change
that the speculation is anticipating. Since the operations involve
payments in the future, the desired effect can be achieved through
operations in the forward market, and, since payment for the foreign
exchange is only made when the forward contract comes due, such
speculation is costless in the interim. If the company is normally
engaged in such transactions it will be difficult to detect the speculative
element, although the banks claim that they do not willingly accommodate such speculation.

When exchange rates were nominally fixed, as was the case in ~development~
most countries from the end of World War II more or less until March
1973, speculative activity reached a peak when it became obvious that
currency values were out of line and would have to be altered by either
devaluation (movement down) or revaluation (movement up). In such
cases it was obvious which way, if any, the currency would move, so
that speculators were faced with a one-way option where they could
win but could not lose. For example, speculators in 1965 were betting
that the pound sterling would be devalued, and while this did not
actually happen until 1967, the pound was certainly not revalued in
the interim. It is hardly surprising that in conditions where speculation
is on a one-way option and has the potential of becoming self-fulfil-
ling, it becomes very widespread, and indeed it was speculative forces
that eventually did in the system of fixed rates. The Bretton Woods
system of adjustable pegs, or more or less fixed exchange rates, broke

down in 1971, and after futile attempts to restore it, was formally abandoned in 1973. With the return of flexible rates, foreign exchange speculation became distinctly more hazardous, but people in charge of corporations' finances are still expected to have as few liquid assets as possible in currencies whose value is likely to decline, and so they still engage in activities in the forward exchange market which try to anticipate exchange rate changes.

Speculation in the foreign exchange market will alter the forces of supply and demand in the market and cause the price of forward exchange to change. Consequently, the covered interest parity condition may be disturbed, thus giving rise to covered interest arbitrage. Going back to the previous example of covered interest arbitrage from Canada to the United States, suppose that speculators feel that the Canadian dollar will decline in the near future, and as a result decide to buy U.S. dollars forward. The rate for forward Canadian dollars quoted earlier was $.8625, and speculators would be selling Canadian dollars forward at this price, hoping that the Canadian dollar would fall in the interim, so that they could buy it at the new lower price, say $.8500, and then sell it at the previously agreed rate of $.8625. However, this increased demand for U.S. dollars forward, or increased supply of Canadian dollars forward, would push down the price below $.8625, thereby widening the differential between the spot and forward exchange rates. Yet it was precisely this differential which gave rise to covered interest arbitrage in the first example, since in percentage terms it exceeded the negative interest rate differential. Consequently, speculation in the forward market in this example would increase covered interest arbitrage, giving rise to an outflow of funds in the spot market and a decline in the spot value of the Canadian dollar. In this way, speculative pressure in the forward market is transferred to the spot market, and the forward and spot exchange rates move together.

If the covered interest parity condition does not obtain, we said earlier that the changes in supply and demand to which it gives rise would bring about a return to parity. However, when the disturbance arises as a result of speculation in the forward market this may not follow. The sale of Canadian dollars in the spot market as a result of covered interest arbitrage would cause the value of the spot Canadian dollar to fall, but the forward purchases of Canadian dollars that are the other part of the foreign exchange swap may not cause the price of the forward Canadian dollar to rise, because they are offset by the demand for forward Canadian dollars from speculators. Indeed, the purchases of Canadian dollars forward by covered interest arbitragers may well be the other half of the contracts for the forward sale of Canadian dollars entered into by speculators. The spot and forward rates for the Canadian dollar will fall in tandem, until the forward rate reaches a level at which speculators no longer think they can profit in the future by buying Canadian dollars in the spot market and then selling them at this rate in the forward market. Once speculation in the forward market stops, covered interest arbitrage will also stop as soon as the covered interest parity condition is reached.

One very important participant in the foreign exchange market remains to be identified. This is the central bank, or in the case of Canada, the Bank of Canada. The role of the Bank varies depending upon the type of exchange rate regime and the view that the Bank takes of what its role should be. When exchange rates were fixed, the central bank had an obligation to supply or demand foreign currency so that its price would remain at the fixed level, or, under the rules of the International Monetary Fund until 1971, within 1% on either side of its pegged value. However, Canada did not adhere to the International Monetary Fund rules from 1950 to 1962, or again after 1970. In such circumstances the role of the central bank depends upon the degree of influence it wishes to exert. From 1950 to 1960, the Bank merely resisted abrupt changes in the day-to-day workings of the marketplace without resisting longer run trends. This is a policy known as "leaning against the wind." Between 1960 and 1962, the Bank intervened strongly in the market, and it has often done so since 1970. This is a policy known as managed flexibility. It can do this by buying and selling foreign exchange in the spot market to directly affect the spot rate, using the country's foreign exchange reserves and operating through the Exchange Fund Account. In keeping with the international integration of foreign exchange markets that operate around the clock, the Bank's traders have been known to be active in the middle of the night in the Asian markets to influence the value of the Canadian dollar. The fact that total foreign exchange reserves are about equal to one day's trading volume in the market clearly limits the degree to which the Bank can set the exchange rate.

Alternatively, The Bank of Canada may try to affect the supply and demand in the market indirectly by affecting interest rates, and therefore the interest rate differential between Canada and the United States. If, for example, the Bank wants to raise the value of the Canadian dollar, or at least arrest its decline, it may take actions to increase short term interest rates in Canada. In the Bank's view[1], this will result in an increased discount on the Canadian dollar forward, as traders immediately adjust the exchange rate differential to the changed interest rate differential in order to maintain the interest parity condition. The decline in the forward value of the Canadian dollar causes it to move out of its normal relationship to the spot rate, and people buy Canadian dollars forward because they take the view that the forward value of the Canadian dollar is low relative to what they expect the spot value to be at the maturity of their forward contracts. As the forward Canadian dollar moves up, the spot exchange rate moves up in tandem to maintain covered interest parity. In other words, the Bank, by increasing short-term interest rates, causes the forward rate for the Canadian dollar to decline to the point where speculation in favour of the Canadian dollar is induced, and this speculation causes the forward Canadian dollar to rise and the spot rate to follow it.

Still another possibility in the face of speculation against the Canadian dollar in the forward market would be to supply U.S. dollars forward to meet the demand of speculators who are betting on a decline in the value of the Canadian dollar. The records show that the Bank has also followed this policy on occasion. The effect of intervention in the forward market in this fashion would be to prevent the Canadian dollar from falling in the forward market, and thus to prevent covered interest arbitrage, which would in turn put pressure on the spot market. The Bank is trading off losses of foreign exchange in the spot market, which are announced at the end of every month, for increased commitments of U.S. dollars in the forward market, which are only made public long after the event.

We see, then, that hedgers, covered interest arbitragers, speculators and even the Bank of Canada are all participants in the forward exchange market, and the price of forward exchange reflects the forces of supply and demand which they represent. However, the difference between the spot rate and the forward rate will never be far from the covered interest parity condition because of the possibility of covered interest arbitrage. Given the short-term interest rate differential, maintaining the covered interest parity condition could involve changes in either the spot rate or the forward rate in order to ensure that this condition obtains and is consistent with the forces of supply and demand in both markets.

## Alternative Ways Of Hedging Against Or Speculating On Changes In Foreign Exchange Rates (against FX risk)

Now that options, futures and forward exchange markets have been discussed, it may be seen that there are several alternative methods of hedging against foreign exchange risk. At the same time these different instruments and markets provide alternative mechanisms for speculation; while we will discuss the various possibilities in terms of hedging, it should be remembered that they apply equally to speculation.

Suppose that a Canadian business had contracted to buy supplies priced in U.S. dollars from an American supplier in three months time, and was worried that the value of the U.S. dollar might go up in relation to the Canadian dollar in the interim. It could hedge against this risk in at least four different ways.

1 First of all the business could, in the traditional manner, buy a three month forward contract in U.S. dollars at the bank. The price the company would be paying for the U.S. currency would be set now, although it would not necessarily be the same as the spot price, and we have seen that it would usually be at a premium over the spot rate. The advantages of taking this route are that the amount of the contract can be tailored to the specific requirements of the company, and the company will not have to put up any money until the contract comes due. On the other hand, the company is obliged to honour the contract when the time comes, and there is no possibility of altering it if circumstances change.

2 Another strategy would be buying Canadian dollar options on the Philadelphia exchange. Since it is concerned about a rise in the value of the American dollar, which is the same thing as a fall in the value of the Canadian dollar, the company should buy a put option on Canadian dollars in terms of U.S. dollars, which would give it the right to sell its Canadian dollars at a fixed price in terms of U.S. currency. In this case, the company could choose the price which it wishes to lock in, since there are different contracts available such as

$.865, $.870, $.875, etc. When the time comes for it to pay its American suppliers it would be assured of paying no more for their U.S. dollars than the rate chosen, if the American dollar had in fact gone up, whereas if the American dollar had fallen in value the company would be able to purchase it at the new lower price, and simply allow the options to expire. The cost of this insurance is the cost of the options plus the commissions the company pays to the brokers. The company may not be able to exactly match the amount of its foreign currency needs with the hedge using this method, since the option contracts come in standard amounts of $50,000 Canadian. On the other hand, this route provides flexibility if conditions change, since the company can simply sell the put options and realize a net gain or loss after commissions.

③ A third method would be to sell currency futures in Chicago on the International Monetary Market of the Chicago Mercantile Exchange. The contract is for $100,000 Canadian dollars and is available for the months of March, June, September and December. The business hedging against a rise in the value of the U.S. dollar would sell futures, since a short hedge protects it against a fall in the value of the Canadian dollar. If the American dollar did in fact rise, the Canadian dollar would fall in value and there would be a profit on the futures hedge, which would offset the higher price of the foreign exchange when the time came to buy it. The company would effectively lock in the price for foreign exchange, but this price would not necessarily be the same as either the spot price or the forward price of foreign exchange, since the price of the futures contract would reflect expectations of future conditions. The company would have to deposit some margin with the broker as well as paying a commission when it closed out its position, and it could always alter the strategy if conditions changed in the interim.

At one time another possibility would have been buying a futures contract for U.S. dollars on the Toronto Futures Exchange. Then the strategy would have been to buy futures contracts so that if the U.S. dollar did go up in value the position could be reversed through a sale of the futures at a profit. The profit on the futures would offset the higher price of the foreign exchange when the time came to buy it. This possible course of action is no longer available, as the U.S. futures dollar contract on the TFE was not able to gain sufficient business in competition with the more liquid futures on the Canadian dollar in Chicago, and has disappeared.

*4* Finally, the company could buy a currency futures option on the Chicago Mercantile Exchange. The contract is for $100,000 Canadian and is available for the upcoming three months. The business hedging against a rise in the value of the U.S. dollar would buy a put option. This would give it the right to sell Canadian dollars in the future at a fixed price, and as with the options discussed above, the cost of the insurance is the premium and commission. The company stands to reap some of the benefits if the U.S. dollar in facts falls in value relative to the Canadian one, since it would simply buy its foreign currency at the new lower price and let the options expire.

The method chosen will be determined by comparing the costs and benefits of the various alternatives, keeping in mind not only financial costs but also the conveniences of flexibility and how closely the hedge can be tailored to the exact amount of foreign exchange risk. An added consideration for speculators is the ease of access to the various markets, since it may be easier for them to trade on the futures and options markets than to deal in forward exchange with the banks. Of course, speculators could operate in the spot exchange market, just as the business could hedge its risk by buying the foreign exchange it will need in the spot market now and investing the funds in the interim. The disadvantage of this method compared with the others outlined is that it requires funds now rather than in the future.

# Note

1   See "Short-term interest rates and the exchange rate." *Bank of Canada Review*. January, 1980. pp. 3-11.

# Further References

Government of Canada. *1964. Report of the Royal Commission on Banking and Finance.* Ottawa: Queen's Printer, 1964. Chapter 15.

Sarpkaya, S. *The Money Market in Canada.* Second Edition. Toronto: Butterworths, 1980. Chapter 3.

Shearer, R.A., Chant J.F. and Bond, D.E. *The Economics of the Canadian Financial System.* Second Edition. Scarborough: Prentice-Hall Canada, 1984. Chapter 8.

"Short-term interest rates and the exchange rate." *Bank of Canada Review,* January 1980. pp. 3-10.

**CHAPTER TEN**

# international capital markets

T HE FINANCIAL MARKETS THAT COMPRISE THE CANADIAN CAPITAL MAR-ket have their counterparts in many other countries, and there are supranational capital markets as well. These other markets provide not only additional sources of funds but also additional investment opportunities for Canadians. Flows of capital into and out of Canada have been relatively free of restrictions over the years, they have always been an important influence on the Canadian economy, and they are rapidly increasing in relative importance as the world's capital markets become increasingly integrated. In recent years, international capital markets have been the source of new instruments and technology.

International capital flows move in response to profitable opportunities and interest rate differentials, but they are also influenced by such things as regulation and taxation. They are recorded for any country in its balance of international payments, and more particularly in the capital account. The balance of payments is a record of all the international transactions a country engages in over a period of time, normally a year. It is divided into the current account, which records receipts and payments for goods and services traded during the year, and the capital account, which records capital flows into and out of the country over the same period.

Capital flows are traditionally divided into long term and short term. Short term flows usually refer to transactions in securities with terms to maturity of less than a year, but this distinction is hard to justify in practice, since the purchase of a long term bond could easily

*direct investment*

*long term flow* — *portfolio investment*

be reversed by a sale in a month's time and turn out to be short term even though it is classified as long term. The long term flows are further divided into direct investment and portfolio investment. Direct investment is the purchase of equity with the intention of gaining control of the operations of a company, and might occur if a foreign company buys up a controlling interest in the shares of a domestic company, or simply sets up a subsidiary operation in the host country. Portfolio investment involves the purchase of equity and fixed income securities solely for the financial return and not for purposes of control.

Since the balance of payments statement in theory records all transactions in a double-entry bookkeeping system, if all international transactions were properly recorded the credit and debit entries would balance, and the overall balance of payments would be zero. If changes in the country's foreign exchange reserves are included as part of the capital flows, then the balance on current account must be equal and opposite to the balance on capital account. Consequently, if a country spends more on foreign goods and services than it sells to other countries, it runs a deficit on current account which must be offset by a surplus on capital account, or, in other words, it must be financed by a capital inflow. Conversely, a country that has a surplus on current account must have a deficit on capital account, or a capital outflow.

Since it is impossible to accurately record all international transactions, the balance of payments never comes out exactly even so that debits equal credits and the balance is zero. Statistical discrepancy is the entry which brings the balance to zero, and while these errors and omissions could be in any part of the statement, it is usually felt that they are more likely to be under short term capital flows.

The Canadian balance of payments in most years has been typified by a deficit on current account, and a corresponding capital inflow. While Canada generally has a surplus on merchandise trade (that is, exports of goods exceed imports of goods), this is usually more than offset by a deficit on services, and in particular the interest and dividends that represent the servicing of past capital flows. From 1982 through 1984, the traditional deficit on current account was replaced by a surplus, which implies an offsetting deficit on capital account. In other words, Canada in those years was a supplier of capital to the rest of the world. However, 1985 saw a return to a deficit on current account, and since 1986 the deficit has been at levels close to $10 billion, with a peak of nearly $17 billion in 1989. This means record inflows on capital account.

Canada invariably registers an inflow of long term capital, while the balance on short term flows has been more inconsistent. In the early years of its history, before there was a very developed domestic capital market in Canada, much of the long term inflow came from England as portfolio investment in the form of bond purchases. Between the World Wars, New York succeeded London as the dominant capital market in the world. Canadian capital inflows reflected this, with the United States becoming the major source, although the Great Depression largely dried up capital flows of any kind. After World War II the United States continued to provide most of the capital coming into Canada until recent years, when Canadian borrowers have turned increasingly to other international markets.

A very important part of the long term capital inflow into Canada has been in the form of direct investment. This was particularly the case for the first three decades after World War II as American companies poured funds into Canada, particularly for natural resource development. However, since 1975 there has been, on balance, an outflow of direct investment. This reflects a reduction in the inflow in response to government measures to screen such investment, a negative inflow as Canadians buy back control of existing foreign operations such as Petrofina, British Petroleum and Gulf, and a positive outflow as Canadian companies buy up and set up operations in other countries. The fact that direct investment flows have been on balance outward does not mean that total long term capital flows have been in deficit, since inflows of portfolio investment have more than offset the outflow of direct investment.

It is more difficult to generalize about short term capital flows. Short term flows were often outward on balance between 1960 and 1974, while since then there have usually been short term inflows. However, the statistical discrepancy is often so large as to dwarf the short term capital movements, and if the statistical discrepancy really is in the short term capital movements, it makes it very difficult to analyze the figures.

If capital, on balance, flows into Canada, the explanation could be that interest rates are higher in Canada than in other countries, or in the case of direct investment the opportunities for profit are greater. Higher long term interest rates would reflect better investment opportunities relative to the supply of savings available domestically, while higher short term rates could reflect the same phenomenon, or a deliberate attempt to keep short term rates higher as a matter of policy to induce a capital inflow. There is a general expectation that the 1990s will bring an increased competition for scarce international capital supplies.

There can be little debate about the high degree of interdependence between the Canadian and American capital markets. Canadian borrowers, particularly the provinces and large corporations, have historically relied heavily on New York. Certainly the yields in the Canadian bond market take their lead from New York. There are numerous connections between the money markets in the two countries. The Canadian stock market normally takes its cue from Wall Street. The movements of prices in stock markets around the world are not highly correlated overall, but the one strong correlation that does show up is between Toronto and New York. As we have noted, many of the prominent Canadian stocks are interlisted on American exchanges. The preceding description of the futures and options markets stressed the competition between exchanges in Canada and the United States, and the use of U.S. derivative instruments by Canadian investors, some of them based on Canadian assets. The large Canadian chartered banks having been active for a long time in New York, and the foreign, or Schedule II banks, many of which are American, have increased their presence in the Canadian market in recent years. However, important as the American market has been and continues to be, the most important development of the past two decades has been the emergence of markets that are supranational— truly international markets that do not really operate in any one country and that are usually referred to as the Euromarkets.

## The Eurocurrency Markets

Eurodollars are simply U.S. dollar deposits held outside the United States. There are other currencies held on deposit outside their country of origin, such as Euromarks, Euroyen, Euro Swiss francs or Euro Canadian dollars, and the markets for all such deposits are called the Eurocurrency markets. The Eurodollar market was the first of these to develop, and it is still the most important.

In a sense, the Canadian banks could be said to be the progenitors of the Eurodollar market, since for a long time they booked U.S. dollar deposits on their Canadian head offices and loaned them out in the United States. For some time such deposits avoided reserve requirements in either country, and this cost advantage was said to be the main reason for Canadian banks having provided nearly half of the call loan money on Wall Street at one time. However, the more usual story given as to the origin of the Eurodollar market involves the Russians, who, fearful that their accounts in U.S. banks might be attached by Americans who had claims against the Russian government, decided to remove them from the United States and deposit them in Paris in the Banque Commerciale pour L'Europe du Nord, whose cable address was EUROBANK. This bank soon discovered that there were parties interested in borrowing U.S. dollars held outside the United States, and the Eurodollar market was born.

The deposits held are term deposits or certificates of deposit, rather than demand deposits on which cheques are written, and in this sense the Eurodollar market is an extension of the money market. It is a wholesale market dealing in large amounts, and much of the activity is interbank lending. The market is most developed in London, but there is activity in other European locations and in Canada, as well as the Caribbean and Far Eastern centres such as Tokyo, Hong Kong and Singapore. It can truthfully be said that the sun never sets on the Eurodollar market.

In the early development of the Eurodollar market in the 1960s, U.S. regulations played an important role in promoting the market's growth. The Federal Reserve System, through Regulation Q, limited the amount of interest that could be paid on term deposits in an attempt to keep down interest rates on mortgages, which were the asset corresponding to such deposit liabilities. Depositors saw that they could get higher rates by booking their deposits outside the country in the Eurodollar market, and did so. During the credit crunch of 1968-9, U.S. banks actively bid for such term deposits through their foreign branches, and the head offices then borrowed these funds back from their overseas branches, until the Federal Reserve imposed a stringent reserve requirement on such head office borrowing. On the demand side, American foreign exchange controls encouraged American firms to borrow abroad as much as possible. The removal of most of these regulations by 1973 cut down the growth of the Eurodollar

market, but the market did not disappear, which indicates that it fills
a need and does not simply exist to circumvent regulations. Euro-cur-
rency markets really serve to integrate the fragmented capital markets
of many of the smaller countries, and they played a prominent role in
the recycling of petrodollars which resulted from the oil price increases of 1973-4. The lack of reserve requirements and the economies
of scale resulting from the wholesale nature of the market allow the
banks to pay attractive rates on deposits and still be competitive in
terms of the interest charged on loans.

When an American, or anyone else, decides to make a Eurodollar
deposit, he ultimately has to write a cheque on a current account
deposit in an American bank to be put on term deposit in a Eurodollar
bank. If the depositor's initial funds are in some currency other than
U.S. dollars, and the foreign exchange risk is hedged in the forward
market, then this is the same as the process of covered interest
arbitrage described in the preceding chapter. Indeed, in the case of
Canada, the best approximation to the covered interest parity condition
is given by comparing the differential between the spot and forward
exchange rates to the differential between interest rates on Canadian
dollar certificates of deposit and those on U.S. dollar certificates of
deposit issued in the Eurocurrency market.[1]

With this deposit, the Eurobank ends up with a demand claim on
an American bank, while the depositor has a time deposit claim on
the Eurobank. The Eurobank may use these funds to make a loan, or
if it has no demand for such loans at the moment, it may onlend the
funds to another bank that does. The rate for such interbank lending
is called Libor, the London inter-bank offered rate, and it is the base
rate for lending in the Eurodollar market, with borrowers paying Libor
plus some fraction which depends upon their credit rating. The rates
on loans are usually subject to adjustment at regular intervals and are
thus variable rate loans, and they may extend for medium term periods
from three to seven years. The loans are usually made by a syndicate
of banks, and the borrowers are large corporations, sovereign governments and quasi-governmental agencies.

It has been suggested by Milton Friedman that if the reserve
requirement in the Eurocurrency system is zero, the potential for the
multiplication of bank deposits is infinite. After all, the deposit
multiplier in the domestic banking system is given by the reciprocal
of the required reserve ratio, and one can see that if this is zero the

multiplier approaches infinity. However, this standard demonstration of all introductory economics courses is also tempered by the proviso that all proceeds of loans must be redeposited and none leak out into hand-to-hand circulation. The corresponding leakage in the Eurodollar market would occur if the proceeds of the loans were used to make purchases in the United States, thereby returning the demand deposit to its homeland, rather than being redeposited in the Eurodollar system. The question, then, is whether this is what usually happens, and the answer is an empirical one. If the borrower does use the money to pay an American supplier, that is the end of the Eurodollar. However, U.S. dollars are the medium of exchange for much of international trade, and the borrower could use the funds to pay someone outside the United States who would redeposit the proceeds in another Eurobank, in which case the process of Eurodollar creation would continue. Alternatively, the borrower could change the U.S. dollars into the currency of his own country, and if the buyer of this currency in the local foreign exchange market turned out to be the central bank, and they in turn redeposited their newly acquired foreign exchange reserves in the Eurodollar market to earn the best rate of interest on them, the process of Eurodollar deposit creation would be further fuelled.

This potential for expansion of the money supply and consequent inflation has worried many commentators, but the empirical investigators seemed to have found less cause for concern. Attempts to measure the deposit multiplier have concluded that it is not very large. Moreover, since much of the Eurodollar lending is to other banks, the really important part of the expansion results from loans made to nonbank borrowers, which appear to be a relatively small proportion of the total. The general conclusion of these researchers seems to be that the expansion of purchasing power resulting from the Eurodollar operations is not that significant.[2]

Notwithstanding these generally sanguine conclusions, the lack of regulation of the Eurocurrency markets raises the potential for unfortunate, and even disastrous, consequences. The closest thing there is to a regulatory body for the Eurocurrency markets is the Bank for International Settlements (BIS), located in Basle, Switzerland, which is the one surviving institutional remnant of the League of Nations. It is largely owned by eight European central banks, but its regular meetings draw central bankers from most of the industrialized countries.

The BIS attempts to estimate the size of activity in the Eurocurrency markets, and suggested a figure of about $800 billion in 1980, when syndicated bank lending was at its height. The BIS tries to eliminate the double counting that is inherent in including interbank lending, but it only has the figures from the eight European central banks and consequently has only a partial picture. As a result of a gentleman's agreement in 1971, these central banks agreed not to redeposit foreign currency reserves in the Eurocurrency markets and further the process of Eurodollar creation. This helps to block one of the possible expansion paths referred to earlier, but only insofar as the participating countries are concerned. Less developed countries may continue to redeposit in the Euromarkets any exchange reserves that they may have, and indeed they have been urged to do so as a way of disrupting the system and thereby increasing their bargaining power in demands for international monetary reform.[3]

Perhaps an even greater worry is that of cumulative credit collapse in the absence of any formal lender of last resort for the system. Since a chain of lending from one bank to another often precedes the loan to the ultimate borrower, a default could cause the whole system to collapse like a house of cards. This anxiety came to the fore with the 1974 collapse of the Herstatt Bank, which was a participant in the Eurocurrency markets, although the cause of its failure was foreign exchange speculation rather than the default of a borrower. In 1974, the members of the BIS agreed to the Basle Concordat, under the terms of which each central bank agrees to stand behind banks whose parent companies are located in their jurisdictions in the event that they experience liquidity difficulties resulting from the abrupt withdrawal of deposits, as long as the bank is otherwise solvent and soundly managed. This lender of last resort facility extends to overseas branches, whereas responsibility is shared in the case of subsidiaries. Still the Concordat lacks the formal status of domestic arrangements. In 1988, under the auspices of the BIS, another agreement was reached between central bankers of the industrialized countries that all banks in their countries would adhere to a common minimum risk-weighted ratio of capital to assets of 8% by the end of 1992.

Eurobanks use currency held outside its country of origin in the form of term deposits, to make variable rate medium term syndicated loans. This was the principal way in which the Eurocurrency markets responded to the problem of recycling the petrodollars which flowed from the oil price increases of 1973-4. When interest rates increased in the late 1970s in the wake of accelerating inflation, the burden of servicing variable rate loans became very onerous, in contrast to the situation in the early 1970s when unanticipated inflation resulted in negative *ex post* real rates of interest on fixed rate debt. By the time of the second round of oil price increases in 1979-80, the credit ratings of many of the oil importing countries had deteriorated greatly and recycling of petrodollars in the Eurodollar market was not as widely-used. Such loans as were advanced by Eurobanks to oil-importing less developed countries were largely involuntary and made only to avoid the less attractive alternative of default.

## The Eurobond Market

Eurobonds are a further important development in the Euromarkets. The Eurobond market is the supranational extension of domestic bond markets. While the terms to maturity of Eurobonds may not differ very greatly from those of the syndicated bank loans of the Eurocurrency markets, the difference is that the bonds are negotiable instruments that are saleable in secondary markets. The bonds are issued outside the jurisdiction of any one country and marketed by an international array of dealers to investors all over the world. From the point of view of a Canadian borrower or investor, Eurobonds may not seem greatly different from bonds issued in the domestic market of some other country. They may have features such as being extendible, retractable, or convertible, just as domestic issues do. However, Eurobonds are usually in bearer form with interest payments made only once a year, and they may have fixed or floating rates of interest.

The borrowers in the Eurobond market are governments, quasi-governmental agencies and large multinationals. They borrow in the Eurobond market because it is cheaper than borrowing in their own national markets. The fact that interest is paid only once a year makes the effective cost slightly lower than it would be if interest were paid more often at the same nominal rate. However, when the Eurobond market began it would usually have been cheaper to borrow in New

York, so that there would have to have been some reason for not doing this. For some time, borrowers were kept out of New York by the Interest Equalization Tax, a measure proposed by President Kennedy and enacted by President Johnson that was designed to stem the outflow of capital from the United States. Interest payable on bonds of foreign borrowers raising money in the United States was subject to a tax so designed that the after-tax return to Americans buying such bonds would be no higher than the return on domestic issues, in this way raising the rate of interest that foreign borrowers would have to pay and thus discouraging them from issuing bonds in the United States. This is another example of how American regulations promoted the growth of the Euromarkets. However, the Interest Equalization Tax was scrapped in 1973, so there had to be other reasons why foreign borrowers would not wish or be able to sell bonds in New York. The disclosure requirements for a prospectus are more stringent in the United States than anywhere else in the world, and borrowers may be reluctant to divulge all this information. The borrowing entity may have a poor credit rating, or may simply not be welcome for political reasons. Alternatively, the issue may be so large that even the New York market would have trouble digesting it without depressing prices. More fundamentally, the United States during the 1980s has gone from being the world's largest creditor nation to the world's largest debtor nation, a change that obviously limits the possibilities of raising money there and has raised the relative cost of doing so.

The lenders, or buyers of bonds, in the Eurobond market are people and institutions attracted by the interest rates and the absence of any withholding taxes. Another popular feature of Eurobonds is that they are in bearer form. This allows the lender to remain anonymous, and enhances the potential for tax evasion. The United States government, in an effort to attract buyers to its bonds in competition with Eurobonds, decided in 1984 to eliminate the withholding tax for foreigners. While the Americans have made the registration requirements less stringent for foreign borrowers, they have not yet moved all the way to bearer bonds in an effort to compete for foreign funds.

The majority of Eurobond issues in recent years have been linked to interest rate and currency swaps, and it is the emergence of the swap market that has been the really revolutionary financial development of the 1980s. Swaps provide for the unbundling of risks and in this way promote efficiency. There are gains for both parties, not unlike the gains from trade according to the law of comparative advantage, because each party has access to a particular market at comparatively better terms than the other party. Moreover, they allow participants to decrease their exposure to risk in the longer run in a way that is comparable to covered interest arbitrage in the short term. Estimates by the Morgan Guaranty Trust Company put the notional total principal involved in swaps in mid-1990 at $US $1.9 trillion for interest rate swaps and $US 520 billion for currency swaps.

Let us look at what is involved in a "plain vanilla" interest rate swap when borrowers wish to switch their obligations from a fixed-rate basis to a floating rate basis, and vice versa, and at the same time reduce their borrowing costs. Suppose one institution has a credit rating such that it can borrow in the fixed rate market at 10%, or in the floating rate market at Libor plus 0.25 percentage points, and its preference is for the floating rate loan. A second company with a lower credit rating would have to pay 11.75% at fixed rates or Libor plus 1% at floating rates, and it prefers a fixed rate obligation. Companies with poorer credit ratings typically face a smaller relative disadvantage in the floating rate market since the periodic readjustment effectively reduces the term of the loan. The companies contract for debts on the opposite terms to the ones they favour and then engage in a swap. The better credit borrows at the fixed rate of 10%, while the poorer credit borrows at Libor plus 1%. Each company remains responsible for its own debt, but through an intermediary the poorer credit pays the better credit, say, 10.25%, while the better credit pays the poorer one at the Libor rate. The better credit risk ends up with a floating rate obligation at the Libor rate less .25%, thereby saving .50%, since they pay the poorer credit only Libor and receive .25% more from them than they are obligated to pay. The poorer credit, meanwhile, ends up paying 10.25% to the better credit plus 1% more than they receive from them to meet their floating rate obligation, for a total cost of 11.25% and a saving of .50%.

Foreign exchange swaps are comparable arrangements where borrowers exchange their obligations in terms of currencies and thereby save money. The deal which is usually felt to have started the swap market in 1981 involved the World Bank and IBM. IBM could borrow at a relatively lower rate in Swiss Francs and the World Bank could get a lower rate in U.S. dollars. They each borrowed in the market where they had the comparative advantage, then agreed to pay each other's principal and interest in the other currency, thereby both realizing substantial cost savings but ending up with the desired funding.

Swaps allow for arbitrage between markets to take advantage of differences in costs, and then allow the participants to separate the risks and offset the ones which they do not want to bear. At first they were arranged between the counterparties by an intermediary, but as the market developed, financial institutions began running swap books and taking on the risks themselves that the participants were trying to offload. If the bookrunners are not able to offset their risks through their own operations, they may use other instruments such as futures and options to reduce their exposure.

Eurobonds provide opportunities for investors to diversify their holdings among countries, and also among currencies. The bonds come in a variety of currencies, although here again the U.S. dollar issues are dominant. The most popular non-dollar currency was the Swiss franc, but this has changed in recent years to the Japanese Yen. Euro Canadian dollars normally comprise about 5% of the market, although this share surged to around 20% in the early months of 1988 as foreign investors were attracted by the appreciating Canadian dollar. Canadian borrowers normally account for the majority of the Euro Canadian bond issues, but foreign companies from Japan, West Germany, Australia, France, Denmark, Sweden and the Netherlands are also participants. When these companies borrow in Canadian dollars they normally engage in a swap to change the proceeds into the currencies they need for their operations.

Other variants available on the Eurobond market are issues denominated in "currency cocktails" such as the SDR and ECU. The SDR, or Special Drawing Right, is an international currency created by the International Monetary Fund, the value of which is based on a weighted average of the value of five currencies: the U.S. dollar, the British pound, the German mark, the French franc and the Japanese yen. There is as yet no corresponding currency available for use in private transactions, but the SDR has gained status as the official international unit of account. Someone borrowing in SDRs gets the proceeds in the currency of his choice at the going rate of exchange between this currency and the SDR, the rates being computed daily; repayment is done by reversing the process. The ECU, or European

Currency Unit, is a similar notional currency used by the member countries of the European Community for official accounting, and for setting the values of national currencies which are fixed in relation to each other under the terms of the European Monetary Agreement. It is based on the currencies of the member countries of the European Community, but dominated by the Deutschemark. Both of these currency baskets provide market participants with some protection against exchange rate changes which might sharply alter the relative value of any one currency borrowed or lent, since some of the currencies in the basket will rise while others will fall in relation to one another.

## Other Innovations

Euro-commercial paper is part of a supranational money market, where one-month, three-month and six-month negotiable money market notes that are like commercial paper are issued by governments, quasi-governmental institutions and large companies. Euro-equities are the stock equivalent of Eurobonds, usually forming part of a larger issue which is simultaneously sold in the home market of the issuing company. The inaugural issue in 1983 was a US$ 43 million issue by Bell Canada managed by the Union Bank of Switzerland.

The syndicated bank loan which formed the backbone of the Eurodollar market in its early years declined after the second round of oil price increases at the start of the 1980s as the credit ratings of the oil importing countries fell. However, large payments imbalances remained to be financed, and corporations found that they could approach the market directly at lower cost than by using bank loans, the banks having also suffered a decline in their credit ratings because of the problems posed by their loans to Third World countries.

The short term arrangement designed for this purpose was the note-issuance facility (NIF) where corporations sold short term paper in the market which was backed and underwritten by banks. If the issue did not sell, the underwriting bank would take up the unsold paper and the corporation would still receive its funds. NIFs were an example of securitization, or disintermediation; in this case the banks were the intermediaries bypassed, but they retained their client relationships and collected fees in the process. This market reached a peak of US$ 34 billion in 1985, but it has since declined. More recently there has been a return to the syndicated loan. This now often comes in the form of a multi-option facility whereby the borrower can get money at a set rate above Libor, or try for cheaper rates by asking for bids to provide the finance in the form of short term advances, acceptances or Euro-commercial paper.

Floating rate notes (FRN) were a longer term response to the problems posed by borrowing at fixed rates during the early 1980s when interest rates were highly volatile. FRNs are a security issued through investment dealers that provide a specified level of financing for the term of the note, which might typically be from five to seven years, at a level of interest that varies with prevailing short-term interest rates. This market reached a total of US$ 59 billion in 1985, but it has also declined. A problem that has arisen with the instrument is that the interest margin is set for a relatively long period and credit ratings may alter during that time. Perhaps the most vivid illustration of this was the collapse of the market for perpetual FRNs at the end of 1986. These securities were issued principally by banks, and concerns about their creditworthiness in the face of Third World debt problems caused the secondary market for these notes to evaporate.

Another arrangement that has become widespread in the new international markets is the forward rate agreement. This is like the forward exchange described in the preceding chapter but applies to interest rates. Banks arrange a contract with customers wherein the two parties agree on the interest rate to be paid in the future on a hypothetical amount of capital. If at the maturity date the actual interest rate is higher, the bank pays the customer the difference times the notional amount, while if the rate is lower the customer pays the bank. There are also interest rate caps, where the bank agrees, for a fee, to limit the interest payable on a specified amount of capital over a designated time period where interest is charged at a floating rate, and floors which provide a minimum interest payable. "Collars" provide both a cap and a floor.

Many other innovations have arisen in the capital markets of other countries. Asset-backed securities originated in the United States, and we saw in Chapter Six that mortgage-backed securities emerged in Canada in 1987. The process has been carried further in the United States and widened to include securities based on car loans and credit card receivables. Organized markets in options, along with futures and options on fixed income securities and stock market indexes have been an important development of the past two decades which was discussed in Chapter Eight.

## The Impact On Canada

There can be no question that these international developments have greatly affected Canada's financial markets. The accompanying table shows huge increases during the 1980s in trade with non-residents in outstanding bonds and stocks and money market instruments; clearly the increases far outstrip economic growth plus inflation. Moreover, the figures for stocks and bonds do not include new issues, and, relative to the size of its economy, Canada raises a significantly higher proportion of new funds on international markets than do other industrial countries. While purchases from and sales to non-residents have increased more or less in tandem, the net flow on Canadian securities is usually positive (a capital inflow), while with foreign securities there is customarily a small outflow. Overall there is still on balance an excess of sales over purchases that is consistent with a deficit on current account. The decrease in the figures for stocks after 1987 reflects the withdrawal of investors from overseas commitments after the Stock Market Break.

The Eurocurrency and Eurobond markets have provided new sources of funds and new investment opportunities for Canadians. While the federal government has not been an active borrower on these markets, it has used them on occasion to augment its foreign exchange reserves. Federal government agencies and crown corporations, on the other hand, have been very active in the international markets, often leading the way in the use of such new technology as swaps. Other levels of government and large Canadian corporations have also had access to these markets.

Many of the innovative instruments just described have found their way into Canadian markets. The most important of these is undoubtedly interest rate and foreign exchange swaps, and many of the large Canadian chartered banks as well as some foreign banks now run swap books in Canada. The federal government entered the swap market early in 1988. Note-issuance facilities have seen limited use in

## CANADIAN TRADE WITH NON-RESIDENTS IN OUTSTANDING STOCKS AND BONDS AND MONEY MARKET SECURITIES
### (millions of dollars)

| | 1980 | 1981 | 1982 | 1983 | 1984 | 1985 | 1986 | 1987 | 1988 | 1989 | 1990 |
|---|---|---|---|---|---|---|---|---|---|---|---|
| **Canadian Securities** | | | | | | | | | | | |
| **Sales** | | | | | | | | | | | |
| Outstanding Bonds | 2,501 | 2,672 | 4,624 | 5,242 | 9,719 | 20,505 | 38,162 | 35,974 | 50,316 | 84,371 | 123,679 |
| Outstanding Stocks | 7,676 | 4,929 | 2,921 | 5,044 | 5,392 | 8,502 | 13,944 | 31,854 | 16,145 | 23,543 | 15,728 |
| Money Market Instruments | 32,655 | 33,005 | 16,924 | 19,876 | 23,277 | 25,714 | 32,842 | 40,140 | 65,696 | 91,341 | 96,325 |
| | 42,832 | 40,606 | 24,469 | 30,162 | 38,588 | 54,721 | 84,948 | 107,968 | 132,157 | 199,255 | 235,732 |
| **Purchases** | | | | | | | | | | | |
| Outstanding Bonds | 1,430 | 1,418 | 4,782 | 4,767 | 5,991 | 17,222 | 30,749 | 33,414 | 42,038 | 75,120 | 120,631 |
| Outstanding Stocks | 6,690 | 6,041 | 3,428 | 5,306 | 5,632 | 7,306 | 13,246 | 27,593 | 18,978 | 20,545 | 17,699 |
| Money Market Instruments | 31,605 | 31,802 | 17,782 | 18,122 | 21,747 | 26,291 | 30,452 | 37,600 | 56,405 | 90,806 | 91,617 |
| Total | 39,725 | 39,261 | 25,992 | 28,195 | 33,370 | 50,819 | 74,447 | 98,607 | 117,421 | 186,471 | 229,947 |
| | 82,557 | 79,867 | 50,461 | 58,357 | 71,758 | 105,540 | 159,395 | 206,575 | 249,578 | 385,726 | 465,679 |
| Net Flow | 3,107 | 1,345 | -1,523 | 1,967 | 5,018 | 3,902 | 10,501 | 9,361 | 14,736 | 12,784 | 5,785 |
| **Foreign Securities** | | | | | | | | | | | |
| **Sales** | | | | | | | | | | | |
| Outstanding Bonds | 407 | 451 | 642 | 2,723 | 11,158 | 24,095 | 31,801 | 63,625 | 33,259 | 48,481 | 50,021 |
| Outstanding Stocks | 5,337 | 6,302 | 5,041 | 7,805 | 9,618 | 12,591 | 21,758 | 33,706 | 20,305 | 25,125 | 24,425 |
| | 5,744 | 6,753 | 5,683 | 10,528 | 20,776 | 36,686 | 53,559 | 97,331 | 53,564 | 73,606 | 74,446 |
| **Purchases** | | | | | | | | | | | |
| Outstanding Bonds | 426 | 470 | 865 | 3,171 | 12,274 | 24,483 | 31,937 | 64,458 | 33,173 | 49,998 | 50,062 |
| Outstanding Stocks | 5,324 | 6,220 | 5,349 | 8,620 | 10,311 | 13,059 | 23,247 | 34,255 | 21,096 | 25,867 | 25,409 |
| Total | 5,750 | 6,690 | 6,214 | 11,791 | 22,585 | 37,542 | 55,184 | 98,713 | 54,269 | 75,865 | 75,471 |
| | 11,494 | 13,443 | 11,897 | 22,319 | 43,361 | 74,228 | 108,743 | 196,044 | 107,833 | 149,471 | 149,917 |
| Net Flow | -6 | 63 | -531 | -1,263 | -1,809 | -856 | -1,625 | -1,382 | -705 | -2,259 | -1,025 |
| **All Securities** | | | | | | | | | | | |
| Total | 94,051 | 93,310 | 62,358 | 80,676 | 115,119 | 179,768 | 268,138 | 402,619 | 357,411 | 535,197 | 615,596 |
| Net Flow | 3,101 | 1,408 | -2,054 | 704 | 3,209 | 3,046 | 8,876 | 7,979 | 14,031 | 10,525 | 4,760 |

Source: Statistics Canada, *Security Transactions with Non-Residents*,
Cat. 67-002, December 1990

Canada. They have arisen in response to clients' requests rather than having been actively promoted, as there is already a well-developed Canadian market in bankers' acceptances and commercial paper. Canadian banks have issued perpetual floating rate notes and were caught in the demise of that market, while domestically the banks and others have issued floating rate preferred shares. Mortgage-backed bonds, if not other types of asset-backed securities, are now part of the Canadian scene, and a host of financial futures and options have been introduced in the 1980s. Admittedly, few of them have survived and the market for these derivative instruments remains underdeveloped in Canada. One of the reasons for this may be that forward rate agreements in foreign exchange and interest rates are well developed here and this allows companies to offset some of the risks that they would otherwise have to hedge in the options and futures markets.

Canadian banks and investment dealers have been active participants in the Euromarkets, but their role has been small and declining as a proportion of the market, even in Eurobonds issued by Canadian companies and Euro Canadian dollar bond issues. The banks may have lacked experience since they were precluded from underwriting securities in Canada until recently, while the investment dealers suffered from limited capital. The structural changes which have taken places, as described in the next chapter, should help to overcome these difficulties, and the merging of Canadian banks and investment dealers may presage the emergence of internationally competitive institutions that will regain some of the lost market share that disturbs the Economic Council of Canada. On the other hand, the opening up of markets to foreign pariticipants has brought competition to Canada, and foreign banks and investment dealers are now part of the Canadian financial landscape, providing conduits for the new technology.

The Economic Council has also expressed concern that the benefits of globalization have been limited to the large institutions and the large financial centres. It feels that the process of securitization can be used to disperse benefits to other regions and customers. With respect to the smaller lenders and borrowers, it is interesting that both foreign banks and investment dealers have pretty well retreated from retail trade in Canada in favour of Canadian-owned institutions, which suggests that there may not be large inefficiencies that can be eliminated through greater competition.

The supranational markets and innovations described in this chapter are part of the process of globalization that has integrated the financial markets of countries, introduced new technology and provided additional opportunities for borrowers, lenders and financial intermediaries. The Stock Market Break of 1987 caused some participants to retreat to their domestic markets and reassess international commitments, particularly in cross-border trade in equities. More emphasis was put on liquidity, and institutions reduced their participation in the Eurobond market where the secondary market lacks liquidity. However, this seems to have been only a temporary interruption. The influx of new firms following the opening up of markets in London in 1986 and in Canada in 1987 has been followed by retrenchment in the face of declining volumes of activity. Nevertheless, even if the increased internationalization of financial markets does not progress at the same heady rate, there can be little doubt that it will continue.

# Notes

1   See "Short-term interest rates and the exchange rate." *Bank of Canada Review*. January, 1980, p.6.

2   See Karlik, J.R. "Some Questions and Brief Answers about the Eurodollar Market," A Staff Study Prepared for the Use of the Joint Economic Committee, Congress of the United States. Washington, D.C.: U.S. Government Printing Office, 1977.

3   See Williamson, J. "SDRs: The Link," in Bhagwati,.J.N. (ed.), *The New International Economic Order: The North-South Debate*. Cambridge, Mass.: MIT Press, 1977.

# Further References

Economic Coucil of Canada. *Globalization and Canada's Financial Markets*. Ottawa: Minister of Supply and Services, 1989. Chapters 3-6.

Hogendorn, J.S. and Brown, W.B. *The New International Economics*. Reading, Mass: Addison-Wesley, 1979. Chapter 5.

Kalymon, Basil A. *Global Innovation: The Impact on Canada's Financial Markets*. Toronto: Wiley, 1989.

Karlik, J.R. "Some Questions and Brief Answers about the Eurodollar Market," A Staff Study Prepared for the Use of the Joint Economic Committee, Congress of the United States. Washington, D.C.: U.S. Government Printing Office, 1977. (Reprinted in Adams, J. (ed.). *The Contemporary International Economy: A Reader*. New York: St. Martin's Press, 1979; or Baldwin, R.E. and Richardson, J.D. (eds.). *International Trade and Finance: Readings*. Second Edition. Boston: Little, Brown, 1981.)

Kennett, W.A. "International Banking — The Challenge for Supervisory Authorities." *Bank of Canada Review*, October, 1980. pp. 3-20.

Morgan Guaranty Trust Company. *World Financial Markets*, 1991 Issue 2, April, "Swaps: versatility at controlled risk." pp.1-22.

## CHAPTER ELEVEN

# efficiency and regulation

Having described the various financial markets in Canada that together constitute the capital market, it now makes sense to enquire as to how well these markets work. They should be efficient and innovative, while at the same time providing a reasonable degree of protection for participants, particularly those who are relatively unsophisticated, thereby maintaining that confidence in the financial system which is a prerequisite for its successful functioning.

Efficiency is promoted by competition, and financial innovation, deregulation and the globalization of financial markets have clearly meant increased competition. On the other hand, greater competition may promote excessive risk-taking and increase the danger of insolvency. Attempts to regulate financial markets must reconcile the desire for greater competition with the need for stability. Widespread failure of Canadian financial institutions in the first half of the 1980s seemed to tip the regulatory balance toward solvency concerns, whereas the increasing global competition of the later 1980s swung it back towards promoting competition.

Regulation of the financial markets involves a myriad of considerations in Canada. Some parts of the system are subject to federal jurisdiction, while others are under the control of the provinces who in turn have differing views on policy. As well, there is an increasing need to co-ordinate regulation internationally. Ownership concerns include the threat of losing control to foreign owners, the degree to which commercial and financial enterprises should be linked and the extent to which financial institutions should be widely-held in order to prevent abuses from self-dealing.

Planning regulation affects market structure by means of rules governing entry into particular sectors of the industry. Prudential regulation attempts to affect behaviour by enforcing rules governing the activities of industry participants and may involve self-regulation or policing by governments. Deregulation in financial markets may be viewed not as an end to regulation, but rather as a reduction in planning regulation with the objective of promoting competition and efficiency, while at the same time increasing prudential regulation in an attempt to ensure solvency.

## Efficiency

To economists, the important type of efficiency is allocational efficiency. When financial resources are efficiently allocated in capital markets it means that those who can make the best use of capital are looked after first, while those who would make the worst use of it are looked after last, thereby ensuring that savings are channelled into the most productive uses. This does not preclude the possibility that there may be overriding social objectives which should be included in the calculation of productivity. For example, different levels of regional unemployment may make it preferable from a social point of view to make an investment in Cape Breton Island that yields a 5% return rather than one in Toronto that yields 10%. In that case, the relative returns in the marketplace could be adjusted by means of taxes and subsidies so that the funds would flow into the investment deemed to be more socially desirable.

There are different aspects to efficiency. Internal efficiency, or operational efficiency, refers to how well the marketplace minimizes the transaction costs of transferring funds from savers to investors, where transaction costs include the costs of obtaining information as well as the costs arising from regulation. External efficiency, which we encountered earlier in the capital asset pricing model, means that prices in financial markets should reflect all available information. While a great deal of attention has been focused recently on external efficiency, internal efficiency is also required in order for financial markets to be efficient resource allocators. The Economic Council of

Canada would argue that another important aspect of efficiency is that the markets be accessible to all.

Research on the Canadian bond market in the 1960s indicated that it was not as operationally efficient as the bond market in the United States.[1] There was an ethic of "gentlemanly conduct" rather than competition in the investment industry, and an understanding that "shopping the street" was not the done thing. Borrowers stayed with the same underwriters, banking groups tended to become ossified, lead underwriters were not changed and the relative places of the firms in the banking groups were jealously guarded. This finding of operational inefficiency in the Canadian bond market relative to the United States was even more worrying when one considered that the exclusion of commercial banks from investment banking in the United States by the Glass-Steagall Act of 1933 is widely felt to have reduced competition and to have led to excessive profits in the bond underwriting business in that country.

These concerns, however, may now be outdated. The development of the bought deal (where a dealer or small group of dealers, acting as principals, buy up a complete issue of new securities at an agreed price directly from the borrower for resale to others) is reported to have reduced flotation costs to about 1%, compared to 2% or more for the more traditional underwriting process. The existence of international alternatives, particularly in the Euromarkets, provides a guarantee of relative operational efficiency for those borrowers large enough and sufficiently creditworthy to have access to those markets. Moreover, there is an "exempt market" in Canada where exemption from registration requirements is given to certain new issues, including government issues, short term negotiable promissory notes or commercial paper greater than $50,000, and private placements where the acquisition cost was not less than $97,000 (increased to $150,000 on July 1, 1987). The rationale for this exemption is that the borrowers are sufficiently well known or the purchasers sufficiently sophisticated that there is no need for extensive disclosure. International competition was provided in this market by foreign firms who, until 1988, did not need to be registered. Foreign securities dealers competing directly in the Ontario underwriting market now need to be registered, but private placements continue to account for a significant share of new security issues, with one estimate in 1989 placing the share of new corporate debt and equity sold in this manner at 30%.

With respect to internal, or operational, efficiency in secondary stock markets, it is worth noting that stock markets in Canada mainly consist of exchanges trading listed stocks, with only limited over-the-counter (OTC) trade. Moreover, the leading stock exchange, the Toronto Stock Exchange (TSE), traditionally attempted to maintain basically a broker market, presumably because it feared domination of the market by dealers. This contrasts with the United States, where there are substantial OTC markets, led by NASDAQ, as well as the "third market" for trade in listed stocks that takes place between dealers outside the exchanges. In trade on the New York Stock Exchange (NYSE), a larger role is played by the dealers who are specialists and who make markets.

A study by Seha Tinic and Richard West in 1974 found that the bid-ask spreads were wider on the TSE than on the NYSE, and the marketability of a TSE security having the same price as a NYSE listed stock was inferior, even if it had the same level of trading activity.[2] They concluded that the price of liquidity was higher on the TSE than on the NYSE or OTC markets. These findings have negative implications for both investors and intermediaries in Canada. The study attributed the higher price of liquidity in Canada, at least in part, to the lack of a well-established dealer market on the TSE.

Increased activity of dealers, as opposed to brokers, reflects the liquidity needs of institutions, which are accounting for an increasing share of the trading, and through their power foment many of the innovations in the markets. As well, in recent years, and especially since the Stock Market Break of 1987, firms are doing much more trading on their own account rather than just for clients. The Canadian exchanges have tried to become more competitive by giving dealers a larger role in the market as principals, in this way enhancing liquidity. The Montreal Exchange led the way by appointing specialists, and the TSE fought back with enhanced market-making capabilities for its registered traders, or "pros." Dealers now account for a large proportion of the exchange trading, and a TSE survey in 1990 was reported as finding that brokers acting as principals accounted for 60% of trading by value, institutions for 30% and private individuals for 10%.[3]

Commission costs for stock trading were consistently higher in Canada than in the United States before the introduction of negotiated rates between the client and agent, which began in the United States in 1975 and in Canada in 1983. The existence of stocks interlisted on exchanges in both countries, as well as the trading in Canadian stock in the United States that takes place on the OTC and third markets, forced Canadian firms to match U.S. commission rates in order to secure business. Even before Canada moved to fully negotiated rates, commissions were negotiable on trades with a value in excess of $500,000. The evidence in the United States since the introduction of negotiated rates points to lower commission rates for both institutions and individuals, while in Canada it appears that the rates at full service brokers have fallen for institutions but have risen for individuals.

The reason for the difference between Canadian and American experience may lie in the reception given to discount brokers in the two countries. Discount brokers simply execute trades without offering any advice or research assistance; it is argued that this gives customers the option of buying and paying separately for these added services if they want them, rather than having their cost included in the commissions. The more acceptance gained by discount brokers, the greater the pressure on rates charged to individuals from full service brokers. In any event, commissions for institutional investors have fallen, and now there is concern with so-called soft dollar deals, where brokers provide institutional investors with research, trips taken ostensibly to investigate investments, or other benefits, in the expectation of having trading commissions directed their way at more than the lowest possible rates.

When markets are international in scope, the presumption is that Canadian institutions operating in them must be efficient in order to survive. For example, transactions in the Canadian wholesale foreign exchange market must be at competitive prices or else they would take place in other countries, since market participants have access to these other markets as well. Similarly, the high degree of international integration in money markets, as exemplified by the Eurocurrency markets, means that large lenders and borrowers have access to alternatives. Canadian intermediaries, at least in their operations in this international wholesale market, have to be as efficient as their competitors in order to survive, and the same conclusion should apply to the domestic market, as long as international competitors have access to it.

There is not much evidence on the comparative efficiency of the rapidly growing options and futures markets. However, there is a great deal of international competition here as well, with U.S. markets listing options on Canadian stocks, and futures markets trading in many similar contracts in Canada and the United States. There is reason, therefore, to presume that Canadians are about as well served as Americans, if they have the alternative of taking their business to the United States. They have done just that with futures contracts in American dollars, preferring to trade in Canadian dollar futures in the more active Chicago market, and with currency options on the Canadian dollar, where Philadelphia outcompeted Montreal on the basis of liquidity.

Generally, secondary markets in Canada are thin and illiquid compared to those in the United States. Fewer buyers and sellers make it more difficult to effect large transactions without significantly altering prices. This can be a problem, particularly for institutions. Spreads between bid and asked prices are typically wider in Canada, or the amounts offered at posted prices smaller. This illiquidity in secondary markets in turn limits the scope of primary markets. To the extent that liquidity is a factor attracting business, the more liquid markets in the United States are able to attract business away from Canada, which of course only accentuates the illiquidity problem north of the border. The increasing integration of world capital markets makes this both less of a problem for large Canadian borrowers and investors and more of a worry for Canadian intermediaries. The Economic Council of Canada has expressed concern about both the declining share of business done by Canadian intermediaries in the international markets and the limited access of small retail lenders and borrowers to the benefits of financial innovation and the globalization of markets.[4]

Nevertheless, the efficiency of Canadian markets seems to be reasonably high and has greatly improved in recent years. Canadians inevitably compare their markets with those in the United States, which are among the most liquid and efficient in the world, rather than with those of other countries of Canada's size where the standards are not so high. However, the securities market in Canada is the fourth largest domestic market in the world, after England, the United States and Japan. The relative operational inefficiency in the bond and stock markets that existed in the past has been reduced in recent years, and the competition from international markets has provided alternatives for large Canadian borrowers and investors, as well as competition for Canadian intermediaries.

## Competition

Competition is a spur to efficiency, and the first thing economists would look at in assessing the competition in markets would be the degree of concentration. Studies of the bond market market in Canada in the 1960s and 1970s revealed a high degree of concentration in terms of the traditional measures of the share of activity of the four or eight largest firms. Since that time the overall number of firms has declined and the share of the top firms has probably increased. However, the makeup of the largest firms has probably changed somewhat—a sign of competition.

This way of assessing the state of competition is not very satisfactory. It not only fails to take account of competition from outside the country, but it also fails to take into account competition from within the country that comes from parts of the financial industry that were previously separated, and this is undoubtedly the most important development of recent years. It is not an entirely new development, however; as the Porter Report noted in 1964, "...the traditional division of the financial business into semi-private preserves has been replaced by a more open system in which virtually no-one feels bound to stay only in the field where he first got his start, and almost everyone is subject to competition from both newcomers and established institutions."[5] Since that time the pace of competition between different sectors of the financial system has greatly quickened.

In Canada, the provision of financial services has traditionally been separated into four functions or pillars: banking, trust, insurance and securities. The logic behind separating the functions is to avoid conflicts of interest. For example, commercial lending is the basic activity of banks, and if banks were able to underwrite securities there would be a danger that they might market securities to help support a firm to which they had already advanced loans, thereby reducing the risk that these loans would not be repaid. Similarly, a trust company might wish to make commercial loans, and could face a conflict of interest if it invested trust funds in the same company to which it had advanced loans. Of course, there may be conflicts of interest within pillars as well as between them. For example, securities firms not only underwrite securities, but also advise and make purchases on behalf of clients, and these firms seldom recommend selling the securities of a company whose new issues they help to bring to the market.

The principle of functional separation implicit in the four pillars approach has been subject to continuing erosion. Trust companies and caisses populaires provide chequing facilities and a wide range of accounts that compete with the banks. Moreover, these institutions now have access to the Canadian Payments Association (CPA) for clearing cheques, as well as membership in the Canadian Deposit Insurance Corporation (CDIC) and the Régie de l'assurance-dépôts du Québec. While the CPA and the CDIC are federal agencies, many of the trust companies and caisses populaires are subject to provincial regulation, and this conflict of jurisdiction in regulation is one of the things which has allowed the trust companies to avoid the requirement of keeping cash reserves at the central bank. The banks complained that the "playing field was not level" since they were required to keep such cash reserves and this raised their costs. In addition, banks have the added cost of premiums for deposit insurance, which puts them at a disadvantage in competing for deposits with securities dealers that offer attractive rates on clients' credit balances, or the short-term deferred annuities issued by insurance companies.

On the other hand, the last three revisions of the Bank Act have brought changes that have enabled the banks to move into areas where they were previously excluded, such as mortgage lending, personal lending and, most recently, leasing and factoring services. The large size and extensive branch network of the major banks has allowed this largest pillar to become the biggest mortgage and personal lender, and consequently any institutions affected by a further enlargement of bank powers fear a similar development. This explains the opposition of the insurance industry to the banks' desire to sell insurance in their branches.

Still another aspect of the division of functions in the Canadian context is that there has traditionally been a separation of the real and financial sectors, which more or less prevented the intermingling of financial business with commercial and industrial operations. This is very unlike the situation, for example, in Germany, where "universal" banks are directly involved in industry. There has been a breaking down of this separation in recent years in Canada as conglomerates with financial subsidiaries have appeared. For example, the Brascan empire is involved in many industries and through Trilon Financial Corporation controls London Life, Royal Trust, Wellington Insurance and other financial companies. Imasco took over Genstar, and in this way the tobacco and consumer goods company gained control of Canada Trustco, the country's largest trust company and seventh largest financial institution.

The policy toward foreign ownership is another factor affecting competition. Foreign ownership of the securities industry in Canada was not a major source of concern until Royal Securities was acquired in 1969 by a wholly-owned subsidiary of Merrill, Lynch, Pierce, Fenner and Smith, the largest securities firm in the United States. Premier Bill Davis announced that the Ontario government believed it was essential that the ownership of investment firms remain substantially Canadian, and Ontario's legislation was amended in 1971 to provide that securities firms could henceforth only be registered if non-residents in the aggregate owned no more than 25% of the issued securities of any class, and any single non-resident owned no more than 10%. Twenty-six firms that were already registered did not meet these requirements, but were "grandfathered," that is, allowed to continue operations exempt from the new regulations but with certain provisos on their rate of growth relative to the industry. As of 1987, when the law changed, there were only four subsidiaries of American firms registered in Canada, so that the new regulations were not only effective in discouraging entry by non-residents into the securities industry, but also resulted in an actual decrease in non-resident participation. However, non-registered foreign-owned firms were increasingly active participants in the important "exempt" market.

The perennial Canadian battle among levels of government for jurisdiction is evident in the financial industry as well. For example, trust companies with national charters are subject to federal regulation, while those incorporated provincially are bound by provincial rules. The regulation of securities markets in Canada, on the other hand, has always been considered a provincial responsibility. On the issue of foreign ownership in the securities industry, Quebec took a very different stance from Ontario, and in 1973 opened the door to foreign ownership. Moreover, in 1983 it invited banks and trust companies to establish securities subsidiaries. In the event, this policy played a key role in the moves in 1986 that determined the new face of the Canadian securities industry.

The erosion of the four pillar concept as institutions within each of the pillars expanded into other functions brought additional competition and benefits to consumers, but raised the spectre of concentration of power. The possible intrusion of foreign competitors into the Canadian securities industry provided additional capital and competition, but at the same time raised questions of continuing Canadian control over what might be considered a "commanding height" of the economy. Innovative financial products, changes in technology, increasing globalization of financial markets and moves toward deregulation in other countries were all affecting Canada. It was obvious by the middle of the 1980s that changes were necessary.

## Planning Regulation

Planning regulation affects market structure through rules governing entry into particular sectors of an industry. In the case of financial markets in Canada, we have seen that there are a number of issues, but the key one has turned out to be the entry of the banks into the securities business.

In the United States the Glass-Steagall Act prevented commercial banks from engaging in investment banking, or underwriting. However, since 1983 American banks have been allowed to engage in securities brokerage and many of them soon began to offer discount brokerage to their clients. In that same year, the Ontario Securities Commission (OSC) followed the American example and decided that the basic core function of the securities industry was underwriting, and consequently that allowing a bank to offer brokerage services did not destroy the traditional separation of functions fundamental to the four pillars approach. As a result, the Toronto-Dominion Bank was allowed to offer its Green Line Service using the facilities of discount brokers, and by 1991 all of the five biggest chartered banks were offering a similar service to their customers. Most of the Canadian banks also had subsidiaries that underwrote securities sold offshore.

In Febuary of 1985, the OSC issued a report entitled *A Regulatory Framework for Entry into and Ownership of the Ontario Securities*

*Industry* (Dey Report). It recommended that non-residents, as well as other Canadian financial institutions, be allowed greater ownership, but not control, of Canadian securities firms. Non-resident firms already in existence, the grandfathered firms, would be registered as foreign dealer registrants, and only registered firms would be able to engage in underwriting in Ontario. Their analysis was based on the premise that there should be wider access to capital for the securities industry, unless it could be shown that this would be contrary to the public interest. The Commission argued that their proposals would provide such access without endangering the policy goals of maintaining the four separate pillars and a substantially Canadian securities industry. The relaxation of restrictions on the regulated sector would be offset by a more stringent control of the previously unregulated sector, and separation by function and by ownership, although watered down, would remain. It appears that the Commission had in the back of its mind the model of the 1980 Bank Act revision, when foreign banks were allowed entry into the Canadian market as Schedule B (now Schedule II) banks subject to limitations on size, in this way bringing previously unregulated operations under control and at the same time promoting competition in the banking sector.

It is interesting to note now that the domestic securities industry, on balance, responded negatively to the OSC proposals at the time. Moreover, the OSC proposals were subjected to criticism by the Ontario Task Force on Financial Institutions in its Final Report (Dupré Report). It argued that foreign ownership was a subject for a formal and open declaration of policy by the Government of Canada that would involve federal-provincial consultation, and that in the meantime the existing 10/25 foreign ownership standard and the current status of grandfathered firms should be maintained. Foreign firms should be allowed to continue to operate in the exempt market, but with much more information required from the participants. However, the Dupré Committee did endorse the recommendation of the Dey Report concerning investment in the securities industry by non-industry domestic investors, including financial institutions.

The federal government also entered the debate with proposals for quite radical change in the financial industry. Responding to the need to bring federal legislation on trust and insurance companies up to date, the Department of Finance in April of 1985 issued a Green Paper called *The Regulation of Financial Institutions: Proposals for*

*Discussion*. The key institution in the Green Paper proposals was the financial holding company, which could in turn own other financial institutions, including banks (to be known as Schedule C banks). In this manner a trust company could own a bank through a financial holding company, thereby getting into the business of commercial lending. With respect to conflicts of interest, there would be a new body to investigate abuses and protect consumer interests, and the activities of the various entities of the financial holding company would be kept separate by "Chinese walls." This type of barrier, which stops information from flowing between the various divisions of a financial institution, exists in the United States to separate the banking and trust activities of certain financial institutions and, perhaps surprisingly, seems to have worked fairly well.

As we have seen, the financial holding company, as exemplified by Trilon Financial Corporation, was already with us in Canada, and thus these proposals to some extent only recognized and legitimized what was already present. But they were designed so as to further erode the separation of the real and financial sectors and of financial and market intermediaries. They provided for new entry into commercial lending, which had until then been the preserve of the chartered banks. Moreover, they allowed for the formation of new banks which, unlike the existing Schedule A banks, need not be widely held. Since the new financial holding companies and banks proposed would be federally chartered, the Green Paper proposals were perceived in some quarters as an attempt by the federal government to centralize regulation of the financial system to a greater degree, perhaps even leading to the creation of a national securities commission, given the provision that a financial holding company could own a securities firm, subject to provincial approval.

The traditional four pillars approach was based on separation of the pillars by both ownership and by function. The general approach of Ontario was to retain separation both of function and of ownership; the federal government position in the Green Paper allowed for integration of ownership through financial holding companies, but attempted to retain the separation of functions; the Quebec position favoured functional and ownership integration, but through subsidiaries so there could be regulation by function.

In the midst of these reports and discussions, events conspired to force policy choices. In November, 1986 the Bank of Nova Scotia announced that it was establishing a wholly-owned full-service secu-rities firm in Quebec, where there were no restrictions on ownership. While subject to federal regulation under the Bank Act, the Bank of Nova Scotia was taking advantage of a loophole pointed out to it by federal officials, which permits temporary ownership of an otherwise unauthorized subsidiary for up to two years.

By this time Ontario was considering expanded limits, up to 49% in total, for ownership of securities firms by other financial institutions or foreigners. Now it had to consider the possibility of losing business to Quebec because of that province's less restrictive legislation. At the same time, many of the securities firms in Ontario apparently had a change of heart and felt that if they were going to have to cede some control in order to gain access to greater capital, they would want the freedom to sell out completely to the highest bidder, including the banks. The banks for their part feared a loss of business from the trend to securitization and wanted access to the securities business. On December 3, 1986, Ontario announced that after June 30, 1987, Canadian financial institutions would be permitted to own up to 100% of securities firms, and foreign interests up to 50%, with the ceiling on foreigners rising to 100% one year later when all foreign firms would have to be registered.

Ottawa agreed to revise the Bank Act to accommodate changes in Ontario's rules, and later in December announced their own policies on financial regulation in a Blue Paper called *New Directions for the Financial Sector*. In effect, competition between banks, trust compa-nies, insurance companies and investment dealers was to be thrown wide open. Consumers would be able to obtain loans and mortgages, deposit and withdraw money, buy stocks and bonds, and obtain financial planning advice from one branch of any bank, trust company, securities dealer or insurance firm. Only the sale of insurance was to remain outside the network. Trust companies with at least $25 million in capital would also be able to make commercial loans. Banks were not to be required to keep non-interest bearing deposits at the Bank of Canada, thus making the playing field more level in this regard.

While banks were permitted to take over all or part of an established securities dealer, large financial institutions were not generally permitted to acquire other large institutions, but had to expand into new areas by creating a new subsidiary. Banks with a capital base of more that $750 million were to continue to be widely-held with no one group permitted to hold more than 10% of the shares. Only those with no significant non-financial interests were allowed to begin new trust, loan or insurance companies. Trust, loan and insurance companies with capital bases of more than $50 million and owned by non-financial interests, along with similar companies without non-financial links but with capital bases in excess of $750 million, were to have at least 35% of their voting shares publicly traded and widely held. The 35% figure was designed to provide protection for minority shareholders through a clause requiring a majority of not less than two thirds of shareholders to implement certain changes to the corporation's operations.

These general principles, while subject to some modifications, remain the basis of government policy and have been embodied in different legislative proposals. The plan has been to amend the Bank Act, the Trust and Loan Companies Act, the Insurance Companies Act and the Co-operatives Act, with the whole package to become law at the same time, the target date subject to continuing revision. New financial institution reform legistation was introduced in 1990 which essentially disbanded all ownership restrictions except for the provision that Schedule I banks were to remain widely-held. Banks, trust and insurance companies would all be able to offer investment advisory and portfolio management services directly. While there is not great controversy over the provisions, the House of Commons Finance Committee did not pass the Trust and Loan Companies Act until March of 1991 and then the legislation died on the order paper when Parliament was prorogued. Thus the proposed time-table for these reforms is still very much in doubt in mid-1991.

## The New Face Of The Canadian Securities Industry

Deregulation of the British financial system in October, 1986 was dubbed the "Big Bang," and Canada had its "Mini Bang" on June 30, 1987. The "For Sale" signs went up on the lawns of the securities firms, and the new face of the industry became clearly discernible.

All but one of the big chartered banks acquired controlling interests in prominent full-service securities dealers. The Royal Bank purchased a 67% interest in Dominion Securities; the Canadian Imperial Bank of Commerce bought a 65% share of Wood Gundy, as well as a 9.9% interest in a new merchant banking joint venture with Gordon Capital; the Bank of Montreal acquired a 75% holding in Nesbitt Thomson; The Bank of Nova Scotia bought 100% control of McLeod Young Weir, taking over the 30% interest previously purchased by the American securities firm Shearson, Lehman; and the National Bank gained control of Lévesque Beaubien and later Geoffrion Leclerc. Meanwhile, the Toronto-Dominion Bank purchased 100% of the discount brokerage, Gardiner Group, as it attempted to consolidate its position in this area of the securities business.

American investment firms generally opted to set up their own subsidiary operations in Canada, and join the already-established foreign securities dealers. The four remaining grandfathered U.S.-based firms (Prudential-Bache, Merrill Lynch, Dean Witter, and Dominick Corp.) were joined by such other well-known names as Goldman Sachs, Morgan Stanley, First Boston, Salomon Brothers, and Drexel Burnham Lambert of junk bond fame. Several giant firms arrived from Japan, including Nomura, the world's largest brokerage, Nikko, Daiwa, Yamaichi, and Sanyo.

Some foreign banks purchased part or all of existing Canadian firms. Security Pacific of Los Angeles bought 30% of Burns Fry, Deutsche Bank bought the small firm of McLean McCarthy, while the Canadian subsidiary of Sanwa Bank of Osaka bought 75% of McCarthy Securities. Other foreign-owned banks set up their own shops, including Credit Suisse and Citibank, while some British securities firms bought into existing firms. S.G. Warburg Group bought 50% of Alfred Bunting, James Capel and Co. purchased 50% of Brown Baldwin Nisker, and W.I. Carr acquired 75% of Capital Group Securities.

Though there is a greater overall foreign presence in the industry, foreign firms have disappeared entirely from the retail side of the business. Four of the Japanese firms paid big prices for seats on the Toronto Stock Exchange, but they do not yet have traders on the floor. The grandfathered firms that had a long history of retail trade are all out of the business. In 1990, Prudential-Bache sold their retail operation to Burns Fry and Merrill Lynch sold theirs to Wood Gundy, while in 1991 Midland Walwyn acquired Dean Witter, thereby becoming the largest retail brokerage in the country. Foreign firms in Canada engage in underwriting, sell foreign stock to Canadian institutions and mutual funds to individuals, as well as Canadian stocks to clients in other countries.

Canadian regional dealers, meanwhile, have merged with larger firms. This has meant, for example, that the head offices of Vancouver's two largest dealers have moved to Toronto. Tassé in Quebec is the only remaining regional firm. Thus there are basically two types of Canadian companies now: the large firms with extensive retail business, whether full-service or discount operations, and the small boutiques who specialize in filling a particular niche. The bank-owned firms dominate, and it is estimated that they do 50% of the business and have 50% of the regulatory capital.

The trend towards one-stop shopping for all financial services that emerged in the United States has not progressed as far in Canada. Merrill Lynch led the way in the United States in offering a cash management account which looks after clients' investments, provides chequing facilities and invests remaining balances on a daily basis in money market mutual funds. To some extent this firm resembles a nation-wide bank, thereby overcoming the legal prohibition on inter-state banking that constrains traditional banks in the United States. Other examples of the financial supermarket concept in the U.S. are Sears Roebuck, whose purchase of the securities firm of Dean Witter allowed the gaint retailer to offer services in savings, insurance, real estate and securities; American Express who acquired Shearson Loeb Rhodes, the second biggest security dealer in the United States at the time; and the Prudential Insurance Company of America, which took over Bache Securities. The jury is still out on the success of one-stop financial centres. Sears has reported that most customers only look for combined financial services when they are purchasing a house, and enter at that time into transactions combining real estate, a mortgage loan, and casualty and life insurance.

Different securities firms in Canada offered cash management accounts to their clients, with Merrill Lynch Canada leading the way here as well when they were in the retail business. The first Canadian one-stop shopping centre for financial services was offered by the Laurentian Group, including the Laurentian Bank which is the only Canadian-owned Schedule II Bank. Starting from a base in insurance, the Montreal-based company took advantage of the deregulation in Quebec to acquire Imperial Life Assurance of Toronto, the Montreal and District Savings Bank, and the Eaton Financial Services arm of

Eaton's (which included Eaton Trust). At one time they acquired a 45% stake in Geoffrion Leclerc, a full-service securities firm based in Montreal, but later sold it to the National Bank and acquired Disnat, a discount brokerage. The Laurentian Group offers integrated services at the retail level from all the four pillars under one roof, primarily in Quebec, but has more recently expanded its presence in the rest of Canada by purchasing the retail offices of bankrupt Standard Trust. Laurentian in turn has financial connections with Banque Indo-Suez, a Paris-based investment banking company, which provides Laurentian with a link to international finance. Clearly the integration of functions has gone furthest in Quebec, where, for example, trust companies can offer insurance and brokerage services. But banks in other parts of Canada now have separate brokerage facilities in their branches, and brokers in some parts of the country can also offer insurance servies, primarily annuities.

## Prudential Regulation

Thus far the discussion of the changing face of the financial industry in Canada in recent years has been largely in terms of changing ownership, new entrants and increased competition. Along with the prospect of greater efficiency, however, increased competition brings a greater danger of insolvency. Public policy has to consider both efficiency and stability, and deregulation can be seen as a reduction in planning regulation coupled with an increase in prudential regulation. This is why the process is sometimes referred to as re-regulation.

Prudential regulation can be undertaken in different ways. Self-regulation occurs when trade associations impose regulations on their own members and clients. Most prominent among these in the investment industry in Canada are the various stock exchanges and the Investment Dealers Association (IDA). Supervision of brokerage firms is shared between the exchanges and the IDA, and some groups, including the Toronto Stock Exchange, have advocated a single national self-regulatory body to increase efficiency and eliminate overlapping jurisdiction. The stock exchanges impose requirements before listing stocks for trading, and demand regular financial statements and notice of any material changes from companies in order to maintain their listings. As well, they establish trading rules designed to protect the public and have special rules to deal with takeover bids made through the exchanges. The importance of such provisions has been evidenced by the recent problems of the Vancouver Stock Exchange, which suffers from a reputation of lax prudential regulation.

The IDA establishes capital requirements for member firms, and in concert with the stock exchanges runs the Canadian Investor Protection Fund which protects clients in the event of any member's insolvency. Customers' deposits have been safe following recent failures of smaller investment firms, but the resources of the Fund have had to be bolstered to ensure that public confidence is maintained, and it is a moot point that they would be adequate to deal with the failure of a major company. The IDA also settles trading disputes in the bond market, maintains trading standards for employees of member firms, and tries to ensure that members observe "know your client" rules and do not engage in unethical conduct. While there has been a longstanding tradition of self-regulation that market participants are anxious to preserve, much less faith is now being placed in self-regulation as a complete solution in the face of increased evidence of wrongdoing.

Government prudential regulation may emanate from either the federal or provincial governments. At the federal level an important control on deposit-taking institutions is the Canada Deposit Insurance Corporation (CDIC) which protects deposits against loss up to $60,000 in the event of failure of such an institution. The institutions fund the insurance by fees, while the government inspects the operations of the institutions in order to ensure that minimum standards of operation are being observed. It is felt that the public, and particularly the small unsophisticated depositors, should have their savings protected, and it is hoped that that this will prevent the sort of financial panic that might follow in the wake of a failure. The intention is to ensure the solvency of the system, but it has been cogently argued that deposit insurance has just the opposite effect, since it both discourages depositors from carefully scrutinizing the institutions with which they choose to do business, and at the same time encourages the institutions to take unwarranted investment risks in order to attract depositors by means of higher interest rates. Certainly there have been more failures and rescue operations since 1967, when the insurance scheme was introduced, than there were prior to its inception. Moreover, the government's decisions to reimburse all depositors when failures have occurred, even for amounts above the insurable ceilings, have exacerbated these negative effects on incentives, which come under the heading of "moral hazard." Such decisions have also resulted in the CDIC itself becoming insolvent, so that the government has been forced to make up the deficit out of its revenues. This, in turn, has produced proposals for higher fees to be paid by the institutions covered, and debates about the wisdom of adding to the costs of well-run institutions in order to bail out poorly-managed institutions. Suggestions for reform include lower limits on insurable amounts with co-insurance beyond these limits, or fees related to the risks taken by the institutions.

The regulation of securities markets in Canada, on the other hand, has always been considered a provincial responsibility. As a result, there is no national securities commission, but rather ten separate provincial and two territorial regulatory bodies. While there has been some harmonization of regulation amongst the various provincial authorities, it is far from complete, and periodically there are calls for a national regulatory agency. In Ontario, the regulatory agency is known as the Ontario Securities Commission (OSC); it administers the Securities Act and is responsible to the Ministry of Financial Institutions.

Among the many concerns of the Ontario Securities Commission in the area of prudential regulation the following provisions are particularly worth noting:

(a)    prospectus requirement. New public issues of securities require a prospectus which affords "full, true and plain disclosure" of all the information surrounding the new issue and the company making it. Provisions have been made in recent years for established borrowers to offer new securities more quickly under the terms of a prompt offering prospectus (POP), and the need to put out separate prospectuses in each jurisdiction in which the securities are being offered has been reduced by co-operation among the commissions. There is also provision in some cases for distribution of stock to the public without issuing a prospectus through the stock exchanges which regulate the procedures.

(b)    purchasers' rights. The purchaser of a new security has the right to withdraw from the contract within two days after the receipt of the prospectus, and has the right to rescind the contract within ninety days if the prospectus contains untrue statements of material facts or omits material facts.

(c)    continuous disclosure. Issuers of securities must notify the authorities in the event of any material change in their business, and must file financial statements on an annual basis along with interim quarterly financial reports.

(d)    proxies. Corporate management is required to solicit proxies from shareholders and to supply shareholders with an information circular.

(e)    take-over bids. The Ontario Securities Act has strict regulations governing any offer to buy shares when the effect of the offer will be to give the offeror more than 20% of the voting shares of the company. The concern is that the minority holders will be fairly dealt with, and there is a provision that when the offeror pays a premium of more than 15% above the market price for the securities he is obliged to make a "follow-up" offer to holders of all other securities of that class, offering a consideration equal to the greatest consideration paid under any private agreement.

(f)    insider trading. Insiders are defined as directors and senior officers of a company along with any person or company holding more than 10% of the voting shares of a company. They must file a report within ten days of the end of the month in which they become insiders, giving information on their holdings of securities in the company, and thereafter within ten days of the end of the month of any changes in their holdings.

(g)    non-voting shares. The OSC has been concerned with the proliferation of non-voting shares and is seeking to regulate the terms of their issue in order that holders of such shares are not disadvantaged relative to the holders of voting shares, particularly in the event of a takeover bid.

This is not in any way an exhaustive list of the activities of the Ontario Securities Commission. Rather it is an attempt to illustrate the concern with the protection of the public which has been behind the growing activity in the area of prudential regulation as the various provincial commissions have become more involved and better funded. Further evidence of this was provided in 1991 by the OSC as it announced new measures covering disclosure rules, valuation reports and fairness opinions, which were designed to protect minority shareholders. The increased activity is in line with recommendations which go back at least to the 1964 Report of the Royal Commission on Banking and Finance (Porter Report), and there is every indication that it will continue to grow as there is less faith placed in self-regulation.

The comparable national regulatory body in the United States is called the Securities and Exchange Commission (SEC). It has greater authority than the OSC, imposes more stringent regulations on disclosure and requires more extensive information in prospectuses for public issues. Canadian stocks listed on U.S. exchanges must meet these requirements, which have to some extent provided a model for Canada to emulate. The SEC in 1988 signed a memorandum of understanding with the three largest provincial securities commissions in Canada (Ontario, Quebec and British Columbia) that provides for joint investigations of securities laws infractions such as insider trading, fraud, improper trading activities and inadequate disclosure. In 1991 there was also an agreement to accept each country's own prospectus requirements for new issues in the other country. As a result, the SEC's newly-promulgated Rule 144a allows foreign and domestic companies to sell to large U.S. institutions securities that are not already listed on a major American exchange without fulfilling domestic prospectus requirements. Underwriters took advantage of this provision to sell shares in the first public offering of Petro-Canada to large American institutional investors. Recently some cracks have appeared in the Glass-Steagall law in the United States, and the investment subsidiaries of Canadian banks that are operating there have now been cleared to engage in underwriting.

On the other hand, interlisted stock and differences in regulatory provisions can sometimes provide a way around domestic securities controls. For example, when the Bronfmans took over Brascan they did so by means of purchases in New York, where they were not constrained by the the 20% takeover rule that exists in Canada. The NYSE does not have the requirement for "follow-up" provisions, either, but it does forbid trading in stocks which have restricted voting rights. Another aspect of rivalry in regulation occurs when trading is suspended in interlisted stocks. Stock exchanges will suspend trading in stocks pending notification of such material changes as the announcement of takeover bids. The objective is to make sure that all market participants are in possession of the same amount of information. However, if the stocks are interlisted, such a ban will only be effective if it is in place at all the exchanges on which the stock trades. The TSE may suspend trading, but if the stock is listed in New York and the NYSE does not go along with the ban, the TSE will only lose business. The NYSE, in turn, will argue that a suspension of trading on the "Big Board" will not be effective because the stock will continue to trade on the over-the-counter market.

While Canadian firms are particularly concerned with U.S. regulation, the increasing internationalization of the investment business argues for harmonization of regulation on a truly international scale. In December of 1988, a new body called the International Council of Securities Dealers and Self-Regulatory Associations was founded in Tokyo.

It would be too much to expect that market wrongdoing would completely disappear as a result of this increased vigilance. A highly-publicized problem in recent years is that of insider trading, with the U.S. Securities and Exchange Commission investigation of Ivan Boesky perhaps the highest-profile case. Boesky profited by using insider knowledge to buy the stock of takeover candidates, and as a result of his indictment he agreed to pay a fine of $100 million to settle civil charges and as well received a three year jail sentence on criminal charges. He in turn informed on Michael Milliken, the man who received a great deal of credit for creating the junk bond market in the United States, and who also received a ten year jail sentence for fraud and conspiracy, along with fines of $600 million. These penalties set new standards for white collar crime. Another recent case in the U.S. involved profits from stock trading based on the leaking of the contents of forthcoming newspaper columns. A variant of insider trading that is also causing concern is "front running," where a trader buys small amounts of a stock knowing that large institutional purchases are forthcoming and that the stock can soon be sold at a modest profit but with little or no risk.

In Canada, there have been moves to tighten the rules and increase the penalties for insider trading, with provisions now for jail sentences as well as an increase in the fine from $2,000 to the greater of three times the illegal profit or $1,000,000. The most prominent case to date involved Bill Bennett, the former premier of British Columbia, who, along with his brother and Herb Doman, sold shares in Doman Industries just before it became public knowledge that a proposed takeover of the company had fallen through, news which caused the price of the stock to fall on the market. Bennett was exonerated in B.C., and the Ontario Securities Commission failed in trying to get him to testify in Ontario where the sales of the stock had actually taken place.

These are some of the ways in which governments and market participants themselves try to police *behaviour* in financial markets. Regulation of the *structure* of markets can also be relevant for concerns for consumer protection. For example, the failure of the Greymac/Seaway/Crown Trust companies in 1983 involved real estate property "flips" which were facilitated by the fact that ownership of these companies was closely-held. Where there is one owner, or a small group of owners, the possibilities are greater for transactions between different companies at less than arm's-length. This is known as self-dealing. A policy of promoting widely-held ownership is one which not only affects the structure of the industry, but also has ramifications for the protection of the public against losses from self-dealing.

Many of the reports already mentioned were concerned with both planning regulation and prudential regulation. There were 22 failures of financial institutions between 1980 and 1985 in Canada. Even more striking were the first bank failures that Canada had experienced since 1923; in 1985, the Canadian Commercial Bank and the Northland Bank were both forced to close their doors. These failures raised questions about the efficacy of Canadian prudential regulation.

The Ontario Task Force on Financial Institutions (Dupré Committee) had a broad mandate to consider the whole financial system in Ontario, and concerned itself not only with issues of access to capital and foreign ownership, but also with more fundamental concerns about solvency in the system arising particularly from trust company failures. In general it argued for much greater prudential regulation. It pointed to a number of recurring factors contributing to the insolvency of financial institutions: self-dealing, lack of diversification, weak management and new entrants. The Committee argued for a prohibition on self-dealing, with exceptions only where a test of market value is possible. It favoured widely-held financial institutions, and wished to maintain the traditional distinction in Canada between real and financial sectors, as well as that between financial intermediaries, like banks and trust companies, and market intermediaries that are unique to the securities industry. It approved of financial holding companies as long as they are registered and regulated, and its response to the concept of the financial supermarket was to recommend networking, the referral of customers from one financial institution to another, with regulators having the power to investigate conflicts of interest.

The Economic Council of Canada issued two major reports dealing with regulation: *A Framework for Financial Regulation* (1987) and *Globalization and Canada's Financial Markets* (1990). In the first report the Council advocated regulation by function, with a separate institution for each function and diversification effected through cross-ownership of financial institutions. A combination of ownership limits, corporate governance and regulatory inspection was proposed to regulate conflicts of interest and self-dealing, as it was felt outright prohibition of less-than-arm's length transactions would eliminate many of the benefits of diversification. The approach of regulation by function was intended to simplify the job of regulators by having each deal only in its area of expertise. In this respect the Council's position was close to that of Quebec, and in contrast to most of the other reports which had favoured regulation by institution.

In its most recent report on the subject, the Economic Council again called for strengthened prudential regulation and the harmonization of such regulation, not only between the various levels of government in Canada but also internationally. Foreign financial institutions should be allowed to enter Canada but be required to operate through subsidiaries which are subject to greater control. The Council feared that increased internationalization had reduced transparency, as cross-border flows were not as well documented. As well, many of the new innovations in international markets involved contingent liabilities that were not recorded on the books. This reduced transparency brought increased risk, and the Council argued that the solvency of financial institutions should be enhanced by tightening the treatment of off-balance sheet commitments, establishing risk-weighted capital requirements for all institutions and further developing safety nets such as the Canadian Investor Protection Fund. In the

Council's view these objectives should be pursued not only domestically but also through international co-operation and co-ordination. Finally, it argued against commercial-financial links, and recommended that all deposit-taking institutions be widely-held.

There have been many other reports dealing with these issues, as well as commentators calling for even more radical change. For example, economist Thomas Courchene believes that in order for Canadian financial institutions to compete it will be necessary to promote not only commercial-financial links (e.g. BCE controls Montreal Trust, having bought it from Power Corp.), but also financial commercial links (e.g. the banks going into commercial business).

In the federal government's Blue Paper of December of 1985 (*New Directions for the Financial Sector*), many of these issues were discussed. Conflict of interest problems were to be handled by greater public disclosure, controls over the spread of information within a financial institution (Chinese Walls) and an enhanced role for the board of directors. To prevent abuses from self-dealing, there were to be restrictions on loans and sales of assets to an extended list of parties not considered to be at arm's length from a financial institution. Such transactions were to be monitored by a committee of independent directors in concert with the institution's auditors. Periodic press reports tell of pressure to change the proposals, and the legislation introduced in 1990 proposed extensive related-party rules. The failure to get this legislation approved means that the policies concerning self-dealing, conflict of interest, responsibilities of directors and financial-commercial links are still in abeyance as of mid-1991. Moreover, there are real concerns about the adequacy of regulation of the markets for derivative products such as options and futures which have not been addressed.

There was agreement between Ontario and Ottawa concerning bank entry into the securities business, but there were continuing differences of opinion between the federal and provincial governments over the division of regulatory responsibilities. Ottawa felt that their jurisdiction over banks included regulation over the subsidiary businesses of banks, including the securities business which had traditionally been a provincial concern. The federal authorities were anxious to ensure that there would not be excessive risk to the banks' solvency from their involvement in other businesses. They maintained a similar stance with respect to applications for entry into the securities business from foreign firms who had any connection with banks, and were also concerned with gaining reciprocal access for Canadian firms in the foreign jurisdictions. However, by March of 1988 the provincial and federal authorities had resolved their differences and signed agreements on regulating the securities industries, although not all the provinces accepted readily the Ontario position.

One other change enacted at the same time by Ottawa was the creation of a new super-regulator called the Superintendent of Financial Institutions, who combined the roles of the Superintendent of Insurance and the Inspector-General of Banks. The Canadian Deposit Insurance Corporation retained its separate identity, however.

While the details of the new regulatory provisions are still to be worked out, more mergers and changes in ownership are sure to occur. There will also continue to be failures, as the recent history of Standard Trust attests. While there can be little question that the Canadian securities industry is now better capitalized and more internationally-oriented, the ability of Canadian firms to compete internationally, the extent to which smaller and regional players in the Canadian capital market benefit from globalization and the system's ability to withstand insolvency and the dangers it presents to confidence are questions still to be resolved. Clearly, the need to balance concerns of efficiency and stability, to choose between greater competition and greater solvency, is an ongoing problem for policy-makers.

# Notes

1   See Peters, J.R. *Economics of the Canadian Corporate Bond Market*. Montreal: McGill-Queen's University Press, 1971.

2   Tinic S.M. and West, R.R. "Marketability of Common Stocks Canada and the U.S.A.: A Comparison of Agent versus Dealer Dominated Markets." *The Journal of Finance*, Vol.39, No. 3 (1974), pp. 742-3.

3   "Many stock market investors are the brokers themselves." *Globe and Mail Report on Business*, February 24, 1990, p. B2.

4   See Economic Council of Canada, *Globalization and Canada's Financial Markets*. Ottawa: Minister of Supply and Services, 1989.

5  Government of Canada. *1964. Report of the Royal Commission on Banking and Finance*. Ottawa: Queen's Printer, 1964. p.108.

# Further References

Department of Finance, Government of Canada. *The Regulation of Canadian Financial Institutions: Proposals for Discussion* (Green Paper). Ottawa: Minister of Supply and Services, 1985.

Department of Finance, Government of Canada. *New Directions for the Financial Sector* (Blue Paper). Ottawa: Minister of Supply and Services, 1986.

Economic Council of Canada. *A Framework for Financial Regulation*. Ottawa: Minister of Supply and Services, 1987.

Economic Council of Canada. *Globalization and Canada's Financial Markets*. Ottawa: Minister of Supply and Services, 1989.

Government of Canada. *1964. Report of the Royal Commission on Banking and Finance* (Porter Report). Ottawa: Queen's Printer, 1964.

Ontario Task Force on Financial Institutions. *Final Report* (Dupré Report). Toronto: Queen's Printer, 1985.

Ontario Securities Commission. *A Regulatory Framework for Entry into and Ownership of the Ontario Securities Industry* (Dey Report). Toronto: Queen's Printer, 1985.

Pattison, J.C. *Financial Markets and Foreign Ownership*. Toronto: Ontario Economic Council, 1978.

Peters, J.R. *Economics of the Canadian Corporate Bond Market*. Montreal: McGill-Queen's University Press, 1971.

Williamson, J.P. "Canadian Capital Markets" and "Canadian Financial Institutions." In Government of Canada, Department of Consumer and Corporate Affairs. *Proposals for a Securities Market Law for Canada*. Vol. 3. Ottawa: Minister of Supply and Services, 1979. pp. 1-133, 719-946.

Ziegel, J.S., Waverman L. and Conklin D.W. (eds.). *Canadian Financial Institutions: Changing the Regulatory Environment*. Toronto: Ontario Economic Council, 1986.

CHAPTER TWELVE

# the 1987 stock market break

O N OCTOBER 19, 1987 THE DOW JONES INDUSTRIAL AVERAGE FELL A record-breaking 508 points, or 22.6%, while the Toronto Stock Exchange 300 Index fell 407 points, or 11.3%. These were the largest declines on record, with the Dow Jones drop almost double that of the 12.9% decline recorded on October 28, 1929.

The bold headlines the next day proclaimed a "crash," which implies complete collapse and invites comparison with the 1929 debacle. As time went on the favourite term to describe Black Monday came to be "meltdown," which conjures up an ongoing process that feeds on itself. The Report of the U.S. Securities and Exchange Commission is entitled *The October 1987 Market Break*, and with the benefit of hindsight "break" may well be the most appropriate term, indicating as it does a sharp fall representing a discontinuity but something less than a complete disaster.

Greater volatility in the markets, as measured by large changes in the market indexes, had been evident in recent years before October 19, 1987. Over September 11 and 12, 1986 the Dow Jones average fell 120 points. On January 23, 1987 it rose by 64 points by 1:39 p.m., and then in little more than an hour fell 115 points. On October 6, 1987, it fell by 92 points. In investigating these movements, the U.S. Securities and Exchange Commission felt that programme trading involving index-related securities played a role in exacerbating the movements.

Programme trading refers to buying or selling a large number of stocks simultaneously and is facilitated by automated order execution systems such as the New York Stock Exchange Designated Order Turnaround (DOT) System, particularly with the DOT List Order Processing System which provides for a specified list of securities to be traded simultaneously. Index-related securities include index options and index futures, which were described in Chapter Eight. These can be used as a surrogate for a portfolio of stocks and their use can both reduce transaction costs and enable large transactions to take place with smaller effects on market prices. Portfolio managers can use these derivative instruments to re-allocate assets in their portfolios as well as to hedge against risk.

As described in Chapter Eight, portfolio insurance is a strategy to protect against loss by rebalancing the asset mix between stock and cash equivalents. Computer-based models compute optimal stock-to-cash ratios at various stock market price levels, and the strategy requires selling stocks on a declining market and buying them on a rising market in order to achieve the optimal mix, with trading in index futures the preferred way of doing this. Index arbitrage, on the other hand, involves taking advantage of differences between the real market and the futures market in the value of the stocks in the index, as discussed earlier in Chapter Eight. Index substitution strategies involve substituting futures for stocks in index funds, with the difference in cost invested in money market instruments to augment the total return. These strategies are, of course, primarily undertaken by institutional investors, or the managers of their portfolios.

In investigating instances of price volatility on the stock markets, the Securities and Exchange Commission postulated a possible stock market collapse resulting from trade in index-related securities. This "cascade scenario" would begin with index futures prices falling in response to bad fundamental news. If the price of futures fell to a sufficient discount relative to theoretical fair value, index arbitrage and index fund substitution could result in stock sales in the real market that would depress prices there. Then portfolio insurance programmes predicated on lower stock prices but utilizing index futures would push prices down further in the futures market and cause the cycle to repeat itself. Plunging stock prices meanwhile trigger stop loss orders and force additional liquidations to meet margin calls, leading to panic selling and a market collapse. The "cascade scenario" does not fully explain what happened in the markets in October of 1987, but it does have some relevance.

In the week preceding Black Monday there was a change in investors' perceptions. The market was widely believed to be over-valued, and while a bullish sentiment continued to prevail there were growing concerns over the persistent U.S. trade and budget deficits and the decline in the value of the U.S. dollar. Moreover, interest rates were starting to rise, and given the decreasing yield on stocks as their prices rose, the gap between the return on bonds and stocks was widening. One report suggested that bond sales by Japanese investors which drove bond prices down and interest rates up, thereby further widening the spread between bond and stock yields, were a causal factor in the break. On Wednesday October 14 came the announcement of a worse-than-expected U.S. merchandise trade deficit coupled with news of forthcoming legislation to eliminate tax benefits associated with the financing of corporate takeovers. Risk arbitrage involves buying the stocks of takeover candidate companies, and the stocks of the risk arbitragers were particularly hard hit as the market reacted to this news. On Wednesday, the Dow fell a then historic 95 points on volume of 207 million shares. Thursday saw the slide continue with the Dow down another 57 points, 53 of those in the last half hour on heavy trading. Friday saw the largest decline yet, 108 points on volume of 338 million shares.

Examinations of the trading on these days show that portfolio insurance played a prominent role. While it was not the cause of the decline, there can be little doubt that it accentuated it. Portfolio insurance strategies dictated sales of index futures, and index arbitrage ensured that the pressure was transmitted to the stock market. While this programme trading did not account for a majority of trading, it was double its usual share and ran as high as 25% of volume at times when there were substantial market price moves.

The knowledge that portfolio insurance strategies were dictating even larger sales meant that market participants faced the opening on Monday October 19 with trepidation. The markets in Tokyo and London that had been open earlier in their respective time zones both had substantial declines, and in New York there were huge imbalances between buy and sell orders by the time the market was due to open at 9:30 a.m. EST. Specialists did not open trading in many stocks until later because of these imbalances, while in Chicago the selling pressure of portfolio insurers drove the S&P 500 index futures to an apparent discount of 20 points. The exact discount was unknown since many of the key stocks were not yet trading in the real market, but as the futures price was taken as an indicator, or "billboard," there was no question that this led to selling pressure.

Portfolio insurers turned to selling stocks directly and added to the institutional pressure in the real market which included sales by at least one mutual fund complex that, faced with large redemptions, had to sell holdings to acquire funds. There was some selling by foreign accounts and margin liquidations, although neither was widespread. Automated order execution systems were overloaded so there were delays, particularly in receiving news of trades and current price information. By the end of the day panic selling had set in, and the Dow finished down 508 points to 1,738, a decline of almost 23%, on a volume of 604 million shares worth just under $21 billion. The S&P 500 futures had fallen 29% on 162,000 contracts valued at almost $20 billion.

The Tokyo and London markets declined dramatically overnight, but Tuesday's opening in New York saw rises in the first hour in both the stock and futures markets. The Federal Reserve Board announced just before the opening that it would provide the financial system with any needed liquidity. Buy-side order imbalances kept many stocks from opening, in direct contrast to a day earlier. The Dow rose 200 points in the first hour, and the S&P 500 futures contract moved up 10%, but the rally was shortlived as selling pressure from portfolio insurers returned. The index futures went to an enormous discount, declining 27%, which at the lowest point implied a Dow level of about 1,400. Earlier in the day the NYSE had requested that members not use the DOT List system for index arbitrage programmes, so that pressure on the stock market from arbitrage based on the futures discount was not as prominent as on the previous day. However, direct selling of stock by portfolio insurers continued and margin liquidations increased.

Trading was halted in many stocks on the NYSE; the Chicago Mercantile Exchange where the S&P 500 futures contract is traded closed for almost an hour just after noon; the Chicago Board Options Exchange where the S&P 100 options contract is traded had closed earlier; and there were rumours that the NYSE itself would close. With the derivative markets closed and their billboard effect muted, the stock market rallied, only to reverse its course after the futures market re-opened just after 1:00 p.m. Rumours of financial failures made a widespread credit breakdown a distinct possibility. Then a number of major corporations announced stock buyback programmes and this turned the stock market around. The roller-coaster day finished with the Dow up 102 points to 1,841, the largest gain on record, on volume of 614 million shares.

While programme trading by institutions involving index-related securities tends to be concentrated in the futures markets, and particularly the S&P 500 futures, the favourite derivative index instrument of retail investors is the S&P 100 option (OEX) traded on the Chicago Board Options Exchange (CBOE). Options markets also experienced great turmoil over this period. Trading halts in the underlying securities on the NYSE as well as delays in receipt of pricing information made trading hazardous, and were reflected in delayed openings and trading halts in the options themselves. Moreover, there were technical problems as many new contracts at different strike prices had to be introduced and the premiums on some outstanding contracts moved into three digits while the computers were only programmed to handle two. The rapid fall in stock prices caused a huge demand for put options, and the premiums for such contracts were both high and inconsistent, as existing contracts were enormously in-the-money and the time values increased greatly. In February, 1988, Amex and the CBOE announced refunds of up to $3 million for customers who traded options on October 20, 1987.

Another key element in the American markets is the specialist whose job it is to promote fair and orderly markets, both by acting as a broker and by buying and selling for his own account. One would expect these market makers to be purchasing stocks on balance in a falling market, and an examination of their activities during the break reveals quite different records, some of them not reassuring. It is possible that their ability to purchase stocks was limited by lack of capital, and it is also questionable how much they can or should be expected to do in the face of overwhelming selling pressure. However, since they are the only ones with access to the book of buy and sell orders for a stock, this monopoly privilege carries with it certain obligations. There were complaints that the specialist firms on the NYSE ignored orders from specialists at the regional exchanges during the October break. Some specialist firms were taken over by other securities firms as a result of the break, and some specialists relinquished their positions in given stocks under pressure from the NYSE.

The over-the-counter market in the United States, or NASDAQ, uses multiple market-makers and trades electronically, but its performance was not particularly good during the break. Retail investors are more important on NASDAQ, and many reported they were unable to make contact with their brokers. Whether this was because the brokers were overwhelmed by phone calls or were simply not answering their phones has not been established. Most of the complaints centred on order execution, problems of confirmation and difficulties with margin accounts. While some smaller broker-dealers were taken over by other securities firms, there were no major failures and no losses to clients for this reason.

From the close of trading on Tuesday October 13, 1987, when the Dow Jones Industrial Average was above 2,500, to noon on Tuesday of the next week when it stood just above 1,700, the world's leading stock market suffered a decline of almost one third of its value. Other U.S. securities markets had similar experiences. Moreover, it was clear that by midday on October 20, the financial markets had approached complete breakdown. Investors, and particularly institutional investors, had counted in their strategies on a level of liquidity that simply was not there under extreme conditions. As someone later commented, "There was no buyer of last resort."

The decline was clearly led by the American markets. There was some stock selling in the U.S. by foreign investors, particularly from October 14 to 16, but this was not the primary cause of the fall. There was also selling by American investors on foreign markets where stocks were interlisted. This was said to have happened particularly in London, where index arbitrage strategies which involved short selling of stocks were not hampered by the NYSE rule that this can only take place on a rise, or "uptick," in price. In any event, the interlisting of stocks ensures that large price movements will be communicated to other markets, and London and Tokyo followed New York down. The fall in Tokyo was limited in any given day by trading halts once prices moved by a given amount, and the peak to trough decline in Tokyo was not as great as elsewhere. Most sensational of all, perhaps, was the experience of the Hong Kong market, where heavy trading in futures on low margins threatened many with bankruptcy and the stock and futures markets closed for four days.

When the stock market did reopen on October 26, it fell in value by a third, amidst a government-orchestrated rescue programme and greatly-increased margin requirements on futures contracts. There is normally only a weak correlation between stock market price movements in the various countries, with the exception of Canada and the United States where there is a strong correlation. Internationalization of capital markets was not the cause of the 1987 break, but when it occurred the stock markets did move together, as shown in the accompanying chart.

Selected Stock Market Indices, 1 September-13 November 1987

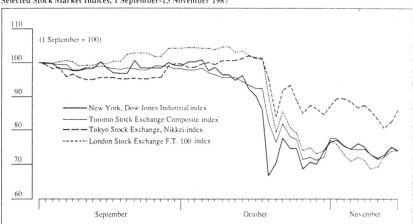

Source: Economic Council of Canada, *Globalization and Canada's Financial Markets*, 1990, p. 159.

The Canadian market was bound to be affected in a similar fashion, even if only because of the interlisting of stocks, and the TSE and other Canadian markets experienced severe breaks. Below are the closing values for the TSE 300 Index, along with the changes in the index and the volume of trade (in millions of shares) over this period.

| *Date* | *TSE 300* | *Change* | *Volume* |
|--------|-----------|----------|----------|
| October 14 | 3719.47 | -40.34 | 26 |
| October 15 | 3674.85 | -44.62 | 28 |
| October 16 | 3598.58 | -76.27 | 34 |
| October 19 | 3191.38 | -407.20 | 64 |
| October 20 | 2977.31 | -214.31 | 77 |
| October 21 | 3246.18 | +268.87 | 67 |

The decline in the TSE from the close on October 13 to the close on October 20 was 20.8%, or just over one fifth, which was considerably smaller than the loss of almost one third in the New York market over a comparable period. The decline in the October 14-16 period was also much smaller, being less than 5%, whereas in New York it was more than twice that. The turnaround did not come in Toronto until October 21, whereas the Dow Jones ended up higher in New York after trade on the 20th, underlining the characteristic lag in the performance of the Toronto market compared with New York.

It can be seen that volumes were more than doubled in Toronto and there were problems in handling orders and transmitting information comparable to those experienced in American markets. What we do not have in Canada is the detailed examination of the trading record that has been undertaken in the United States. It would seem unlikely, however, that programme trading played the same role in exacerbating the situation in Canada that it did in the United States. Index futures are not as highly developed in Canada, and the most widely-traded futures contract, on the TSE 35 Index, was only introduced in May, 1987. Moreover, controls limited the size of programme trades to 10 futures contracts per firm every five minutes, and there were also limitations on price movements in the futures contract.

What have been the effects of the crash/meltdown/break? Many, remembering 1929, felt that the stock market collapse would usher in recession, if not depression. There were logical reasons to expect that this could happen. When the value of stock portfolios falls, people have less wealth and if they rein in consumption as a result of this "wealth effect," then the decline in expenditures can cause a slow-down. Moreover, companies find it more difficult and expensive to raise money by selling stock, and are less inclined to want to invest. They also typically suffer a decline in the value of their pension funds without a corresponding drop in their liabilities. In the event, any brake on economic activity was hardly noticeable, and some commentators even said it was a welcome development insofar as it helped to counter an overheating economy.

Perhaps it was the securities industry itself that was most adversely affected. Many firms suffered large declines in their capital as their inventories fell in value. Trading volumes declined sharply after the break, new issues were down and portfolio insurance programmes were abandoned. Layoffs became widespread as a result of falling profitability and of retrenchment in companies that had expanded in the face of deregulation.

There have been a number of examinations of exactly what happened to U.S. financial markets in October, 1987. The two most prominent are the *Report of the Presidential Task Force on Market Mechanisms* (Brady Report), released in January, 1988, and *The October 1987 Market Break, A Report by the Division of Market Regulation, U.S. Securities and Exchange Commission* (SEC Report), which came out in February, 1988. They argue that portfolio insurance strategies coupled with the interaction between the futures market and the stock market through index arbitrage accelerated and exacerbated the fall in stock prices. On the other hand, reports from the derivative markets in Chicago and the Commodity Futures Trading Commission (CFTC) stressed the problems arising from the fact that the cash and futures markets became disconnected when stock prices were not posted and the markets were temporarily closed.

The Brady Commission emphasized that the stock, options and futures markets are all intimately connected and really one market, and that consequently they should be regulated by a single agency. Their suggestion was that the Federal Reserve Board might be the proper authority, since the Federal Reserve Board already had the authority to set margin requirements for stocks, and the Brady Commission felt that margin requirements should be consistent (but not necessarily the same) between cash and futures markets. The Brady Commission also recommended the installation of circuit breaker mechanisms such as trading halts or limits to price movements.

The SEC Report suggested that a special trading post for baskets of stocks might be established on the NYSE floor complete with its own specialists, and it was also concerned about the higher leverage in the derivative markets; it wondered whether the losses from reduced liquidity if margin requirements were raised might not be outweighed by gains from reduced volatility. The SEC was not enthusiastic about price limits to reduce volatility, but suggested later openings for trade in derivative products to reduce their price leadership effects. The SEC Report also investigated in detail the role of specialists, the over-the-counter and options markets, capital adequacy, information systems, order execution and confirmation, clearance and settlement, and customer complaints. In subsequent discussion, the SEC favoured unified regulation for the various markets, and advocated that it take over regulation of financial futures from the CFTC.

In the event, few radical changes have been made in the wake of the market break. The futures exchanges put limits on price movements of stock index futures, while the NYSE limited access to its DOT system if the Dow Jones moved by more than 50 points in one day (the collar). Both of these remedies work to sever the link between the markets that normally operates through index arbitrage, and are opposed on these grounds by those who feel they ultimately work against the market and reduce liquidity. Under pressure from customers, some large New York securities firms have announced that they were refraining from engaging in index arbitrage, either entirely or for their own accounts. In 1988, circuit-breaker mechanisms were introduced whereby trading on the NYSE was to halt for one hour if the Dow Jones moved by more than 250 points on any given day, and if upon resumption it moved by more than another 150 points, trading would be halted for two hours. Trading in the S&P 500 futures contract on the CME would halt if the price moved by more than 30 points, and for a longer period if it subsequently moved by more that 20 points.

These circuit-breakers have not really been tested, although extreme volatility in the market has not completely disappeared. The Dow Jones declined by 140 points on January 8, 1988, the day the Brady Report appeared, and it fell by over 100 points again on April 14, 1988, in spite of "the collar." On Friday, October 13, 1989 the Dow Jones average fell 190.58 points, and the circuit-breaker on the CME futures market was tripped and trade halted for a half-hour. Afterwards this was credited with creating market chaos rather than a cooling-off period, as trade continued on the NYSE. As one wag noted, the best cooling-off period was the weekend, and on Monday the Dow rose by 88 points. This episode brought renewed pressure on the securities firms to stop programme trading, and they complied, at least temporarily. It has been suggested, however, that this trading still takes place, but it is simply done off the exchanges.

With the benefit of hindsight, the October 1987 market break is looking increasingly less important. The markets quickly recovered from their post-break lows. In New York the Dow-Jones has gone to new highs above 3,000, while in Toronto the TSE 300 Index has risen, but not to the levels of 1987 before the break. In terms of the historical record, 1987 does not look much like a repeat of 1929. The chart of the gyrations of the Dow Jones average since 1887 illustrates this very dramatically. The chart is drawn on semi-logarithmic paper so that equal distances show equal percentage changes, and certainly 1987 looks insignificant when compared to 1929 and its aftermath. It contrasts nicely with the short-term perspective of the other chart on page 213 which looks only at a two and one half month period in 1987.

The correction that did occur in October, 1987 was compressed into a very short time, and the role of programme trading in promoting this is what is perhaps most unique about the event. Increased short run volatility seems to be a permanent part of the new environment.

## DOW JONES INDUSTRIAL AVERAGE

### 1897 – PRESENT

Source: R.B.C. Dominion Securities.

Portfolio insurance may be on the decline, but the technology for programme trading is here and will not disappear. The interconnection of the international markets was dramatically illustrated by the events of October, 1987 and that is unlikely to disappear either. Finally, it may be worth remembering that investment dealers are finding trading a bigger source of profit than commission work, and while investors favour stability, traders thrive on increased volatility. However, volatility of the dimensions experienced in October 1987 drives investors away from the markets, threatens the solvency of dealers and is not in anybody's interest.

# Further References

Economic Council of Canada. *Globalization and Canada's Financial Markets.* Ottawa: Minister of Supply and Services, 1989. Appendix C.

*Report of the Presidential Task Force on Market Mechanisms.* Washington, U.S. Government Printing Office, 1988.

United States Securities and Exchange Commission. The October 1987 Market Break, A Report by the Divison of Market Regulation, U.S. Securities and Exchange Commission. Washington: U.S. Government Printing Office, 1988.

# index

182-5, 189, 191, 195, 200, 201, 207ff.

## V

Vancouver  105
Vancouver Stock Exchange  105, 106, 113, 136, 143, 197
variable rate mortgage (VRM)  90
"variation margin" (futures)  126
vendor take-back (mortgages)  91
Victory Bonds  54

## W

warrants  59-60, 96, 100
"wealth effect"  214
Wellington Insurance  188
West, Richard  183
W.I. Carr  194

Wilson, Harold  153
Winnipeg  125, 128, 130
Wood Gundy  76(note), 193
World Bank  171
World War I  46
World War II  46, 81, 153, 163

## Y

Yamaichi  194
yields  8, 10-26, 35, 38, 58, 73, 101-2
yield (stocks)  17-18, 98, 101-2, 113-4
yield curves  20-3

## Z

zero coupon bonds  8, 16

Printed in Canada